Teaching Literature

"My name is Mr. Collins. I'll be teaching you English literature, and I'm armed."

Teaching Literature

Writers and Teachers Talking

Interviews edited by Judy Kravis

Cork University Press

First published in 1995 by
Cork University Press
Unversity College
Cork
Ireland

British Library Cataloguing in Publication Data
A CIP catalogue record for this book is available from the British Library.

ISBN 1 85918 025 6 hardback
1 85918 026 4 paperback

Typeset by Seton Music Graphics, Bantry, Co. Cork.
Printed by ColourBooks, Baldoyle, Co. Dublin.

For literature students, past, present and future

Contents

Judy Kravis

Peter Morgan

Judy Kravis was born and educated in England. She has published poetry and fiction, including *Rough Diamante* and *Tea With Marcel Proust*, as well as a study of Mallarmé. She has given readings, some with film and music, in Europe and the US. Her opera libretto *Hot Food With Strangers* was performed in Ireland and London in 1991 and 1993. Judy Kravis has taught French literature at University College, Cork since 1974. In the breaks between teaching and writing she is usually gardening.

Introduction

> What remains to be 'understood' is that books are not written so that my son, or daughter, or young people, may comment on them, but so that, *if their heart is in it*, they may read them. (Daniel Pennac, *Reads like a Novel*)

THIS BOOK IS about our strange efforts to teach literature, because, in various ways, literature is our life. We have some long love of words, even dependency on words read, written, declaimed. 'Don't forget to take your anti-declamatory pill today,' I overheard on the subway in New York. We all forgot.

Most of the contributions are the result of interviews, some on the phone, one by correspondence, most of them live. The contributors are teachers who write, writers who teach, writers who don't teach, writers whose books are taught. The teaching they describe ranges from prison to primary school, from PhD to remedial. Their writing includes fiction, poetry, theatre, journalism and biography. I chose to interview, rather than to invite written contributions, because I wanted the book to have a talking tone, or rather, a series of different talking tones – as students experience a series of teachers. Teaching happens mainly through talking, yet the language of the classroom – like the language of literary comment – is often far from the language of conversation, particularly in universities.

Have teachers been duped into an elevated teaching language by literature itself? Do they raise their diction with their defences? Teachers can be very exclusive creatures, none more so than university teachers, whose ivory tower is full of anxious captives. Some teachers fear literature as the goalie fears a penalty kick, and muster their defences in the form of critical distance, metalanguage and analysis. What are the reverberations of that fear on students, whose impulse in the turbulent time between age twelve and age twenty-two is to define, to know, and to pass the exam? Certainly it removes pleasure from education and literature from the humanity of those who wrote it. Should we talk about books as we talk about love or gardening, as we argue about politics and religion? Should those who talk about books sound more like those who write them? Clevinger, the Harvard man in *Catch 22* who 'knew everything about literature except how to enjoy it,' warns us of the dangers of knowing too much about too little.

Literature is taught in primary school under the simpler names of reading and writing, at secondary school, where it separates itself from language, and at university, where, at worst, it separates itself from life. At primary and secondary level, it is taught by people who have had teacher training and who usually teach at least one other subject. At universities, literature is taught by academics and writers who don't have teacher training but have fame or a PhD – or both. In Western culture there's a dwindling relation between the scholarship on which academic reputations are built, and the ability or desire to teach. It may have worked in Ancient Greece, where education was clearly for an élite and teaching was the visible face of wisdom, but democracy has fogged the position of the teacher in the late twentieth century – to say nothing of the face of wisdom. Higher education is still for an élite, though it pretends otherwise, while globally speaking, all education is for an élite. There is little time or energy for thinking about how to teach in societies whose governments don't back their fine words about education with money. Already stymied by comments like 'those who can, do, those who can't, teach', the teacher is pushed into the half-light of productivity; whereas after a couple of World Cups run by the media, we now talk of a football ethos and there's no argument.

Teaching is, as everyone who's ever been to school knows, a very hit-and-miss affair – with more misses than palpable hits. Where fifty years ago anyone was pleased to leave school knowing how to read and write and do sums, even reckoning a certain pride in a firm copperplate hand or a good head for figures, school-leavers and graduates now prefer to have a knowledge of business practice and keyboard skills. Literature is not uppermost on any government agenda; the arts in general come under 'good causes' likely to benefit from lottery money. In this climate, literature looks archaic, and teachers of literature look like Flann O'Brien's society of one-legged men, united the world over in their cultish preservation of the arcane. So much the better, say some teachers, literature should be hard to find, it should be rare and strange and the result of a personal quest, not a slot on a syllabus, a text with a test and then oblivion.

A curious vista opens up: in the distance, luminescent and complete, is literature, mostly written by dead writers, kept in libraries, catalogued and shelved, or in more remote areas of bookshops, usually in uniform series, so that the browser gets that *frisson* of respect. Closer to hand but still exclusive, contemplating and competing, the scholars live in privileged relation with literature; for them the jangle of contemporary fiction in the bookshop is either invisible or the stuff of entertainment. In the foreground, the jobbing teacher faces diminished respect and huge classes who are motivated mainly by the vision of the job that literature might help them acquire – not teaching, they hope.

Can we reshape this vista? What are the relationships between writers and teachers, between literature and teaching? In Ireland, where I have taught since 1974, there's a certain respect for writers, whose earnings from their creativity are not taxed. A writer in a recently oral culture still has some magical powers. There's also a tacit acceptance that writers are as qualified as academics to teach; they're in line with storytellers and heroes as holders of a heritage. Ireland is the land of saints and scholars and, latterly, poets and musicians. It's also an island, and in island society, icons are important. But traditionally there has been – and often still is – great suspicion between writers and academics, both in the United States where creative writing is widely taught, and in Europe where it's less common. Is it the inevitable battle between two sides of the same coin? The same ego and the same fulfilment through an audience? There's nothing overtly public-spirited about being a writer, whereas a teacher is bound in a contract with the students: the teacher is paid to teach; the students pay to be taught - or their parents, or governments, pay for them.

The academic can easily forget that reading is not always a natural activity for students, whereas the writer – who's used to being thought unnatural – is above all aware of having to get people to read. When a writer is teaching, students have a line inwards to the book and how it was made, what choices were involved, as well as a line outwards to the public world where the writer lives and publishes books which all sorts of strangers are currently reading. The writer/teacher personifies the whole process of the book, not just the product or book-as-tomb. On the other hand, as representative of the university exam system and the university administration, the academic is a remote figure. Scholarship is for other scholars, as difficult and as remote as great wealth but not as desirable. Where the writer represents freedom, waywardness and sometimes subversion, the academic represents the status quo – and prefers it to be in Latin.

Writers who teach tend to write the kind of literature which might be studied, the kind that has not earned its author a sufficient living – that's often the practical motivation for teaching. They need to keep the head unfettered in order to be able to write. They know how to perform on the page and can often perform in the classroom too, which raises doubts in some academics: it's fine and even necessary to seduce as a writer, but to seduce as a teacher is fraught with difficulty. Where is the line between dangerous charisma and infectious enthusiasm? Between passion and smothering?

The writer may be curious to know what the academic says about his or her own work, but can easily dismiss it as parasitical, derisory, or simply wrong-minded. For the academic, the writer's book was first of all a riveting read – we hope. It touched a chord. The writer may well be dead, and fair game for reinvention by the academic; or alive, living down the road, subject to the same everyday world and yet totally out of the academic's control, each new book a new chapter in the critical work the academic is preparing, and potentially a new slot on the salary scale.

In Western society the teacher is a civil servant and has to recognize productivity parameters and economic viability. The more centralized education becomes, the more it resembles business. Should students be told about the phenomenon of 'publish or perish' so that they understand why there are so many secondary texts in the library? If the teacher is writing criticism during holidays and sabbaticals, is it hypocritical to tell students that the primary text is really what matters? The authority of the teacher mingles with the authority of the critical text she or he is writing or quoting, and forms a higher zone which students see as absolute. Should university libraries call a halt and only stock primary texts and see if they come up shining? The student arriving at university from a non-literary household sees the books in the library as united by size, seriousness and strangeness. A library with only primary texts would be an honest library.

But, argues the academic, biographies of writers are fascinating, they are works of fiction in themselves. Philosophical essays about literature can be as moving and as exciting as poems. Shouldn't university education train the intellect, lengthen the attention span and focus the concentration of the student? We can't do that by simply encouraging them to read fiction and poetry. And, since the late twentieth century is the era of international collage, of postmodern rape and pillage, shouldn't we also teach comment on literature, theories about literature, structures for literature?

Literature crept on to the school teaching curriculum, encroaching on the domain of grammar, handwriting, punctuation and letter-writing, not long after literature started looking at itself. The earliest of the 'isms', like symbolism or futurism, reflected the dilemma of writers in the world. The later ones, like formalism, structuralism, deconstruction (which significantly doesn't need an 'ism'), reflect the dilemma of the critic in the tower, the theorist in orbit, the secondary person with a primary ego anxiously eyeing the tenure track. The most fine-tuned and persistent of literary theory seems to have come full circle and reads like a branch of fiction. Some academics with an eye on the full span of their activities are now publishing intellectual autobiographies which set literary theory on the kitchen table next to the salt. How much of this extraordinary spectrum can or should a student absorb?

When literature was less taught it was more sought after. It had the wholeness of a pleasure or a need; it did not need justifying, proving, or having its sources checked. We're desperate not to be exclusive these days, not to say the wrong thing. But you have to trip to walk. You have to digress to arrive. The truth is crooked, as Nietzsche knew. Education happens on the street corner as well as in the classroom. The canon – or not – is less important than the way you present the books you choose to teach, how you think about your students, how well you remember the riotous condition of being young.

When asked which teachers they remembered, contributors usually told tales of the riveting, the ghastly and the mundane. Some had no memories of teachers, only of a certain sense of distance, greyness or fear. Most commonly they remembered teachers' passions and mannerisms, phrases they bequeathed, potent combinations of love and scorn. Many teachers were remembered as great readers-out-loud, performers of various kinds. Teachers who stick in the memory are usually those who are eccentric or generous in manner, who don't just talk about literature but also clothes, or potato clamps, or what they saw on the way to the classroom, teachers who seem less to represent literature than the stuff of their own lives in which literature is included.

Teachers I admire include some who have not taught me but whose books I have read – like John Berger, Jorge Luis Borges or Cynthia Ozick – and some who have taught me, like George Craig, who came as close as anyone could to talking out of the back of my brain when I was twenty-one. Or Mrs Pipe, who taught me Latin when I was sixteen, and incidentally poetry, when she read out a line of Virgil about sleep-giving poppies and exclaimed, 'Isn't it beautiful!' then read it again. She had plump vowels and a good ear for a dead language. I remember the manner of teachers whose words I've forgotten, like George Steiner talking off a blackboard left from the previous maths lecture as a warm-up for his talk on difficulty in literature. Or A. J. Ayer talking about language, truth and logic. I understood absolutely nothing after the first thirty seconds. He seemed to speak from further and further away, and grow taller and taller. Or the maths teacher at school who, to illustrate relativity, drew pictures of Jim Hardy shooting from a train. We photographed him surrounded by a big group of us sixteen-year-olds at his desk; he was holding the needles and the wool and we were teaching him knitting.

Students I admire include the boy who felt that a French *nouveau roman* was an insult to his intelligence, got very angry about it but persevered, and ended up discovering he enjoyed the book. And the girl who, from the middle of strong, mass bewilderment in a large class, asked of a poem by Artaud, 'What have this guy's ravings got to do with us? Why do we have to read it?' 'What has Hannibal Lecter, psychopath and screen idol, got to do with us?' I asked. 'Why are we all trooping down to the Cineplex to see *The Silence of the Lambs*?' I would like to be able to add that the discussion was long and noisy, but in a class of a hundred students this is hardly possible.

Teaching at its best is liberation and a two-way event; at its worst, insidious imprisonment, first for the students and then for the teacher. The percentage of readers per head of population may well be little different now compared with a hundred years ago. Is this what Gutenberg imagined when he developed the printing press and assured the future of reading? The work of art in an age of mechanical reproduction is fraught with paradox.

There are certainly more writers among those readers now. Can you only teach reading through writing and writing through reading? All teachers of literature also write – criticism, theory, stories, diaries, essays and poetry – as well as comments on students' work. All teachers of literature also read. We began as readers and scribblers. We practised like mad. Literature came into our lives in a rush of emotion. We have stayed with it for years as teachers, writers, readers. We can teach out of that old rush of emotion. It is still there, isn't it? On good days.

I was reprimanded for reading in a Cork pub because, as the publican told me, 'reading is an anti-social activity'. It was an unkind but accurate remark. How can that solitary involvement translate into teaching? This is an age of very *intéressée* seduction, full of tacit promises about self-advancement. How can literature compete? The Irish novelist, Joe O'Connor, had a teacher who thought reading should be demonstrated in front of large gatherings, like gymnastics or cooking. In some primary schools, silent reading is performed in front of the class, to give the children the idea that reading is a valued activity because it is an internal moment, an enhanced solitude. The Western preoccupation with the physical and external – war or sport or wearing the health club body as the ultimate costume – makes people wary of the internal and solitary. It sounds too much like hard work without any moral satisfaction or even the admiration of others.

What happens to the teacher's first, solitary encounter with the book as it is taught over and over again? For what does the teacher give marks in essays and exams? Should we give credit to students for their questions as well as for their answers? If you know how to ask a question, do you know how to answer? In England/Ireland we dignify some homework with the name of essay. In the USA it's an assignment or a term paper. In France it's a *devoir*, a duty, it's an *exposé* or an *explication*. An essay is a try, which is honest. There is also the homework that happens by serendipity: the way you suddenly understand Beckett in an empty car park, or on the bus. Should poetry be taught in the context of nonsense? Do teachers talk too much? Do they trust enough? Their students? Themselves?

We can, we may, we should, teach literature as the breath of life – or at any rate the breath of virtual reality. Once upon a time we discovered we couldn't live without it. Let's remember that. We chose it. It chose us. We can talk about books as part of our relationship with the world, part of our intimacy. We know them in the same way we know people, with warmth, familiarity and strangeness. Books are intimate. Teaching is intimate – in small classes – like conversation. With large classes, teaching is performance, which puts literature into the realm of ritual and exaggerated intimacy, like disco-dancing or drinking. Most books are internal, ambiguous, searching, mysterious, paradoxical, private, public, cerebral, visceral creatures. They can plunge us into contradiction, chaos and catastrophe. These are the qualities that first attracted teachers and writers to books. They're also the qualities most echoed in the lives of young readers.

The reality for most teachers of literature is that they are introducing books to people who are not attracted by books.

Where we were seduced by words, students are seduced by moving images. The wonders of the world have moved. Few teenagers are turned on by the Pyramids or the Taj Mahal. They have not heard of the Hanging Gardens of Babylon. They have not heard of Babylon unless they're Rasta. In France, eating has been introduced into the primary school syllabus because the French gastronomic heritage seemed in danger of succumbing to fast food, and the liberty of children's palates along with it. In America, children are being taught in school how to distinguish a friendly expression from a hostile one on someone's face. If roots of life like food and the expression on a face are taught in schools, how radical must we be to teach reading?

Gabriel Josipovici

Gabriel Josipovici was born in Nice in 1940, of Russo-Italian, Roman-Levantine parents. He lived in Egypt from 1945 to 1956, when he came to England. He read English at St Edmund Hall, Oxford and, since 1963 has been on the faculty of the University of Sussex, where he is now part-time Professor of English in the School of European Studies. He has published over a dozen works of fiction and five critical studies, including *The World and the Book* and *The Book of Good: A Response to the Bible*. His plays have been performed in London and Edinburgh and on the BBC and German radio. His latest novel, *Moo Pak*, was published in 1994.

What is the Point of Your Grandmother?

SUSSEX HAS CHANGED enormously in the time I've been here. Last year in the first term, instead of twenty-five students that I might have had, that is twelve tutorials with two students in each, I had seventy-five students. Those of us who still believe in the tutorial system have simply been working huge hours. I'm fortunate in that I teach part-time – I teach two terms out of three – so I don't feel too bad. But it hasn't essentially changed. The first course I do with freshers is 'Historical Approaches to Shakespeare'. I think it's wonderful to make them do Shakespeare when they first come. The thing to do is to get them away from the two Shakespeare plays in two years they've done at A level, so we go through about thirty Shakespeare plays in the first five weeks. They look absolutely stunned for the first week when I say, 'I want you to read six early comedies and write an essay on them.' But in about four cases out of five the therapy actually works, and although they're shattered, they realize that they can work harder than they thought they could, and through this saturation process they do actually start to respond. I had the most wonderful response from a mature, not very old student – she was twenty-five or so – who went to see *The Winter's Tale* in about the fifth week and said, 'My God, it was absolutely wonderful, for the first time there were no barriers between me and this play. The language wasn't difficult, nothing was difficult, I was really responding to it.'

So my feeling is one must get them reading as hard as possible and not directed in any particular way. I really try to get them to forget ways of doing things they've learned at school, to forget prejudices and start thinking for themselves. Prelims are always a problem. They were a problem for me when I was a student. I don't think Oxford solved it particularly well. That Shakespeare course is excellent because Shakespeare is difficult enough for people – there is a bit of a struggle. On the other hand, they are familiar with quite a bit of it, and they can go and see plays performed. I set two topics a week which they choose on the spot, so that I know there will be two different topics. These might be, for example: 'Why do we feel the need to stand up and clap at the end of a comedy (but not of a tragedy)?' Or: 'Shakespeare's comedies contain many heroines but few heroes. Discuss.' I try all the time to shake them out of their conventional attitudes, so that if we're doing tragedy we will do *Titus Andronicus* as well as *King Lear*, since both are called tragedies. So they have to rethink their Bradley or whatever they've done at school. They always talk at first in terms of character and morality. I hope that by reading a group of plays together they will start to see Shakespeare as more like Bach than George Eliot: someone exploring the possibilities of given forms, taking delight in what the tradition has given him and what he is able to do with it.

My own way of dealing with Shakespeare goes back to my student days when I never felt I got anywhere with him till I was put in for a Shakespeare prize, and decided to read every single Shakespeare play in the canon. I realized the best way to understand one play is to read all the other plays, because, in the case of any massive author, it is a matter of becoming acquainted with not just their language on the page, but the whole language of their trade, and the only way to do that is to subject yourself to it.

These first-year students would be doing one other course at the same time. And if they're in the School of European Studies, they would be doing a language. We used to have an 'Introduction to English' course, a version of which they do in their second term, where they can choose a play, a novel, a long poem, a kind of genre approach which I no longer teach, I don't like it. But I think that what is important is really getting students to see that they *can* read, and to think about reading and preferably to reread rather than rushing to secondary work. There are times when I'm inclined to say, oh God, standards are falling, and then you get a year – like last year, for example, I had a wonderful lot, I had half-a-dozen who I think will probably go on to get firsts. One can never tell.

Now that we have a lot of EC students at Sussex, as well as a lot of American students, it is obvious that our own students are less educated than their EC counterparts. When I take these students for medieval studies, say, and we do Chaucer, I know that the French students will already have quite a background in medieval French stuff, and they will have read some Boccaccio and maybe a bit of Dante. The Italians will have read some Dante, some Boccaccio and some Virgil. The Greeks will probably have read Virgil and Homer. All right, they haven't done it very well, perhaps in a rather 'question and answer' fashion, but they have got under their belts Montaigne's essays and things which somehow people wouldn't dream of doing the equivalent of here. Who reads Bacon's essays or anything like that in school? Some people I encounter when I do admissions interviewing have done A levels which consist of *no* early literature; it's all twentieth-century except for the odd Shakespeare play. They have no grounding in anything outside their own century. Also they don't know how to spell and they don't know how to construct an essay and so on. One might say that the French do it too mechanically, but nevertheless they have at least got something, some tools which can help them.

I take in a couple of essays a term from each student in all the courses I teach and then discuss these with them. Quite often what that consists of is not really discussing the content, but spelling and strategy, always with the notion in mind, not of some ideal essay, but of what is the best way of saying what you're trying to say about these books. My approach doesn't radically change after the first year. If I teach the medieval period, which is a two-term period paper they do in their second year, or European Foundations, which is a one-term course also in the second year, again I think of these as text-based courses where students are becoming familiar with the material by reading. Obviously I might suggest with earlier literature a few more critical or scholarly works, to help them get a context, but it is mainly a question of getting them interested and excited. I get them to go and listen to tapes of readings of Chaucer or Dante, so that they can see that this is something you *hear* as well as just reading with your eyes. When I'm teaching medieval English, in the third week, having done a couple of quite hard weeks, we do the medieval lyric and I get them to choose one lyric from an anthology and read it aloud and talk about it. It does look unfamiliar and frightening at first, and some of course are more willing than others to take the plunge, but once they do, they realize that it actually is easier than it looks on the page.

My teaching is mainly through tutorials. When I started teaching I may have been more enthusiastic and maybe a little less patient, but I don't think there are really skills for that kind of teaching. I was taught tutorially, so it seems the natural way. I have since discovered that there are different ways of doing it than my tutors did it. It isn't always a good idea to have people just reading out their essays; that's why I take in essays. In some cases I don't ask for any essays, but we read out bits of difficult texts. I go around the group and then discuss what we've read. So one can vary it, but I've been doing that for a very long time and I don't feel it's really developed. As far as lecturing is concerned I suppose I've got more relaxed, I get less anxious and therefore prepare a bit less and perhaps know a bit more, but on the other hand there's still the sense that sometimes you've done rather good ones and sometimes you haven't, and that doesn't always have to do with the content.

I haven't consciously gone against the kind of teaching I received myself. When I was a student, I felt quite privileged to be where I was and grateful to my teachers, although I felt that they were part of a culture and part of a tradition that I didn't understand or really have much inwardness with. After all, I'm not English and only came to this country at fifteen, with experiences behind me that are nowhere dealt with in this literature. Sussex was wonderful because I felt able to talk about the things I'm interested in talking about. The lecturing was often rather bad at Oxford. There were marvellous people who simply were so terrified of doing this that they read nervously from proofs or from antiquated lecture notes and never even looked up. One was amazed that people who had known that their lives were going to be spent doing this kind of thing had never taken the trouble to think of an audience. Of course there were exceptions, but partly it was the fault of the system that at Oxbridge it was written into your contract that you must give two sets of lectures a year. I thought one of the beauties of Sussex was that that was never the case. One lectured when one felt one had something to say, given of course that every year we do have a Modern European Mind series, and a Shakespeare series and so on, and those must keep going, but you're not forced to push out the stuff, which means that there isn't this thing of simply recycling dead material or just reading it out. I haven't ever been to a lecture in Sussex which has just been read out.

On the other hand, the tutoring at Oxford was very good. There was one tutor in particular, Rachel Trickett, whom I invited down to Sussex last term. It was a wonderful occasion. I was asked to organize a series of European lectures – we have these series which are meant to unite the School of European Studies – and I was asked to do one on a slightly earlier period. Rachel was a great friend of Philip Larkin's and Andrew Motion's biography and the *Letters* had just come out. She told me how very strange it was that here was a man who was a good friend and an excellent librarian and a good minor poet, and then when he died his private papers made people say, 'Ah, but what he really was was a sexist, racist – whatever.' In no previous century would people have ever thought the private somehow annulled the public in that way. I suddenly thought it would be wonderful to do a lecture series on public and private in the pre-industrial world. One can ask historians, art historians, music colleagues, all sorts of people to contribute. I asked Rachel to come and she gave the last lecture in the series. The extraordinary thing, going to these tutorials in her room – tutorials which used to last for about two hours – was that there were practically no secondary books at all. She would just go to her shelf and pick out some essay by Bulwer Lytton, or Emerson, or whatever, which was absolutely relevant. For her, I think every writer in English from Chaucer to James is a living presence. She would say something like, 'Next week we'll do Wordsworth. Read the collected works and read Mary Moorman's biography.' Mary Moorman's biography is two volumes of five hundred pages each, but one went away and did that and then one had a serious, long, long discussion about the ins and outs of Wordsworth. It was marvellous.

I think what one learns from one's teachers, and what I find even when I go to colleagues' lectures for instance, is not so much the content or what they say but an *attitude*, a sense of relation to the past and responsibility to scholarship and so on. So I think that was important for me. I was also taught in my first year by an American medievalist, Del Kolve, who is now very distinguished, and who became a good friend. He was just a research fellow then and he introduced me to John Berryman in 1960 when he was hardly known over here. So I think I was perhaps very lucky because I know some contemporaries at Oxford really had rather miserable times. It could be a problem when you had one tutor or two for three years. If you feel that the teacher is passionate and wants to convey that passion, then it's not a question of whether or not they are particularly good with students but that the passion comes across. With the tutors I had, I think there was this sense that talking about literature was something perfectly natural.

Sometimes of course there are some wonderful secondary works which can be illuminating in themselves and indeed this man, Del Kolve, has a brilliant book on the Miracle plays, which is much more than just about that, it's a whole book really about the Middle Ages. When we get around to doing the Miracle plays, I stress to students that this is the book they should look at. I'm very, very selective about the secondary reading I recommend. I don't send them to critical theory at all. I don't believe in it as a realm. I never wanted to teach in the critical theory MA. I think a lot of it is pseudo-scientific, an attempt somehow to put the understanding of literature on scientific lines, and I find that not very interesting. It's very popular for a very clear reason, it seems to me. It seems to provide a key. Young people grow up with no clear sense of where they are, and then there's this barrage of stuff coming at them, and they're asking, 'What on earth is it? Where should we stand?' and suddenly somebody is saying, 'Look, this is what it's all about.' The more confused people are, the more likely they are to grab it. I think the pull of that is enormously strong. I do find quite a few students resist it and of course the best students know how to make use of it when they need to. Some students become obsessed by it.

I think in literature there aren't any keys. And really this is the thing about tutorials, even in rather big tutorials, we can discuss a great variety of issues. Obviously students often ask if there are one or two books which could tell them what is the key to all this, but a course like Modern European Mind, for example, is designed precisely to make them discover that that's the wrong sort of question. Rather than giving them something which one feels is false or inadequate, one tries more to make them see that asking that question is something they have to grow out of – towards what, it's hard to say. One of the things I liked about Oxford was that, unlike Cambridge, it wasn't suffused with this Leavisite approach, which I think is what you now get in cultural studies and the new historicism, but which to my mind goes back a long, long way in English culture, to a sort of Puritanism, a belief that somehow you know there must be a reason for these things and a morality, and that if there isn't, then it's *frivolous*. This division between the serious and the frivolous I think is still very much there. Luckily in Oxford people seemed not to feel that this was an issue. It seems to me that if one reads the great writers, one doesn't feel that's an issue. If you're reading Proust or Shakespeare, the two things go together – ethics and aesthetics. I think it's such a boring kind of thing when people say, 'Well, what's the point?' It's like saying, 'What's the point of your grandmother?' I remember somebody ringing me up when there was some crisis about funding little theatres and saying, 'Can you justify little theatres?' and I said, 'Well, can you justify life?'

I really try not to think about the education I'm giving people and what they do with it later. Part of me has always felt: this is absurd, I shouldn't be doing this. I shouldn't be teaching literature, I shouldn't be getting paid for teaching it, they shouldn't be studying it. Then part of me feels: well, I like doing it, I feel at a local, individual level it actually is worthwhile. But I really have no views, or at least totally conflicting and confused views, about Education with a capital E, particularly in the humanities and particularly in literature. From the beginning, I've been thinking: What is the point of this? Probably all the most cultured people I know are self-taught, so that isn't the issue. People come to you – particularly mature students – and say that being at university will help them, that it's better to study books with other people. Well, my feeling quite strongly is that one reads books by oneself and that often talking about them is not the best thing to do.

When people then start talking about jobs and productivity and all the rest, then I really don't know what the answers are, but certainly I believe in education; that's why I did go on to teach despite the occasional doubt. When I was taught by Rachel Trickett, it was at quite an important time in my life. It was in my third year at Oxford and I had always rather despised academic beings and thought, no, that's the last thing I want to be involved with. But somehow her presence and what she did, made me feel that it might be worthwhile, that I could do it, and maybe that would be a way of earning my living relatively seriously and in a worthwhile way while giving myself time to write. Of course a lot of people think that.

When I came to teach at Sussex, for the first three years I dried up and I really thought I was going to have to leave because I just couldn't do my own writing, partly because I was living with masterpieces. I then had a term's leave, ostensibly in order to write a critical book, but I was in a real panic. I felt that if I didn't write the novel I wanted to write then, I never would, and I didn't know what it was I wanted to write, but I did know that I wanted to do something bigger than the very small things I'd been doing. I was absolutely scared to death. Every single morning I would wake up in a cold sweat. It was wonderful, it broke through all sorts of barriers. I wrote this novel, *The Inventory,* and once I had written one, I began to get confidence and people at the university accepted that I had other things in my life as well as teaching and writing criticism. But there's always this problem that if you spend a week writing poetry or fictional things it might be a total waste of time, whereas after a week preparing a lecture or writing a review, even if you don't get very far, you feel even for yourself – never mind the world outside – that you've done something. So of course in one way it's always much easier to do that. Part of the difficulty of teaching in the early years was finding a balance, and I must say Sussex was wonderful because there were people like George Craig and Stephen Medcalf who had a kind of openness and generosity and not the awful professionalism of the academic world, which made one feel that this was worthwhile. And when I realized too that I actually didn't function properly as a human being if I wasn't doing my own writing, and therefore I was not going to be a good teacher because I was going to be restless and cross and so on, I began to justify my own writing in that way and say, okay, maybe I'm not going to be such a good teacher but that's how I am. There were terms, it's true, where I cut all sorts of corners, and when I talked to students later who'd attended courses that I did in that mood they said, 'You seemed to be asleep all the time.' I wasn't asleep, I was just trying to work out what the next sentence or paragraph or chapter was going to be. But eventually I did find a sort of balance.

I don't think that there's any close link, good or bad, between writing and teaching, except perhaps I have a little more inwardness with writers I teach than people who don't write at all. I have a sense of what it's like to be a writer, to have produced these things, especially with particular writers that I feel close to, like Proust. But the other way around, I certainly don't think that it gives anything at all. If occasionally I have started work on something of my own with, as it were, ideas culled from books I've read or whatever, it's never worked out. I do worry at times and think, oh dear, one shouldn't be doing this thing, but then one has to do something unless one wants to go freelancing, in which case there are other sorts of pressures which I don't think I have the psychological capacity to cope with. The problems raised by teaching and writing are quite separate, and part of the solution of the problem is to keep them separate.

On the other hand, being involved in both teaching and writing means that it's easier to talk about books with students as one would with one's friends. Though if one is doing five tutorials on Shakespeare in the week because of numbers having risen, inevitably one isn't going to approach the fifth with the openness of the first. I think that's a problem, yes, and I don't know the answer.

I have in front of me this enormous *doctorat d'état* which was done on my work two months ago. The chap came to see me, a very nice young man, and asked if he could come and talk to me and he did, and then he asked if he could come again. I didn't really feel that I wanted that, but then they invited me to go to the *soutenance.* I'd been reading this book about Pinget and heard that he went to *soutenances* of theses on his work, but I thought that was the last thing I wanted to do. I didn't want to go and hear somebody talking about my work. It's very pleasing to know that people are reading it, but I don't really feel I would learn anything and wouldn't particularly want to either. Occasionally if people have come here and have done theses on my work, I certainly have refused to supervise them because I don't think there is a link, and anyway I am rather against students doing research on modern topics because that doesn't seem to me to be research. But that's my prejudice. Scholarship should help bring the past to life, but with modern literature what you want is modern with some culture, some sense of the past, and an openness of mind. The odd article is fine – but theses and books!

I'm rather against the whole PhD thing, I think it's part of a nineteenth-century *Wissenschaft* idea which Nietzsche knocked on the head and led out for good. But institutionally it's now necessary, which is very sad. I was very lucky when I came here, David Daiches said, 'How's your research going?' I said, 'Very badly,' and he said, 'Well, do you think there's a book there somewhere?' and I said, 'Well, maybe,' and he said, 'Well, you'll have plenty to do preparing for our courses.' So I then spent twelve years teaching and thinking and I then probably wrote a better book than I would have otherwise. *The World and the Book* has just gone into its third edition. That wouldn't have happened if I'd tried to write it at twenty-two.

Hermione Lee

Jerry L. Thompson

Hermione Lee grew up in London and read English at Oxford. She has taught in the US, Liverpool, and is currently Professor of English Literature at the University of York. She is well known as a critic, broadcaster and reviewer. From 1982 to 1986 she presented Channel Four's first book programme, 'Book Four'. She has written books on Virginia Woolf, Elizabeth Bowen, Philip Roth, Stevie Smith and Willa Cather, and edited *The Secret Self*, anthologies of stories by women. She is now working on a new biography of Virginia Woolf and has been commissioned to edit the *Oxford Book of Women's Verse*.

Free Exploratory Space

As a child I wanted to teach or act; I didn't know which. But from the age of eight or nine onwards my main activity was reading. I had (and have) a very literary, largely self-educated mother. She published a couple of children's books and has a great passion for writing and literature. She's enormously well-read, especially in history. She left school at fifteen and went into publishing for a few years and then married and had two children, of whom I was the younger. My father, a GP, also wrote books for children, and he reads when he's not listening to music, or carpentering. So it was an extremely literary (and musical) household. That was the formative influence, and I've never reacted against it. There was no censorship. My mother would never say, 'No, that's not very suitable dear.' I do remember picking up *What Maisie Knew* thinking it was going to be like *What Katy Did*, and being horribly taken aback on the first page. But most of my childhood reading was a sort of hoovering up of nineteenth- and twentieth-century fiction.

I'm the product of exactly the sort of school system which is now thought to be very bad for you. I narrowed down my studies very early. I went to the French Lycée and then to London grammar and private schools. I did Oxford entrance exams before my A levels (in English, Religious Knowledge and Greek). I dropped all science subjects as early as I could, and I'm scientifically illiterate and innumerate. I'm not proud of this, but it was that route which led to teaching literature. And then I had that peculiar English degree course at Oxford in the 1960s, when you started with Anglo-Saxon and Milton and didn't read anything beyond about 1850. Bizarre, of course, but interesting. It gave me two experiences, one of which was acquiring English as a foreign language, going back and reading *Gawain* and Malory and Chaucer and seventeenth-century poetry, as one would learn maths or Latin. (And you had to do Latin as part of the Preliminary course.) What I got from that was a sense of doors opening on to linguistic riches I hadn't known about.

The other feature of Oxford was tutorials, which meant you were at the mercy of your particular tutor. I was only seventeen when I arrived at St Hilda's. I had Anne Elliot, a Spenserian, as my first tutor. A remarkable teacher, who scarcely said anything. She would eventually comment, and it would be very much to the point, but by then you would have babbled yourself into some kind of incoherence. I always wanted to be able to teach like that, to wait and listen. And I was taught by a famous, outrageous old Oxford gentleman called Hugo Dyson, an extinct breed. He used to compliment us on our coloured stockings and suggest that we do essays on the femme fatale in Romantic literature and tell us extraordinary stories about people he'd known. He was erudite and funny and encouraging and he made one feel that there was a great deal of fun to be had from spending a life with books. But he also typified that fatal smug frivolity that goes with the Oxford tradition. And I was taught Shakespeare by Stephen Wall, who became a friend, and who made me think about the relation between text and performance. Then I went on to do the BPhil. in nineteenth- and twentieth-century literature and I didn't make much of it. I don't think I knew quite what I wanted from it, and I don't think Oxford then was very helpful to its graduates.

But what Oxford did teach you was intellectual inventiveness and self-reliance. If you could think of something to write each week and come back with it, you would have an interesting conversation. And if you hadn't done any work or thought anything through yourself, that was it, you wouldn't get anything back. So you learnt that it was up to you. Of course the examination system was ridiculous – regurgitating three years in a week, on Disprin and adrenalin. That's changed now, and one of the best developments in educational methods in the last twenty years has been the growth of continuous assessment.

My first job after Oxford was teaching in America. I had a Woodrow Wilson teaching fellowship and I spent a year in Virginia at a traditional liberal arts college, William and Mary, where I taught freshman composition and a sophomore survey course (‘*Beowulf* to Beckett’). Large classes, starting at eight in the morning. I learnt to organize material and to communicate, but I didn’t know how to deal with students who hadn’t read anything. I was spoilt by Oxford; I wasn’t accessible enough. After that I spent seven years teaching at Liverpool University, in a very friendly department, where I learnt how to do the job, and since 1977 I’ve taught at York.

For most of my teaching life I’ve also been doing other things, either writing, or in the media. Obviously this is not uncommon. It’s a very prevalent pattern in this country. I reviewed fiction and then other books for *The Observer* for about twelve years, and then for the *Independent on Sunday*. When Channel Four began in 1982, I presented a series called ‘Book Four’, which I did for about five years, mostly interviews with writers. Channel Four had an educational remit then, and I strongly believe that media work, talking about books on radio or television, or literary journalism, shouldn’t be different from what you do in the classroom. I don’t accept the need for two completely different languages, one which is technical and one which is accessible and general. There are uses for a technical language of criticism, but it should always be possible to translate into a language for the ‘common reader’. If my working-life has any meaning, it’s to do with explaining, making available to other people my enthusiasms or my interests. The books I’ve done – a critical biography of Willa Cather, work on Elizabeth Bowen and Stevie Smith and Philip Roth, anthologies of stories by women writers called *The Secret Self*, work on Virginia Woolf – have been meant to convey enthusiasms. I once heard Edmund White say, ‘The great enemy of art is indifference.’ I have it written above my desk. I think teaching, as well as writing, is a form of countering indifference.

I think it’s good for one as a teacher (quite apart from the pressure of research ratings!) to be doing something other than teaching and administrating. It’s good for the students, too. When I was doing the television programmes in the eighties, the students were interested – they used to come and tell me whether they thought I’d got it right or not, and have arguments with me about the writers I'd been talking to. We're all so much under pressure now that it's much harder to find space for university teachers to break their routines, even to go to conferences, or to change direction. But it's important to keep flexibility and interest in our working lives.

You can't talk about teaching literature without talking about the political context in which universities exist. Obviously things have very much changed since those balmy days when I sat in Hugo Dyson's study reading 'La Belle Dame Sans Merci'. The basic idea of a three-year degree in the humanities is under threat. What we can teach and at what level is changing very fast. With a prescriptive, centralist national curriculum and the underfunding of schools and public libraries, there is less range of reading and less opportunity for school-teachers to encourage wide reading. And so there's a system which bolsters indifference, makes it less likely for children who *don't* have a privileged home background to be adventurous. At the same time, the ideology that universities should become more accessible isn't being backed up by funding. So expansion without investment means bigger classes, fewer books in the library, more pressurized staff, less attention to individual students. If we're now teaching students who have read less than they might have done twenty years ago, it's certainly not their fault. We are having to take on more students who may not have read very much and may not be in the habit of studying literature. And we're having to adapt to this without any backing – or indeed without much respect for our profession – from the government. So the way we teach has to change. It becomes much more like teaching American undergraduates. We can't make assumptions about how much people have read.

But, in spite of the pressures, one of the things I desperately want to hang on to is the principle of small group teaching. York is a relatively small university with a collegiate structure. Though it has grown in its thirty years, it still has a relatively intimate and friendly feeling to it. When I began teaching at York in the late 1970s, we had seminars of seven or eight and tutorials of two. Now it's tutorials of three to five and seminars of fourteen to twenty. That's still small group teaching, though, and I think we need to hang on to that. I think it's educationally powerful, not élitist. The more students you get who are not coming from a specialized literary background, the more you need to talk to them as individuals and the more they need to hear their own voices. The problem with big class teaching is that it's fine for the bossy, aggressive, exhibitionist, confident students who will leap from their seats and speak out, but it's incredibly hard for the students who are unconfident, which is still very often the girls in the class.

At York we do three kinds of teaching: lecturing, two-hour seminars or colloquia, and tutorials. Like many academics, I'm a closet thespian, and have spent a great deal of time in the past doing amateur theatricals. The lectures I remember at Oxford were all great performances: Christopher Ricks on Tennyson, Helen Gardner on T.S. Eliot. They were inspiring – because they had performed, because they had gripped you. I still can't divide my sense of teaching from my sense of theatre. I do think lectures should have some performance element about them.

That's one kind of communication, but I think this slow, careful, close-up tutorial teaching is more important. In those situations I do a lot of close reading and putting of texts into some kind of context. I want to make sure that students are reading enough to see why something is being written when it's written, and what it comes out of. And because I'm also a biographer, I want to make dead authors come to life. If I was talking about *To the Lighthouse*, there are several things I would try to do. First, perhaps, I'd plunge into the middle and ask people how they respond to a page or a paragraph, to the tone of voice; what they think is going on, whether they can understand it – because Woolf is quite difficult. Then I'd want to ask why the book is this shape, why it looks as it does, why it doesn't look like *Middlemarch* or *Emma* – why it's got the structure it has and what that has to do with the 1920s in England. And then you also need to ask: why is she so interested in painting? Why is she so interested in philosophy? Why has she chosen this particular family? Why is there so much ambivalence about family life? How much does this have to do with something personal? And what is this extraordinary line down the middle of the book? What is this break? And then you might start talking about *To the Lighthouse* as a post-war novel which is dealing with Victorian materials. So you might build it up like that.

How do you teach? Do you tell people things, or do you ask them questions? When you're teaching something you know extremely well and have been researching, you sometimes teach it less well than a work you're curious about and are discovering with the students. The temptation to tell people things when you are already in possession of a lot of knowledge is very strong. But you have to hold back. It's much slower if you're asking the questions and not giving the answers. But it has to be slow because people are trying to work out what they think. And because your own view is not necessarily the right one. You have to keep asking the questions and waiting for the answers and seeing whether the next answer doesn't go a little bit further. I hate those kinds of classes where there is clearly a hidden agenda, and you can see in the students' eyes that they're thinking, if I get the right answer, I'm going to 'win'.

It's not that I think that in teaching literature 'there is no such thing as a right answer'. Of course there can be right answers – about a date, or a bibliographical fact, or the words in a poem, or the life of a writer. There can be places where you say, 'No, I don't think so,' or, 'Try something else.' But I hate it when the students think that there's an ideology or a code they've got to conform to and if they can locate it then they'll be ok. I think teaching should be much more open, more eclectic and various than that. So I suppose that I try not to be coercive. Which fixes me as a liberal humanist and a respecter of differences – which we all know is its own kind of tyranny.

About coercion. I am worried about and frightened of ghettoes in teaching. I resent the possibility that at some point I may not be able to teach, say, Henry James because he's a dead white male, or because I'm a woman. The graduate applications I get now are almost all for women writers, from women students. And women's studies is partly responsible for that. We have a flourishing women's studies graduate programme at York which I've taught on in the past. But I prefer teaching in the mixed context of an English degree – to be able to teach Woolf and James together, or Cather and Hemingway together. For some students – mature students for instance coming back into academic work – women's studies can be the most fulfiling kind of course. But I am afraid of certain sorts of appropriation. I want to be able to teach male writers *and* women writers *and* Black writers *and* queer writers. I don't want to feel that there are rooms I can't go into, just as I don't like feeling that teaching literature must conform to set procedures.

I think there should be an element of serendipity, accident, wandering, for students and for teachers. Virginia Woolf hated the idea of university lecturing on literature, because she loved serendipitous, self-educated, second-hand bookshop, public library kind of readings. Inevitably the university teaching of literature must make people read according to a structure. At York the structure provides a large number of options and relates English literature to a foreign literature (it's called the Department of English and Related Literature) or to art history. And so within that structure it allows for great variety and flexibility. I've had a lot of colleagues who are very adventurous readers, unusual teachers. There's a great deal to be said for eccentric teaching, wilful teaching – leaping off at tangents, introducing unlikely references, roaming through ideas. I don't think I do this – I think I'm probably rather a straightforward and sensible kind of teacher. But I like the possibility of all those free spaces and explorations.

That kind of eccentricity is precisely what doesn't lend itself to teaching appraisal, now that we're falling into line with the business model of targets and accountability. And if we're thinking of students as clients, then that's the proper thing to do. But it doesn't allow for the unexpected. Teaching appraisal suggests that there's only one way to do it, and I don't think that's right. People say: what is the point of teaching English, and how can you possibly justify a non-vocational degree? There is a very clear answer to that which has to do with the vital importance of making people aware of their language and their history and their culture, how to write better and think more clearly. These are not luxuries. They are practical advantages to life which equip you for a number of professions. But there is a less clear and just as important answer which is that you give people a free exploratory space in their lives, a period when they have internal adventures. That sort of justification is not much valued. It sounds unrealistic and élitist: 'you come into this privileged space and you don't have to earn your living and you can just muck about in your mind.' But if you turn this hostile version on its head, what you are providing as a teacher of literature is an opportunity of great value, where the students encounter new and difficult disciplines and set themselves ambitious internal tests.

But where accountability and appraisal are a good thing is in raising the teacher's own awareness of how she or he behaves. I don't see any point in a teacher being aggressive or scornful or sarcastic. You sometimes want to be, of course, and everyone is at times. You get impatient. It is infuriating to set reading which doesn't get done, and then to try and have a conversation about something which hasn't been properly studied. But if students say, this person is always grumpy, or doesn't tell us anything, or talks all the time and doesn't listen, then that has to be a useful corrective.

When I'm talking to students about what to read, my priority is always the primary text. So, to go on with this imaginary tutorial on *To the Lighthouse*, I'd much rather that they go away and read *A Room of One's Own*, *Mrs Dalloway*, *Orlando* and maybe two of her essays on modern fiction and came back with that, than if they used my book on Virginia Woolf, or Lyndall Gordon's biography, or Louise de Salvo. But once we had talked about those primary texts, I would always offer a range of critical and biographical readings to pursue. Most students are suggestible and easily influenced, and if they start by reading the critical texts they won't see it for themselves. Of course I want the students to read good critical works too, but I don't teach by using primary texts very sparingly, or only in short extracts. You have to discuss how to read the secondary material, not just treat it as a feeding bag. For instance, you could use part of a seminar to get five different students to read five different critical essays on the same text, and each make a report on that, so the class is aware of different possible readings. But one of the things I've been criticized for as a teacher is that I ask people to read far too much. I taught a course on Henry James and I asked the students to read nine novels in nine weeks. Although they'd had the reading list for about a year, of course it was too much, and we ended up doing maybe four or five of those books. You have to be increasingly careful not to overload people. All the same, it's best of all when students read avidly. That's the best reward for a teacher.

It's important to be alert to changes in the canon, and to select books for teaching so as to incorporate these changes. Nineteenth-century American literature, which I've taught for years, is a good example because the canon has shifted so much. Ten or fifteen years ago you'd have taught Emerson, Thoreau, Poe, Twain, Melville, Whitman and Emily Dickinson. I still want to teach some of those people because of their huge value and importance and excitement. But now I would teach them with Frederick Douglass's slave autobiography, Charlotte Perkins Gilman's *The Yellow Wallpaper*, Louisa May Alcott's *Little Women*, or Harriet Beecher Stowe. I remember the first time I put *Little Women* on the course and one of my more austere (male) colleagues said, 'What, you must be joking!' As though this women's novel *were* 'little' – trivial, inferior, silly. But as social history, as propaganda for female behaviour in nineteenth-century America, as a female version of New England thinking, it's extremely interesting. Or, in a twentieth-century period paper, it's useful and suggestive to put next to each other a great classic of modernism like *Ulysses*, and works by writers who have been read (or unread) as minor and eccentric, or whose reputations are shifting, like Ivy Compton Burnett, Dorothy Richardson, May Sinclair, or Henry Green. The structure of our courses at York allows for this sort of variety and freedom, which I like very much. To an extent, the students can construct their own courses, and it is possible to do a non-chronological course, or a mainly twentieth-century or mainly medieval course, or a variety of joint degrees for instance with art history. Or they can follow a more straightforward chronological path.

I'm learning to teach a course which raises other challenges, on post-colonial writing. Here I start with readings and rereadings of Conrad's *Heart of Darkness*, and I might teach Achebe, Ngugi, Gordimer, Bessie Head, Desai, Rushdie, Atwood, Alice Munro, Kincaid, Walcott. I can range over the world by selecting a few contemporary texts. You have both an enormous advantage and a disadvantage teaching contemporary literature. The students are already interested and excited about reading authors who are alive or immediate, but it can sometimes make it more difficult to sort out critical judgement or to place a book in a tradition. It makes it harder to *see* it. The twentieth-century is hugely popular with students at the moment. British Academy applications are overwhelmingly to work on a writer such as Angela Carter, rather than on Pope or Dryden. Eighteenth-century undergraduate courses are hard to fill. This phase we're in now troubles me a bit. I suppose I'm biting the hand I feed myself with, but I don't want students to read only twentieth-century literature. You have to make an interventionist effort to make sure this doesn't happen.

Why do I teach? When I was doing the programme on Channel Four several people said to me, 'I'm sure you're going to give up teaching now and go freelance.' But I'm glad I didn't. Teaching is the only place in your life when you spend an hour, or two hours, talking about a writer. In average conversation, the most you can ever bend peoples' ears about a book you're reading is about seven and half minutes. (That's about the limit now on television and radio book programmes too.) So there's that. And the fact that it keeps you in touch with what people of the next generation are thinking and talking about, which, if you don't have your own children, is very important. It keeps your mind working actively, it prevents fixity and indifference. It's good to talk to people who are reading things for the first time. I like it when they come and say, 'Whitman is amazing!' or, 'I can't bear *Ulysses*'. . . . And then you start talking and arguing again about these works, which otherwise would have been settled and fixed in your mind, like museum pieces.

Ron Padgett

George Tysh

Ron Padgett's recent books include *The Big Something, Great Balls of Fire, Ted: A Memoir of Ted Berrigan,* a translation of *The Complete Poems of Blaise Cendrars, The Adventures of Mr & Mrs Jim & Ron,* a collaboration with artist Jim Dine, and a translation of Apollinaire's *Poet Assassinated.* From 1969 to 1978 he taught imaginative writing to students of all ages. For two years he directed the Saint Mark's Poetry Project in New York, before becoming publications director of Teachers & Writers Collaborative, for which he has edited many books on the teaching of imaginative writing. In 1996 David R. Godine will issue Padgett's *New & Selected Poems.* Padgett lives in New York City.

The Pleasures of Fried Shoes

When I started teaching imaginative writing, I had no experience as a teacher. But I had a lot of experience as a student, which helped me flip the coin over and become a teacher. Most of my teachers had liked me. That was what I responded to most, that they liked me and they treated me well and they praised me and told me I was very smart, but the ones that I liked best weren't necessarily those of the subjects I was interested in.

For instance, when I went to junior high school at the age of twelve, I wasn't what you would call a reader. I was smart, I'd done okay at school. But I was more interested in sports and girls and being popular. There are probably many reasons why I became a reader. One of them was puberty. It suddenly changed my way of looking at things. The whole world looked different and I think I became a little more introspective. Also my eyes went bad at that point. It was quite crushing for me because I couldn't be as active and I had to wear these horrible objects on my head. At that time wearing glasses was associated with bookishness, which may have actually contributed somewhat to my becoming introspective and self-conscious. But also I had a wonderful teacher, Miss Lily Roberts, for three straight years. Not an easy teacher, but she loved her subject. She loved writing, books, poetry, punctuation, spelling, sentence dia-gramming – she idolized it all. And it was as her student that I began to read books.

She was probably using the same techniques that the other teachers were using. At that time most of the teachers seemed to use the same methods. It was the attitude she brought to the material and to the students. She liked students. She really was rooting for us to do our best and I took a great fancy to her and started reading.

The first year she gave each of us a little chart called the reading wheel. It was a circle divided into pie wedges cut into it with a little tiny circle in the middle. Around the circumference of the circle, next to each wedge, was the name of a different subject category – sports, humour, non-fiction, poetry – and each of these wedges was filled with little circles. When we read a book, we would have to decide which category it fitted into. And we would choose a circle inside that wedge, put a number in the circle, and then key it to a list outside the circle in which we put down the title and author of the book. Her requirement was that we read . . . was it three books in a year? Something like that. That was asking a lot of some of the students.

In grade school I had read excerpts from books in our class readers, but I had never been required to do any independent reading. In Miss Roberts's class we chose the books ourselves, but we were supposed to develop a balanced look to our reading wheel, not just read books about sports, or we would be all lopsided. So the graphic display of the wheel had an effect on me. The first year I read the minimum three books, one of which I'd actually read the year before, about a baseball hero of mine. But early the next year, all these little reading wheel circles started getting filled in like crazy. And in the final year it was just overflowing. I'd gone from reading a dog story for children to reading the *Iliad* two years later. So that was where I really took a big leap forward in my reading. I also read books about science and mathematics, biographies, and poetry.

By the time I was sixteen I knew that I wanted to be a writer. I had discovered contemporary literature: Jack Kerouac's novels and Allen Ginsberg's poetry. And then very quickly the so-called San Francisco renaissance poets, and then writers such as Robert Creeley, Charles Olson, the Black Mountain poets. And then suddenly it all branched out very quickly to other contemporary writers, such as Frank O'Hara.

It is so unthinkable that any of those writers could have appeared in the high school curriculum. In my senior year in high school I did a book report on Gregory Corso's *Gasoline* and the teacher just sat there with her jaw hanging open. She had no idea what I was talking about. What, is this poetry? I mean, Corso was using images such as 'fried shoes'. She had probably read Yeats and Frost, but when I read aloud lines like 'I pumped him full of lost watches,' she just said, 'It sounds very interesting, Ron.' She hadn't the foggiest notion what it was all about.

I really caught fire when I read *On the Road* and *Howl*. I knew their authors were alive right now. I had started to subscribe to magazines, rather fugitive little magazines, and saw the brand new work by these people coming out. And then at the age of sixteen I just really lost my mind and I decided to start my own literary magazine. I wrote to Allen Ginsberg and two weeks later got back a wonderful long poem 'My Sad Self' submitted to my magazine with an encouraging letter. Robert Creeley, Gilbert Sorrentino and others responded the same way. So I felt immediately in touch with the writers. On the one hand they seemed kind of god-like for me, on the other hand they didn't, because they answered my letter, they licked the stamp that went on the envelope! As opposed to, say, Dylan Thomas: he was dead and already in some kind of strange pantheon.

Of course it cuts both ways. With the pantheon, you can get a kind of strange awe and respect for what you're reading, which has its uses. But if you remain in awe of literature, you can't write it. You can't ever imagine that you too could write anything of any value because there is no way you could equal, say, John Milton, whose language is remote, whose diction is strange, and whose subject matter is alien. It doesn't have anything to do with *you* when you're looking at it from that point of view.

One idea behind Teachers & Writers Collaborative is that if we can get kids writing at an early enough age and really enjoying it and seeing that there is something rewarding in it for them, they see the relevance of it. They won't be easily put off by a great writer because they're writers too. The students in our programmes come out of the whole experience saying, I'm a writer. But if you don't write, you don't ever see the connection between reading and writing. You can't. If you're smart you guess it, but you don't really feel it.

In the university, students are asked to write about the great pieces of literature, but they are expected to write about them from the point of view of the professor and not from their own, as if they were proto-professors struggling to recreate certain intellectual structures, using a certain level of discourse, aping the kind of writing you'd see in scholarly journals. Unless your intention in life is to be a professor, there really isn't much point in it.

One of the most valuable lessons I had in college about of writing about literature was with a professor who actually wasn't a very good teacher. His remarks on seventeenth-century English literature weren't very edifying, and he had a kind of hang-dog manner. He was a Milton specialist and he was very bright, I knew that, but in class he just didn't come across very well. However, when it came time for us to write about literature, he didn't assign essays and term papers the way all the other professors did. He said, 'I want you to write a little bit about every author we read in this survey course. I want you to keep a sort of diary. Don't worry about spelling. Just keep it legible. You can say absolutely anything you want. All I want is your response to what you read, your genuine response. You can write a little bit or you can write a lot. But I would like you to write about every writer we read. And every two weeks I want you to hand in these things, just so I can see that you've done it. I may not even read them. You're not going to get a grade on them. You're going to get an overall grade.'

And that really did something for me. I loosened up and let go. If there was an author whose work I really didn't like, I would write things like 'This is the most boring pile of shit I've read all year.' I would actually write something that blatant! The other professors were asking me to write formal essays, which I was slowly learning how to do, while the teachers scrutinized every word, every paragraph, making you sweat. They were also introducing me to the idea of intellectual rigour which I hadn't really encountered before. They were actually very keen people, but they were fostering a writing style that didn't interest me very much. But when this guy gave us a fairly loose *modus operandi*, it carried over into the formal writing I was doing and all of a sudden I could write formally with a lot more ease and pleasure. Instead of trying to please the professor, ape him, write something that had a certain intellectual tone, I could actually say things that I was interested in saying.

My Shakespeare professor was like Miss Roberts: he made me crazy about Shakespeare, because he was crazy about Shakespeare. He loved Shakespeare. He was a short chubby man, wall-eyed and with a pointy nose, and he would burst into long quotations such as one of Juliet's soliloquies and you'd find yourself swooning at this short, fat, ugly Juliet. It made you actually just go crazy for her. But that was what it was about: professional enthusiasm and love for the work.

In my experience as a travelling poetry teacher, I learned that it isn't whether or not the teacher is young or hip or liberal, as opposed to old and square and conservative, it was just how much that teacher really liked the subject. I have gone into classes whose young attractive teacher has got a contemporary poetry anthology in the hip pocket and assumed that it is going to be great to work with her kids. But really she was wearing jeans because everybody else was, she had the anthology because she thought she should probably know something about it because a poet was coming into the class, and the old frumpy teacher's class often turned out to be a lot better. And even if her taste wasn't the same as mine and she thought that, say, Robert Frost was the greatest poet who ever lived and I didn't happen to agree, it didn't matter because what matters is she thought poetry was great, she loved it, she found a way to let it show in the classroom.

I guess there are a lot of teachers who never read out a line and say 'this is mysterious' or 'this is wonderful'. They read out a line and say 'Which part is the metaphor?'

I started working with young children because I was asked to. Kenneth Koch, who had done some extraordinary pioneering work for a year, called me up and said there's this school of little kids I've been teaching and it's been wonderful and I'm going on sabbatical and I want somebody to come in and substitute for me. I'd just been out of university a couple of years myself and I never wanted to get back in school as long as I lived; it was the last place on earth I wanted to be. My whole life had been in school and now I wanted to get out into what we call life. But Kenneth was very persuasive and talked me into going over to visit the school with him, and I loved it, just loved it because really there was excitement and pleasure in the work they were doing.

Later, when I started teaching older students as well, I used the same ideas, adapted, of course. I found that the older the students, the more difficult it was to teach them. High-school students tended to be suspicious, resistant, tradition-bound. They'd already been convinced that they weren't imaginative, that writing was boring and difficult. I never got any resistance from a eight-year old child: I could walk into a room and ten minutes later we were all writing poems together. High-school classes, you walk in the room and two to three days later they *start* to loosen up. They're a tough group.

There are a lot of ways to make the students see that literature is in fact relevant to their lives. Here's an example. Years ago I was working in a junior high school in a small town in South Carolina. The students were twelve or thirteen years old. It was the first time I'd worked with them. I started talking about vacations, how great it was to be out of school in summer and even better if you could go somewhere you always wanted to go, and I started talking about places I had always wanted to go to – Mongolia, for instance, or Ireland. I mentioned these places and how I had recurring fantasies about going there, what it would be like there and how nice it would be to just get up and go. This intrigued the students, partly because I was an adult talking about something personal and not teaching them anything! When they had warmed to the subject, I started to talk about certain writers who had written about this and I told them I'm a writer and I'd written about the fantasies of going somewhere and wanting to take somebody with me.

'Think about somebody you're really crazy about and how nice it would be to invite that person to go with you to this place,' I said. 'Recently I was talking about this idea with some kids in New York and we wrote about it, things like, "Oh come on, let's get in our big white Cadillac and drive to Las Vegas!"' I read them some student examples about going to exotic places and doing all these things, and in the midst of these examples I read them Marlowe's 'Come live with me and be my love'. I read in the same tone of voice as I'd read all the other examples and then I said, 'Okay, everybody, listen, you've got some paper there, write down something like this, just inviting somebody you like to go some place great with you, let yourself really go.'

They wrote some good pieces, which I read aloud. At the end of the class I took the Marlowe poem out and read it to them again and asked, 'Who do you think wrote this poem?' The class guessed that it was by a friend of mine in New York. It was so thrilling that they would think that Christopher Marlowe was a friend of mine in New York. If I had gone into that classroom and said, 'Christopher Marlowe is one of the great writers of English literature. I want you all to listen to this very carefully because I'm going to ask you some questions about this later.' Test, test, test. They'd have frozen up, they'd have felt that the poem was alien, outside their experience.

It's the old John Dewey child-centred education. Who are these people you're going to teach? And how are you going to teach them if you don't know who they are? This is particularly important for teaching younger students. With older students, straight lecturing, in which the teacher in no way accommodates the students, can also be memorable. I had one college professor whose every class period consisted of his reading a lecture. There were only thirty of us in the class, and his lectures were wonderful. He would get carried away with his reading, and you could see the spit flying off his lips, his enthusiasm just spilling over. He got very excited about his ideas, which in fact were pretty good ones. You could always tell which was the concluding sentence to a paragraph by the kind of momentum he slung into the idea; you could feel the flow of the syntax in his voice and the way he moved his body. It was wonderful. Of course he was talking about all these works which were terrific – medieval English literature – so that helped too, but again it was a question of style.

Kenneth Koch had a different style. He was teaching one course he had just invented called Twentieth-Century Comic Literature: Gertrude Stein's *Tender Buttons*, Joyce's *Ulysses*, Jarry's *Ubu Roi*, Firbank, Svevo, Machado de Assis, etc. Few of these books had ever been taught in the Columbia English Department and Gertrude Stein had never been taught anywhere in the university. Kenneth invented the course because he liked the books, but he was breaking new ground, so he did a certain amount of thinking on his feet. It was always very interesting to watch him get to that point in his thinking when he didn't know exactly how to say what he wanted to say, and you'd see him scratch his head, his eyes would roll up to the ceiling as if he was looking for an idea up there and you could actually see him thinking up there around the ceiling. It's a pleasure to be a student and to see somebody have an idea. It's one of the great things to be with someone who says: 'I've got an idea!' The same thing happens when you see somebody thinking, you see them light up; it's great.

Younger students tend to think that teachers know everything and have always known everything. It's the same with printed books. I've found that many students assume that printed books are perfect and that whoever wrote them wrote them down exactly the way they look there, that to write a book you first write a title and then you just write the rest till it says The End. The idea of revision doesn't occur to them. They think the book has sprung full-blown from the head of its author. Imagine the awe it would inspire to think that somebody wrote a book that way from start to finish.

Recently there has been a more progressive element in American education with regard to teaching writing. When I was doing a lot of work in the classroom with little kids, between 1969 and 1976, I and some other teaching writers began to realize that our discoveries were localized and that we should offer some writing courses for graduate students in education, the people who were soon going to be teaching little kids. The teachers we were encountering in schools were intimidated by the idea of dealing with 'original' writing. So we were hoping to offer a course in graduate schools. But the schools would have none of it, because, although we had artistic and literary credentials, none of us had doctoral degrees in education.

I suppose it's more of the old creative versus the academic syndrome. For instance, you can go to Columbia University for four years of undergraduate work and you can do graduate work there too. But now there's also a division called the MFA Programme, in which you can get a master's degree in writing, poetry and fiction. As I understand it, there has been a certain amount of wariness between the English and the writing departments. The English department of the college has tended to be suspicious of the 'creative' stuff on the grounds that it's not really a proper English programme. It's an arts programme. It's loosened up there a little, probably because Kenneth Koch teaches some creative writing courses in the English department. But I do know that around the country there's traditionally been a suspicion and rivalry between English departments and writing programmes.

I began by talking about a teacher I had in junior high school, but she wasn't the real reason I became a reader. The real reason I became a reader was because my parents, who were not literary people, were very generous in buying me comic books, and so even before I went to school I knew how to read. From comic books I learned that you went from left to right and that in those balloons the things were words and that they said things and the talk related to the pictures. It wasn't just that I could read; I really loved those books, I loved the way they looked. They were so beautiful. I loved the characters in them: little Nancy and the house her friend Sluggo lived in, and the transparency of Caspar the Friendly Ghost.

It was reading comic books that made me really like reading. They were not only a lot of fun to read but they were given to me as tokens of unconditional love. My parents bought me as many of them as I wanted. So I always had this great supply of them. I remember once when I was ill in bed, my father came in with a stack of about forty or fifty comic books – he'd driven all around town and collected them from different places – and just plunked them on the foot of my bed and said 'Here,' and then left. He didn't say, 'Reading is good for you, I hope you like these, and maybe we can go from this to reading real books, or serious books.' There were no strings attached whatsoever. I was ill, but I was in heaven.

Anne Waldman

Anne Waldman is a poet, performer, teacher, editor, translator and video-maker. For many years she was director of the Poetry Project at St Mark's Church In-the-Bowery in New York. She has worked with musicians, composers and dancers, and has twice won the Heavyweight Champion Poet award at the Poetry Bout sponsored by the Poetry Circus in Taos, New Mexico. She currently teaches at the Naropa Institute in Colorado, as well as performing in both the US and Europe. She has published many books of poetry, the most recent being *Iovis Omnia Plena.*

A Living and Breathing Organism

I TRAVEL AROUND to many colleges and universities as a guest of other writing programmes and notice that the Jack Kerouac School of Disembodied Poetics – the creative writing programme under the wing and auspices of the Naropa Institute – has a very different and often radical approach. Allen Ginsberg and I founded the poetics programme at the inception of Naropa in 1972, to represent, honour, contain, and continue the lineage of what I call the 'outrider' tradition. This is a tradition of experimental, outrageous, visionary poetics, honouring Sappho, Blake, the Sahajiya (India's erotic-mystical tradition of poetries), the Surrealists, troubadours and trobairitz (female troubadours), H.D., Gertrude Stein, the Objectivists and so on, to name a few of our poetic reference points. Of course we took this up to the present and have brought together over the past twenty years writers of many of the so-called 'schools' of the past half century – Black Mountain, New York School, Beats, San Francisco Renaissance. The sense at the Kerouac School is that you cannot hope to write anything of interest without reading, studying, honouring the wonderful iconoclasts of the past and the current masters who are alive and active right now. And the current poet's role is to preserve and guard those traditions, saving them from extinction, as well as be an active cultural worker in these post-modern Dark Ages. Naropa is based on Buddhist and contemplative principles and we take seriously the Boddhisattva's vow to 'liberate all sentient beings'. The study and writing of poetry can be a liberating path and is a skilful means to *gnosis*. We had some very distinct ideas about the premise for such a programme, one being Ezra Pound's adage about not taking criticism from anyone who has not written a notable work of art him- or herself. We also appreciate William Carlos Williams's 'no ideas but in things' which can ground the student in 'minute particulars', 'luminous details', close to the nose experience as a source for writing.

So most of our classes are reading as well as writing classes. We are not beholden to the workshop process, which seems self-referential and myopic. The writers who teach here teach their specialities. When Allen Ginsberg is in residence he teaches Blake, Whitman, Kerouac. Anselm Hollo, a poet and translator originally from Finland who is fluent in many languages, teaches a translation class, and Surrealist/Dada poetics and poetries. Andrew Schelling, poet and essayist who translates from the Sanskrit, teaches a class on the poetries of India, as well as a class on Pound's *Cantos*. Bobbie Louise Hawkins, who heads the prose track, teaches Colette, among others. Jack Collom teaches a class called Eco-poetics which looks at world literature in terms of an ecological bias. I work a good deal with the writing of Gertrude Stein as a challenge to students, a goad to them to break through their linear message-bound thinking. Ethnopoetics, the poetries of other cultures, is an important component here. I like to make huge, what I call 'resonant leaps' in the reading. We might be studying H.D. and her so-called 'imagism' and flash back to Sappho, or ahead to some of the lyrical poems of the contemporary poet Diane DiPrima.

We imitate some of the writers we study. We get close to them. I've taught a class over the years entitled 'Shapely Writing' where we look at and write in traditional forms. We start with the Greek ode – which was originally a sung and danced poem – and trace it from Homer and Pindar to the Chilean poet Pablo Neruda, who wrote a collection called *Odas Elementales* – odes to natural things. Then we might look at Frank O'Hara's odes, which are quite freewheeling, yet still retain a celebratory, high tone. So you get a sense of progression from grandiose poems honouring returning heroes and warriors to a poem dedicated to the poet's socks.

Then we write odes ourselves. Or we might look at the Ubi Sunt form of François Villon and write our own laments on the theme of 'Mais où sont les neiges d'antan?' We might study the history and form of the sonnet, the villanelle, the pantoum, and so on, with the intention of writing them ourselves. Then the discussion of the creative work is more exciting, and scholarly, for that matter. I want students to use the library! We have a new library at Naropa, named for director emeritus Allen Ginsberg, and we take our poetry holdings seriously – they are there to be *used*!

Although the tastes of the faculty vary, our commitment to the act of reading as well as writing is strong. I appreciate my own undergraduate education which was at Bennington College in Vermont, where I worked with writers such as Howard Nemerov and Bernard Malamud. Nemerov taught Blake from the point of view of an active poet. We had close readings of texts and the feedback on the work was also strong. Bennington was useful in that it made use of the 'don' system. The idea of apprenticeship is important in creative work. You work with particular people who hold a particular wisdom rather than work with particular structures. We want our students to be familiar with the lineages we try to honour and continue. The books are teachers as well. All the folk who teach at Naropa are comfortable with this approach. They don't set themselves up in any pretentious way. A bit like master and novice, but not as heavy-handed as the traditional guru-student situation. I personally experience the study and writing of poetry as a spiritual path. And certainly the Buddhist backdrop of the Naropa Institute is commensurate with this approach.

We give grades to our students, but we also give written, personal feedback as well as conversational feedback. I often give a page or two of criticism on the manuscripts students present at the end of a semester for my classes. They each make a book. This is often a handsome production, hand-sewn, illustrated. It anticipates the required thesis of creative work they complete at the end of two years. All our faculty meet with students on a regular basis. During the summer session, students meet one to one with guest faculty for a critique of their work. Some of our students want to go on to further graduate work, so grades *do* matter from that point of view, but the intimate feedback is perhaps the better response, and most useful. We also have several works-in-progress gatherings each semester in which students present their work orally – in spoken performance, as it's called – for critique. Students are also quite responsive to each others' writing, and there are many outlets around town – readings, series, publication – to be involved with. I grade on the creative work, the research work, the class presentations.

We are moving towards offering classes in creative non-fiction as well. Charles Olson's book on Melville, *Call Me Ishmael,* or Susan Howard's *My Emily Dickinson,* are luminous touchstones in this area. I think this kind of writing is as vital as creative fiction and poetry. The creative or investigative essay may be elucidating in the way poetry is. Wrestling with ideas, facts, luminous details is rigorous and stimulating. It's good that students understand that writing a critical paper can be a creative event and that it should be passionate. One of our students investigated the very experimental, somewhat unsung writer Mina Loy, who was active in the 1920s. She was British, led a fascinating life, was married to Arthur Cravan, the surrealist poet and boxer, then disappeared into relative anonymity to Aspen, Colorado. Hedy Berger, our student, wrote a very personal response, working directly with Loy's work and what other people had written about her. She unearthed a taped interview which she transcribed. She somehow got close to Loy's own voice in her work. It was a passionate piece of work, which also influenced Hedy's writing in a positive way. Another student, Eleni Sikelianos, took a similar approach in her study of Lorine Niedecker. I like research by poets. It's lopsided. It can be built upon. It is not a closed system of scholarship, dry and analytical. If our students are working with contemporary writers, we encourage them to make contact, arrange to interview them, correspond, unearth unpublished documents. Sometimes the personal, passionate, gut response may be problematic. We had one student who was too far over an edge in that direction. He was trying to 'crack' Blake, taking hallucinogenic drugs and reading Blake and masturbating into a bonfire. I really drew the line. His research became indulgent and confessional and not that interesting ultimately. Allen Ginsberg's poem 'Sunflower Sutra' – his vision of hearing Blake's voice – arrived after masturbation, so you never know. There was obviously some resonance there.

I encourage students to work with writers who have not been written about to death. Secondary sources are obviously useful, but we want students to do their own thinking, make the connections themselves. The whole thing is not just dependent on other people's opinions and views. If you're just regurgitating other people's opinions based on their research and a lot of their opinions are already third or fourth hand, you're not learning anything. It's hard to describe how you teach people the skill to trust their own opinion, to be honest about what's really their reaction and what's someone else's. It's hard to teach creative thinking, to show someone how to reach insight and realization about a piece of writing. I remember at Bennington the most exciting work I did was when I felt I was making the connections, when after exhaustive reading and rereading, suddenly I understood. Some students never get there and you can't really tell them how to get there. You can just give them somewhat of a map. You can give them a sense of what it is to live with the text, by reading, rereading it, getting inside it, following the writer's allusions and references and looking things up. Close reading in that way is incredibly exciting, working with etymological dictionaries, with other languages or with a whole tradition. There are so many underpinnings to some of those texts.

Zukowsky's *A*, for example, or Olson's *Maximus* poems. There are so many directions you can go. William Carlos Williams's *Paterson* is an excursion into a real place, a mythological place and also the poet's mind. It's a collage of other voices. Out of our reading of this comes a range of writing experiments. I have students research their home towns, their family lineages. I have them recount dreams, overheard conversations. I have them pick up on other languages, interview their parents, and so on. I have a list of hundreds of writing experiments. Study the planet Mars for a year, write a poem that looks like a pyramid, write in the same spot at the same time of day every day for a week, ride a bus and keep writing, go to a museum and sit in front of a painting for an hour and write. All these experiments are designed to have you interact with the phenomenal world and get you out of your neurotic ego-mind which is often churning up stale reruns, stale clichés, confessional doldrums. Wake up!

Our American system has made poetry anathema. You never experience the poem. It's rarely read out loud. It's paraphrased. You dissect it, you don't live inside it. That's why we have our students get up and read the work aloud. A poem is a living and breathing organism. That's the universe, that's the event. Not what you extrapolate and sum up and paraphrase. You do need handles however, you need permission to explore poetry and poetics in this way. You need creative writers and teachers who can point the way so that you can trust your own mind and sensibility to get inside the poem and understand that it's not just an obscure item that some poet is trying to torture you with.

There are various ideas I've tried for helping students get inside a text. Cannibalizing Proust, for example. I get students to perform chance operations or permutations off a text. For instance, maybe every tenth page, from the last ten lines I will pick out a word at random, whatever my eye lands on, and try to make some sort of sense of that, or see what I freely associate with that. Or you can pick a column of words down the page, surround them with blank space on a page, or repeat them like a chant. You can intercut with other texts. William Burroughs's and Brion Gysin's book *The Third Mind* is an interesting guide here. John Cage, Jackson MacLow and others have been quite active with these kinds of approaches. Responding with one's own imaginings was also encouraged in the workshop. I often feel like I am having a dialogue with other writers, others texts, in my work, in my head. A dialogue with a whole world of language! You might randomly spot a word in a dictionary which leads into vast meditation, conversation. My long poem 'Iovis' (literally 'of Jove') is a lengthy argument with male energy in all its guises.

I was working recently with a group of MFA students who wanted to pursue more radical experiments. We were working out of my home, just six students; it was a real luxury. Sometimes I just put on a tape and just said, 'Respond to this.' Or we'd look at a form and dissect it or deconstruct it in a way, do an upside down villanelle, or play around on top of structures. Or we'd use the idea of a found object or a found text, take something very mundane out of a *Popular Mechanics* magazine or a magazine on medical practices, or some text that's not your own and has its own distinct vocabulary and frame of reference, and then take it apart or get inside it in a way that you devise or intercut it with something of your own. Or take a Shakespeare sonnet and intercut it with some really innocuous text.

Students don't lose respect for Shakespeare or Proust by doing these sorts of experiments. They are certainly smarter than that. There's a sense, however, of being able to challenge the so-called canon, or of getting inside it, raiding it to understand it. To add to the continuum. Great literature is often presented in a sanctimonious fashion which is off-putting. From the point of view of many younger women, it's also male-dominated, that canon. I often joke about stealing the poet men's secrets and dancing on their corpses singing my own song! I am against annihilation or appropriation, or appropriation that doesn't cite sources, doesn't engage in a 'play' of sorts. A writing that doesn't acknowledge its debt is spurious. These are strange times, difficult times. These are also multicultural times. Can one write anything new? It's a good question. The need to deconstruct, experiment, is healthy. To shift gears, to get off the Eurocentric schema is healthy. I remember teaching Shakespeare in a Black ghetto in Philadelphia many years ago. How was it relevant to experience in that world? We played with the sound, with the richness of the language. It's still a question, although something worked since we acted out scenes in this case. The postmodern Dark Ages is a time for bards and seers to think creatively about ways to keep certain flames alive and to engage in an exalted expression themselves that is rooted in sound and the oral tradition and the magics of language. And that alleviates suffering.

Many of our students aspire to be writers, and many of them, whatever comes of their own writing, will have careers or lives in the field of writing and literature, in teaching, editing, publishing, translating, performance, video, arts administration, social action network activities. We have an Outreach programme where students do writing workshops in prisons, in homes for the elderly, with the homeless, with AIDS victims. Everyone has a story to tell. Our students take the experiments we work with at the Kerouac School into many different arenas. What we are achieving, I think, is a sense of community as writers, as artists, as investigators, as cultural workers. Everyone who comes through here has, in a sense, taken a vow to poetry as an *engaged practice* which entails study, reading, writing and taking something of the inspiration out into the world. We can be active in the world. Our graduates stay in touch, they stick around, they return. The webwork out of this nexus is extensive. The vision of keeping the world safe for poetry is extremely compelling.

Kenneth Koch

Kenneth Koch taught schoolchildren to write poetry in a New York public school in the late 1960s and early 1970s and wrote two books about it: *Wishes, Lies and Dreams* and *Rose, Where Did You Get That Red?* He has taught at Columbia University for many years. A new book of his poems, *One Train* and a selected poems, *On the Great Atlantic Rainway* were published in 1994. Kenneth Koch was born in Cincinnati, Ohio, but for most of his life has lived in New York City.

The Butterfly and the Rhinoceros

THE FIRST TIME I taught a poetry writing workshop was at the New School for Social Research. It was long before I taught at Columbia and the students who came to this workshop were adults which meant they were anywhere from eighteen to seventy. To some extent when I started to teach I was teaching people to write from the point of view of a style that John Ashbery and Frank O'Hara and I wrote in. It wasn't exactly a common style, but we had something in common. I wanted to bring into the workshop the experiences I'd had outside of school which had helped me to be a better poet, such as reading other poets and being influenced by them, trying new forms, using ways of writing that brought unconscious experiences in, such as my dreams, and so on.

Then I got a job at Columbia and within three or four years I was teaching a writing course there. I used the same kind of techniques I'd used with the adults at the New School. It was after I'd been doing that for a number of years that I taught in the schools. I used very few texts outside of those that the children wrote. I would tell the children to write a Wish Poem and I'd get them excited about their wishes and then I would use the Wish Poems of the fourth graders to interest the second graders, the Wish Poems by the second graders to interest the third graders and so on. Later I found a way to bring already written great poetry by adults into the classroom. I taught Blake's 'The Tyger'. I read the poem aloud. I explained everything in it that the children didn't understand. I dramatized it a little bit so that they would understand it more. I got to where Blake says: 'What immortal hand or eye / Could frame thy fearful symmetry?', and nobody in the sixth grade knew what symmetry was. I started making up a drawing on the board: symmetry is when something is exactly the same on this side as it is on the other, and then I got a bright idea. I said, 'I have good news for you, you're all symmetrical, try it out.' I don't think anybody's been so excited about symmetry since Blake. So the very things the children didn't understand were exciting to them.

After we'd gone through the whole poem, including the penultimate stanza which I never completely understood – I don't think it's fair not to teach things one doesn't completely understand, if, after all, one has gotten a lot out of them oneself: 'When the stars threw down their spears, / And water'd heaven with their tears.' I'm not sure I know what Blake's talking about there. I presume he's talking about the end of the war in heaven. But the kids in the sixth grade had a pretty good idea and they said, 'Well, it sounds like, after God made the world, it rained so that things would grow, and the spears are like lightning.'

Then I told the children to write a poem, like Blake's, in which they imagined they were talking to a mysterious beautiful creature, even a dangerous sort if they liked. For a magic moment they could communicate with it, they could ask it anything they wanted. They asked if there could be more than one animal and if the animal could answer back – one of the points of Blake's poem is that the animal doesn't answer – but I said yes, because that it would make it more enjoyable and seem more real. I think that there are three or four poems inspired by Blake's 'The Tyger' which show that the children had a better reading experience of Blake than most people do in college classes, mostly because they paid so much attention to the details of the poem, and to feeling like it and writing like it. Some of the poems they wrote are really good.

Children learn more from participating and acting than from merely listening. There's a lot they didn't understand about Blake but there's a lot that they did. You know when you're about ten years old you're closer to believing you can talk to a dog. Children are much closer to Blake in one way than adults are. After I taught this poem, I looked in a textbook, a ninth grade textbook which had Blake's poem in it, and above it in bold black letters much larger than the type of the poem it said: 'The tiger is a symbol of God's wrath. Now read this poem.' That's really something to take the experience away from the children.

I had a very touching experience when I was teaching children. There was a little Black girl named Fontessa Moore in third grade and Fontessa was obviously a lively, spirited little girl and she was eight years old and she wouldn't write a poem. All the other children were writing and I tried to cajole her into writing too. So in the second or third class the subject was colours. I had told the students to write a poem about the colours of things that don't really have colours. I said, 'Close your eyes' and I'd whistle and say, 'What colour is that sound?' and they'd say, 'Red.' 'Green.' 'Blue.' Fontessa wrote a technically perfect poem about how Black and white people might be different outside, but they're really the same inside and they should love each other. I thought she'd probably copied it out of a book or a magazine. But it would be silly to accuse her, an eight-year-old, of plagiarism. I said 'Fontessa, this is a perfectly made poem but this has been said so many times, don't you think it's sort of corny, it doesn't seem very interesting, it seems kind of boring and I think you're very funny, why don't you write poems that are more like you?' So she said, 'You mean I can write a funny one' and I said 'Yes.' So then Fontessa began to write in other classes and a lot of words were spelt wrong and obviously she hadn't been willing to write because she was very bad at spelling.

David Frost used to have a weekly show and he found out about my work and invited me and four or five of my star students on to his show. Fontessa was there and he admired her very much and actually invited her back on the show a second time. When she was in sixth grade, in emulation of my book *Wishes, Lies and Dreams*, she made up her own book of poems which she made copies of and a dedications page on which she thanked people, and she said, 'I want to thank my parents, I want to thank Mr Ron Padgett but most of all I want to thank Mr Kenneth Koch. I used to think I never would amount to anything, but he taught me that spelling didn't matter and I love him for that.' It makes me very sad when I think of it, you know, the harm it's done to children in school, putting spelling before expression. So somehow you have to avoid that trap. I tell the children, 'Don't pay any attention to spelling or anything like that when you're writing. At the end of the term I want you to turn in a notebook of your poems; by that time you can find out how the words are spelt.' Another thing I do is if I collect the poems, the children know in advance I'm not going to make any marks on them. It's hard for teachers to resist marking misspelt words. Also, you don't want to write comments on all their poems because even if you write 'this is wonderful' the kids will know you're lying. Sometimes they're not wonderful and you don't want to write 'this is stupid' so I try to get it all done in class. The kids read their poems, we respond to them, and it's all over.

Someone wrote to Wallace Stevens one summer when he was in his fifties or sixties and said, 'What have you been reading,' and he wrote back and said 'Well I haven't really done much reading but I've been doing a lot of writing which seems to me a very intense form of reading.' At Columbia I teach a course in modern poetry in which students do imitations of four or five of the writers we study every term and they all think it's the best part of the course. You know one can talk for a long time about inscape and sprung rhythm and so on but when you have to turn into Gerald Manley Hopkins and crowd all those words into a line you really know what it feels like. You feel the excitement and you read him better; you get the music.

Another course I teach at Columbia is called 'Form in Poetry.' I start with ballads and then go on to sonnets by Wyatt, Sydney, Spenser and Shakespeare. Then I do Shakespeare's songs, Campion's songs, Jonson's songs, John Donne, and I go through the Romantics on my way to modern poetry and the subject is the form of poetry. So we talk a little bit about pentameters, rhyme schemes, stanzas, but the interesting thing about the course is that instead of writing papers the students do a lot of poetry writing. They write extensively in the style and in the form of every poet that we study and it seems a wonderful way to learn literature.

I do have them write an essay at the end of the term because it helps make them organized, but I have them pick one of the imitations that they've done or write a new one and write a piece of bogus scholarship in which they claim they've discovered this manuscript and demonstrate whether or not it's genuine – that is, genuinely by Keats, Shakespeare, or whomever. I let them have one page to be silly and then they have to write five or ten pages in which they're serious.

You do whatever you can to make literature something that belongs to students rather than something that is distant, remote. One way to make it belong to them is to have them write it and not to treat it with so much respect that it's unapproachable.

Of course, there are limits to students' – or anyone's – ability to write like the poets I was teaching, but these limits are instructive, too. In my Form in Poetry class I was having the students write sonnets in the style of Shakespeare. First I had them practise writing the first lines of sonnets – you know the first lines of Shakespeare's sonnets are like trumpet calls – 'Let me not to the marriage of true minds' or 'When to the sessions of sweet silent thought'; they're very grand. Then I taught them how to write the couplets, the sort of soft thoughtful conclusion and how to construct the whole thing, and one young woman said after having tried, 'There's something that I'm finding it very hard to get and that's that he seemed so confident, with the world so much in his control. The world doesn't seem to me that way.' I thought that was brilliant. It led to some very interesting perceptions of Shakespeare's poems.

If I taught an introduction to poetry, I would start off with a few poems that I like and I would let everybody have a copy of the poem and I would read the poem and say, 'What do you think?' Poetry is written in a different way from the way almost all other things are written. Poetry is deliberately suggestive rather than definitive. You don't read poetry to find out how to get to the door or how to open a can or how to play tennis. You read poetry for some other reason. Therefore the language may seem vague and may make you excited, happy or unhappy, or thoughtful without your knowing why. The first response to a good poem is certainly not to understand it intellectually. The best way to understand one poem by Yeats is to read ten poems by Yeats. The same thing with a new friend who starts talking to you and you don't know if he's serious, if he's joking or what. You find out after you've talked to the person for a while. So, I'd say to the students, 'I'd just like you to listen to this poem. I'll read it twice – it's almost impossible to understand a poem the first time you hear it or read it. Then you just tell me something you like about it because the first step in understanding a work of art is to like it, to get pleasure from it, because art is constructed so as to give pleasure, that's the nature of its construction. A good analogy is music. If you listen to a piece of Mozart or Stravinsky and you don't feel pleasure, either Mozart or Stravinsky is not any good or you're not understanding what's going on, you're not hearing the harmonies or dissonances that are supposed to make something happen to you. Sometimes I can read a poem and understand it immediately and even imitate it. But it takes a long time to be able to do that and there are still poems by Wallace Stevens and even Yeats that I don't understand.'

We were reading a very difficult early poem by Yeats, 'The Rose of the World' in my class at Columbia once: 'Who dreamed that beauty passes like a dream? / For these red lips, with all their mournful pride, / Mournful that no new wonder may betide . . .' To me, and later to my students, the poem is close to incomprehensible. Poetry is so seductive, it's so pretty on the surface, that it's very hard to understand what it says, there's this dazzle, it's like trying to see what the sun is made of. We read the poem and I said, 'You may not understand it, it may be incomprehensible at first, but is there anything you like about it?' Finally somebody raised his hand and said, 'I like the way this guy talks as though what he's saying is very important.' That seemed to me a wonderful perception about Yeats's style and tone and a good way to start talking about his poem.

When I read the beginning of *Paradise Lost* to my fifth and sixth graders, I said 'What do you think of that: Of man's first disobedience, and the fruit / Of that forbidden tree'? Some little girl in the back row raised her hand, a very skinny little girl, and she said, 'It sounds like the preacher.' I thought this simply stated version of a recognition of the ceremonious nature of Milton's language was awfully good.

But to change education is really tough. I thought I was making a big difference with my work in teaching children to write poetry and it's made some difference but sometimes I felt it was like being a butterfly trying to influence a rhinoceros. It's tough. I had a friend who worked in the Southampton Library – Southampton is a pretty sophisticated community – but she said that my book *Wishes, Lies and Dreams* had come up for purchase by the library, but they decided against it because in it I said that spelling shouldn't matter for children when they wrote poetry.

In my modern poetry class at Columbia I used to give one long paper at the end of the term. But there were so many flaws in these papers – it's hard to write about poetry. The first and most natural response to reading a good poem is not to write a critical essay about it. The most natural response is to write a poem or call up a friend and read the poem, or read more poems or be excited but certainly not to write a critical essay, although it's wonderful to write clearly. But it's not easy. So I changed my assignments because I was getting papers at the end of the term in which the writers didn't know how to give evidence and didn't know what they were supposed to say about a poem. What I'm doing currently is having the students write three or four short papers. In the first they take a poem that we haven't discussed in class and do a prose paraphrase of it, and then write a two page essay saying in detail which version is better, the prose paraphrase or the poem, and why. The students learn a great deal about what you can't get into a paraphrase. Of course what the essay turns out to be about is what the way in which meaning is communicated by line, metre, repetition, transitions, strange juxtapositions and so on.

I teach some poets in translation. I resisted this for years. People say you don't get anything from poetry in translation; poetry is lost in translation. Nonetheless I don't know ancient Greek and I can still get something out of Homer and anyway twentieth-century poetry is international. I mean if you don't know Rilke and Lorca and Pasternak, you don't know what's going on. A number of my students know a foreign language, so one assignment I give them – which is voluntary – is to translate a poem of which there are two other translations. They give me the three translations, theirs and the other two and the essay of five to ten pages is on why their translation is the best of the three. One question I always have on the modern poetry exam is this: I print a poem ('Leda and the Swan', say) and ask the students to imagine that three other poets have also written poems on this subject. Describe their poems, quote from them as much as you can and justify your opinion. So I give the students a chance to be creative in exams. I have to make the exams interesting otherwise it's very tedious to grade them.

Another question that I like a lot is I take for example a poem by Yeats, 'Among School Children' and I write a rhyming-couplet version which makes the main idea extremely clear. The question I ask is: which version of Yeats's poem do you prefer and why? I try to develop the students' taste. I am always asking them how they like a particular poem. I tell them some things that could conceivably be wrong with it: isn't Lawrence in bad taste, a bit vulgar, corny? Isn't Hopkins a little over-excited? because I want them to participate in the whole thing.

When I teach poetry writing, I never give people grades on the works that they write, I just write comments and in my academic classes where the students write poems as sort of a sideline, I don't give A, B, C, and I don't lower a student's grade because he or she doesn't write good poetry. Spelling and punctuation wouldn't have any effect on my grading of the writing of poetry or stories but it probably would have an effect if I were teaching a course like teaching people to write simple prose. One has to train people to go out into society and be effective; they have to learn to spell and punctuate, though a course in modern literature is hardly an appropriate place to do that. It makes it hard to enjoy literature.

Eoin Bourke

Eoin Bourke was born in Dublin in 1939. He first studied architecture at University College Dublin and then worked in London as a hospital porter. He travelled through Europe, worked as an English teacher in Spain and settled in Munich where he worked as a postman, actor and radio broadcaster. He is Professor of German at University College Galway and has published widely on a variety of themes. He is married to the poet Eva Bourke and has three children.

To Activate the Crowd

IN THE GERMAN Department of University College Galway student numbers are still manageable. In a first year lecture there might be sixty, in a second or third year lecture about thirty. Even with the larger groups of sixty I try to provoke personal responses from the students to avoid the situation of purely passive note-taking. I put the students in a small theatre which has banked seating, so that their faces are all clearly visible. Initially, I have a problem urging them to move down from the back benches to the front so that they're within speaking range. It takes about three or four lectures to get them to do so, but eventually when their faces are more or less at eye level, or slightly above it, quite a lively discussion takes place. They respond a lot – indeed, sometimes I can't hear the individual contributor because they're all talking together. I'm delighted about that. That's the way I like to do it, to activate the crowd. I don't know if I would call it a technique. I go about it in a simple way.

My literature hour with the first year is a poetry lecture, for want of a better title, or rather a poetry discussion hour, and poetry gives rise to a specific problem of its own because the students come in to college having crammed Yeats's 'Sailing to Byzantium' and other texts which they don't understand for their Leaving Certificate, and as a result they often have a deep hatred for poetry. This is particularly true of the male students, who consider poetry slightly sissy and associate the wrong things with it – they think it's to do with 'lofty' things, sentimentality, love and death. So I begin with texts which are completely off-beam and nothing like anything they would have seen before. I use an author called Rudolf Otto Wiemer who wrote texts – you can't even call them poems – which masquerade as grammatical exercises. One of them is entitled 'Temporal Clauses' and begins:

> When we were six we had the measles.
> When we were fourteen we had war.
> When we were twenty we had love problems.

The lines are all of exactly the same structure with only two words changing in each: the age and the complaint. But the complaints operate on different levels and the students can grasp that pretty well straightaway. I ask them is there something strange about referring to measles and war in one breath in exactly the same kind of syntactical framework? Through this they get an idea of stylistic registers and the difference in scale of the problems being focused upon. And the text continues:

> When we were thirty we had children.
> When we were thirty-three we had Adolf.
> When we were forty we had air-raids.
> When we were forty-five we had rubble.

Then I ask who are these 'we'? Of course the key line is 'When we were thirty-three we had Adolf', and then the coin drops. The one thing everyone knows is that Adolf Hitler came to power in 1933. (Students know an awful lot about Hitler; they're fascinated by him.) So they deduce that the 'we' are some group whose age is coincidental with the years of the century and therefore what is meant is modern German Man, if you want to use that word. So I bring them straight into the text like that. I think it's very important not to give any introduction that might pre-empt independent thinking on their part.

Then some of them want to know more about Wiemer because they are used to a biographical approach to poetry, and I say that I know nothing about him, but that we can deduce from the text some things about the way he thought. Then I contextualize – that's the next step. I give them the date of the poem, which is 1972, and tell them about the years preceding it, from the Auschwitz and Treblinka trials of 1963-64 to the student rebellion of 1968, as a way of illustrating why Wiemer's generation became so critical of their fathers' generation in the course of the 1960s.

I try to draw the information out of the students by inducing them to read more attentively than they're used to. I try to get them keyed into the idea of reading a text closely and deducing meaning by going out from the text to the context. I say that the biography of the writer isn't necessarily all that important. Poets use codes to signal that there's something beneath the surface-text and I try to get the students to pick up those signals and to decode them. This Rudolf Otto Wiemer piece is very good for illustrating the difference between surface-text and sub-text. The surface-text is a grammatical exercise, but they all quickly realize that it's in fact a historical critique of the German people, which then becomes the sub-text. I ask them, 'What's the first signal that there is a sub-text?' 'Well, Adolf, and 33.' So you can teach a lot on the basis of this terribly simple text. (I use very few texts, maybe three very short ones in the space of an hour.) Needless to say it's very helpful that it's immediately comprehensible to first-year students. I tell them what I mean by 'sub-text' by putting a diagram on the board with a surface-text surrounded by different layers of context, like an onion, the individual circles forming the autobiographical context, the socio-historical context, the literary context. Signals (metaphors, images etc.) light up in the surface-text, travel out to one or more of the contextual layers around it, bounce off and down to a sub-text beneath. To get a full picture, you have to be acquainted with the contextual layers too.

I choose texts for first year with an eye to their syntax, their simplicity and their accessibility. Then I begin to peel away the layers and show that in fact it's a more complex text than they thought, but I do it so gradually that they can accompany me on the way. I don't go too fast or overload them with too much information at any given moment. But the main thing is to go out from the text to the context. And of course they see that the reason I choose a text like that is to break down their stereotypes of poetry. On a few occasions I sent them away from the first session telling them to bring back a definition of poetry for me. I said they could go to the reference section of the library if they wanted or they could do it out of their own head. Those who came up with their own definitions were exactly like those who'd found one in the reference section – they defined poetry as lyrical and sublime and to do with beauty, nature, transcendence – and of course they all think that poetry is extremely personal and confessional. So I give them a text like Wiemer's and ask, 'Is this sublime? Is it a poem about the poet?' Or, 'Who are the "we"? Is the poet the spokesperson of that group?' And they come to the conclusion that he's not; he stands outside them and dissociates himself from them. The 'we' is a persona, the collective persona of the post-war German people whom the author despises and criticizes for their undifferentiating and unanalytical view of recent history. And so the students begin to relativize their prejudices about poetry and see that it can have a more immediate bearing on reality and that there can be more fun attached to decoding it and searching through the layers of meaning for the sub-text.

I always project the texts on to screens. That way we're all looking in the same direction, we're all looking at the first line as we're talking about it. I can effectively say, 'Where in that line does something strange happen?' if we're all looking at it, whereas if the students have the text in front of them they're looking down at their desks and I'm talking to the tops of their heads. I show them concrete poems which are quite witty and unconventional, or nonsense poetry, or *Lautgedichte* – that is, aural poems that depend on recitation to make sense. A good example of this is the kind of text written by the eccentric Austrian writer Ernst Jandl, who does things like taking a polysyllabic word of some import, breaking it down into its components and jumbling them about with the result that the word is stripped of its significance and is made to sound ridiculous. I preface this by saying that when I was a child and had nothing to do, I would occasionally repeat my own name over and over and over again until I had reached the point where it sounded so ridiculous that my identity seemed to wither away or disappear and I'd be left wondering what kind of ridiculous noise people had put on me and ask myself, 'Am I that noise?' Jandl does something similar with Napoleon's name in a text called 'Ode to N'. It only dawns on the listener at an advanced stage of the reading that N is Napoleon as the text begins with bizarre and jumbled segments of the name:

lepn
nepl
lepn
nepl
lepn
nepl
o lepn
o nepl
nnnnnnnn
lopn
paa
lopn
paa

and goes on for three pages like that. If you want to derive a subtext from this, then it's probably anti-heroism, making the French national hero and conqueror of the world sound utterly absurd. Jandl does the same with the word 'philosophy', extracting highly incongruent meanings from its components:

viel
vieh
o
so
viel
vieh
o
so
vieh
sophie

This, at its face value, means 'many cattle, oh so many cattle, oh so cattle, Sophie'. I ask the students what could the author have intended with this fragmentation of the word. Presumably, Jandl is making anarchic fun of the loftiness of philosophy or of people being too academically serious or élitist about anything.

I usually have worked out a programme for a well-rounded hour to give the students the feeling that they're going away with some new experience. A lot of them respond. Some of them even come up and say, 'That was fantastic' or, 'That was great fun.' I go to the extent of making a fool of myself, shouting out the mad sounds 'paa – noo – paa – noo – papaa – noo – nonoo – nononoo – nonononoo – paa' etc. There's a famous text by the same author called 'schtzngrmm' which is entirely devoid of vowels and begins:

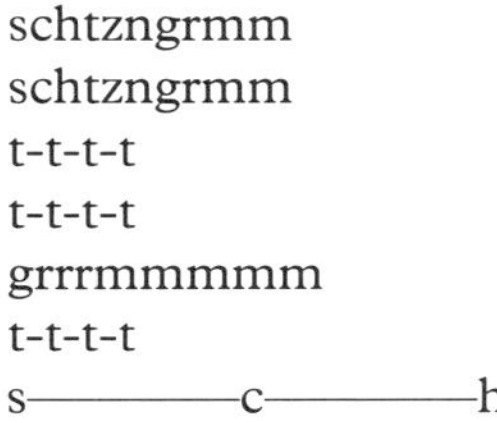
schtzngrmm
schtzngrmm
t-t-t-t
t-t-t-t
grrrmmmmm
t-t-t-t
s———c———h

After reading it out, I ask the students, 'What was that?' On the page it doesn't look like anything, it's just a series of letters, but when they've heard it they realize it reproduces the sound of warfare, and I ask, 'What kind of warfare?' 'Well, the older kind of warfare.' Then I reveal to them that the title is a distortion of the word *Schützengraben* which means a trench, a war trench, and the text is a critique of war. Even the lack of vowels conveys the metallic coldness of war. The piece ends up with the sound 't-tt'. I ask what could be meant by that, what vowel would you supply in the context that we've been discussing to make sense of the last word-fragment? And they immediately come up with the word *tot*, dead, perhaps meaning that the person listening to all these sounds in the trench has lost his life in the last line, thus bringing the 'poem' to an end.

About half those lectures are unexaminable and the other half are examinable. For instance, the 'grammatical exercises' by Rudolf Otto Wiemer are examinable: you can put three on a page and ask the students to search for the sub-text. I tend to alternate between serious and examinable lectures (Wiemer, Enzensberger) and unexaminable 'fun' lectures (Jandl, Morgenstern). That way I bring a bit of play and adventure into things. That's particularly important in the first year to soften them up and break down barriers, but also to combat the exam-orientation of the students. I try to bring poetry off its hieratic pedestal, to make it more accessible. This year, for instance, I gave them a whole series of semantically very simple poems by German guest workers – Turks, Italians, Lebanese, Yugoslavians, all writing in German about the situation of the so-called *Gastarbeiter* in present-day Germany. I grouped the poems in such a way that one group is about the dread of German bureaucracy and of receiving the letter from the authorities that you're being expelled, and another one is about the contempt of German co-workers for your native language, as if it were an inferior language, and the demand that you should speak in German, and that kind of thing: everyday alienation and racism. And so, having shown them a text and discussed with them what it means – one or two of them will have been in Germany and will have picked up some sense of this aspect of German life – I bring a lot of my own personal history into it.

I lived in Germany for thirteen years, and when I went there first, Ireland was not yet a member of the EEC, so I had to go along to the police station every year to get my resident's permit renewed. Sometimes they would arbitrarily decide that it wasn't going to be renewed, or even summon me and tell me that I have to leave the country immediately because I was discovered to be working and studying at the same time. I tell them about that experience to make the texts more experiencable. I give them background information about the number of *Gastarbeiter*, the reasons why they were fetched in the first place – and they were actually fetched to cater for the needs of the German economy, they didn't go there of their own accord. I give the students a detailed history of the *Gastarbeiter* problem and they respond very well to that. This is a new part of the course, and of the two questions that I put on the exam, some ninety per cent answered the one on Gastarbeiter poetry because they identified very closely with it and saw that it was 'poetry with a purpose' as a means of coming to terms with an intolerable situation.

I've always talked about my own experiences to students. I expose my soul a lot. I don't care. I know most lecturers wouldn't dream of it because they fear a loss of dignity. It has never had any adverse effects on me, I mean the students have never abused the situation in any way. Telling personal anecdotes makes the otherwise rather distant thing called 'German Culture' more intimate and human. It also takes the students' minds off the ever-present 'Damocles' Sword' of the exams, if only for a moment, and of course it improves teacher-student relationships.

In the first year I try to teach students close reading and lead them on the adventure of a 'journey into the interior' of texts. In second and third year I prefer to use literary texts as documents of history. I approach an entire problematic and then show them literary texts which demonstrate what I'm saying in a far better way than any other text can. Literary texts are generally the most culturally resonant, the most seismographic of all texts when it comes to reflecting the *Zeitgeist*. The students begin to see the point of literature as something which illustrates a problem larger than itself. For instance, I treat the topic of the history of the German Jews. This is a course that I've been doing for years now and I've always been trying to replace it by some other topic but the students won't let me, it's so fascinating to them. I begin with the history of the early medieval persecution of the Jews. I tell them what texts to read and to get going on the texts in the meantime. These are fictional texts with a strong basis in historical reality, not part of the canon. One text I do is an absolutely magnificent one: *Post ins Gelobte Land*. I doubt if it's on any literary course in Europe, because the author, Anna Seghers, was a communist. I begin with the revelation – and it is a revelation to the students – that the persecution of the Jews didn't begin with Hitler's assumption of power, but rather in Central Europe in 1096, when the first Crusaders coming from France hit the Rhineland and thought they were already in the Holy Land, and on finding that they had a long way to go yet and were starving and cold, they expressed their frustration by falling upon the well-to-do Jews that they found in the towns of Worms and Trier. There followed a whole series of antisemitic myths: the desecration of the Host, for instance, or the so-called blood libel – the myth that Jews slaughtered Christian children as part of their rituals – or that they were the cause of the plague by poisoning the wells with magical concoctions, etc., etc. Then I go into the psychology of prejudice and scapegoating, and we move on to the texts. The first one is by Heinrich Heine, *Der Rabbi von Bacherach*, the first German-language text by a German-

Jewish author which deals with the whole history of the Jews. And then I move on to late medieval times, through to the Enlightenment period and the French Revolution and eventually the modern period, using the Seghers text to illustrate the period from the Russian pogroms of the late nineteenth century to the Third Reich.

In these classes, too, I activate the students. I say at the first lecture, 'I want you to tell me what the "blood libel" means, or the significance of the plague in the history of Jewry.' And I take them by the hand, so to speak, and I bring them down to the library. We have a marvellous *Encyclopaedia Judaica* there, and I say, 'You can look it up in that or you can go to the *Encyclopaedia Britannica* or other sources if you want.' In some cases this is the first time the student has entered the college library since beginning their studies a year previously. Each student has to write one page on a different topic and when I reach that point in the lecture, I call upon the individual student to tell us what she or he knows and they say a few words on their topic and hand out copies of their page of information so that the others can insert them in folders. So the students have all got a whole body of information by the end of the lecture, information they have dug up themselves. This makes them feel that the lecture is a two-way process of mutual education. And then I supplement their information, of course, in the lectures.

There's a medieval poem by an author called Süßkind von Trimberg, who is thought to have been a Jewish minstrel because he describes himself in one of his poems as wearing the pointed hat and the long cloak of medieval Jewry. I show them slides of that outfit and point out to them that the wearing of such clothes was enforced by a decree of the Christian Church in order to single out the Jews and distinguish them from Christians, and also that the Yellow Star of David of Nazi times had its origin in similar decrees in the Middle Ages. In this way the isolation process began, as well as the ghetto. The word 'ghetto' comes from Venice, but the institution stems from the Archdiocese of Gnesen where the Bishop dictated that the Jews should not only live separately but have themselves enclosed. So I show the origins of the persecution of Jews as being Christian and the students are amazed by that, they've never heard the likes. They begin to see Christianity in a somewhat different light.

I tell them that if the university doesn't shake you up a bit, change your stereotypical thinking patterns, then it's no good for anything. I don't try to offend them but I do confront them with uncomfortable historical facts, saying that one has to face them and cope with them. I use a lot of literature written by Jewish people to illustrate the horror of the pogroms in Russia, and also Yiddish texts, translated into modern German, and bring them right up to present day with short texts, often written by very obscure Yiddish authors or even Polish Jews from the Warsaw ghetto. They love that course because it surprises them and makes them think about hypocrisy, about the dangers of stereotyping and the various forms of scapegoating of minorities in history.

More often than not, I use texts from outside the literary canon. I would never spurn a text from the canon which is good and illustrative of something important, but I wouldn't place a canonical work on the programme simply because it's recognized as one of the great works of literature. It wouldn't disturb me to have a whole programme which is entirely non-canonical. I think it's more important to involve the students in an educative, mind-broadening exercise, and I'd take any kind of text for that. In certain cases it's true that the canon can be extraordinary. Shakespeare is a fantastic experience. You can't say the same of Goethe, though, but all German curricula throughout Western Europe would somewhere have Goethe on the course because literary education is considered incomplete without him. I personally wouldn't weep many tears to see Goethe disappear. Anyway, I think a curriculum should be constantly changing and one should experiment continually.

I tend to choose texts that are manageable sizes; I think that's important. I choose novellas, short stories, poems. Often you're hoodwinking yourself into thinking that the students are going to read tomes like Thomas Mann's *Der Zauberberg* in the original. The odd outstanding student will, of course, but by and large they're going to buy an English edition, and so we try to forestall that by using manageable texts which are sometimes read together in tutorials.

I began a course last year on 'das kritische Volksstück', which means a critical folk play, as against the kind of folk comedies that are still very widespread in the south of Germany and operate on a village hall level and are basically affirmative of southern German rural life. In the twenties some writers began to base their plays on these but transformed them to show up the problems of country village life. This trend was revived in the sixties and these plays appeared on the big state theatre stages. I like to use these texts because they touch upon an awful lot of problems which the students would be acquainted with from their own villages. They often come from places in Kerry, Donegal and Roscommon and they would recognize in the plays quite a few of the problems that are coming to light in rural Ireland now and being discussed in the media for the first time ever. For example, oppressive family situations, incest, the brutalization of the young or the marginalization of outsiders, the handicapped and illegitimate. Most of these German plays were written in the Catholic south, Bavaria or Austria, so the Catholic Church plays a role in them as well: the priest as a power figure, the local mayor – every village has a mayor – and the local gombeen. The plays depict power struggles in the micro-structure and that goes down well. So I give the students six or seven critical folk plays, which is a manageable number. They're short texts, although they fill an evening when performed.

My ideas about teaching don't exactly come from the education I received myself. I studied in Germany and it was a completely different, utterly different world. First of all, the students are all older. They come into college at the age of twenty-one, they leave at the age of thirty or so, already balding when they get their degree, and they've got a different attitude to learning. They're there for intellectual enrichment and are very competitive. Learning is largely seminar-based and only partially lecture-based. There's no curriculum as such; you choose your own seminars and lectures, and lectures are not examined. When I tell our students that I ask, 'What would you do if there were no exam at the end of this lecture? Would you continue to come?' and they usually chorus, 'No way!' I tell them that in Germany there were no exams at the end of the lectures and nobody paid any attention to whether you attended or not, and yet you couldn't find a seat in the lecture hall, it was so packed. They can't understand that at all. Few are interested in intellectual enquiry for its own sake; most want simply to get as good a BA as possible. When they come back from their year in Germany they're more sophisticated and mature and they get interested in study for its own sake, but first- and second-year students straight from Leaving Cert. are still completely exam-oriented. So the atmosphere in Germany was utterly different, and I just have to gear my teaching methods to the realities here.

I suppose I stage my classes really, and I get extraordinarily depressed if it doesn't work; I feel my day is ruined if a lecture doesn't work. We place a lot of emphasis on theatre here. The students put on one to two plays each year and get great kicks from it. I have done a lot of acting myself and that is very much part of the way I teach, in the sense that I act out lectures and invest quite an amount of feeling into them. I suppose I proceed from a point of view that if you don't pick texts you can make into a real experience, then you may as well be talking to the wall. You have to affect the students in some way personally and sometimes I stand on my head to do that.

I didn't start off my studies wanting to be a teacher. I studied architecture first and made a spectacular mess of it, very spectacular. I was a very bold boy as a young student, so I have an understanding for the wayward students. When they come to me crestfallen at their own failures, I say, 'By the way, I went through exactly the same thing – if anything, I was far worse than you.' That bucks them up. My studies were such a momentous failure that I was kicked out of home and had to leave the country and set up on my own in England as a Paddy. So I went through the Paddy experience as a hospital porter and building-site worker and all that (an experience I draw from when teaching *Gastarbeiter* literature), then saved up enough money to get out of both Ireland and England with the intention of never returning to either of those countries for the rest of my life. On my way to Israel – I wanted to join a kibbutz – the money ran out in Munich and so I got a job first as a hospital orderly and then a postman, began to make friends and started learning German in the evenings after work. Then I was persuaded to take up studies again because I was a voracious reader and had already acquainted myself with a lot of German authors, such as Thomas Mann and Franz Kafka, in translation. I then began to read them in the original, reading as much as I could get my hands on and enjoying nothing else like it. And I gradually landed on my feet by co-founding a theatre group and discovering that I could act comic roles quite well.

While studying German and English literature at Munich University, I and a Welshman together founded a literary discussion group called the Critical Society, because such a thing was missing in the university. We used to meet every Friday evening for years. It was entirely voluntary; there was no membership or anything like that, anybody who wanted to come along could take part, the agreement being that each individual would prepare an agreed text like 'The Flea' by John Donne or *Endgame* by Beckett, and would talk for up to half an hour about it and then everybody else would join in the discussion. The participants would all have read the text. I learned an awful lot from that. It was entirely non-hierarchical: if lecturers took part, as they sometimes did, they did so on a completely democratic basis, out of interest. The group ran for years. Even marital partnerships were founded on it.

The way we talked to one another at these discussions was completely different from the way people spoke at the university. German seminars were based on the same idea of discussion, but the students were generally trying to shine, to impress the professor and to outdo the other students. Most of the discussion at university level was quite haughty, quite abrasive and very competitive. This Friday evening thing was utterly non-competitive. Everybody was allowed to make the stupidest of comments and would still be taken seriously and have their contributions discussed for whatever potentiality they had.

Also at that discussion group we talked in very everyday language, which is how I like to teach now. I throw very little theory at my students unless it can be explained on the basis of a text. One of the concrete poems that I show them on the screen is about words:

WORTE
WORTE
WORTE
WORTE
WORTE
WORTE
WORTE
WORTE
WORTE
WORTE
WORTE
WORTE
WORTE
WORTE
WORTE
DU WORTE ICH

I show them this picture first and ask them to keep it in mind while I show them the next one:

WORTE WORTE WORTE
WORTE WORTE WORTE WORTE
WORTE WORTE
WORTE WORTE
WORTE WORTE
DU WORTE WORTE ICH

'What is it about?' I ask them. They immediately understand. In the first text the words form a barrier between 'you' and 'me' and in the second they form a bridge. I explain that in a lot of professions, such as those of lawyers or economists, the experts do the first: they use language as a barrier rather than as a bridge in order to make themselves sound more knowledgeable and inaccessible and therefore more indispensable. Academics tend to do the same thing to increase their importance; they often mystify rather than clarify. I tell the students that I am not going to do this, that they should stop me any time I say something which they feel is above their heads. I also say to them when I want them to comment on a text, that they can begin with the most elementary observation and then we build on that. No observation is so simple as to be unhelpful.

The problem of whether or not to suggest they read secondary literature is solved for me by the fact that most of it is in academic German and is too difficult for first- and second-year students. When I first started teaching, my courses were based on the works of one author such as Kleist or Heine. I've come away entirely from that and moved to focusing on a social or a historical problem, such as the explosive urbanization of Germany at the end of the nineteenth century, and examine literary texts by different authors which illustrate the problems of urbanization most sensitively. If we were to treat Heine, then of course I would make a desk reserve supply of books about Heine available for students. But I generally try to get them working on texts for which there is little or no secondary literature. My main interest is in the historical contextualization of texts. Sometimes one author lends him- or herself, like Heine, to characterizing a whole epoch, but then there are other writers who in combination with Heine do it better than Heine alone, so I usually use combinations of different authors and text-types. But you can't expect the students to buy sixteen different books; indeed they often have so little money that they can hardly even buy the prescribed texts. So I use a lot of photocopied handouts to cover larger numbers and variations of text.

A lot of the students are locked into the damaging position – learnt at secondary level – of trying to catch the lecturer's gems of wisdom as accurately as possible in order to regurgitate them in the exam. I tell them that I want them to read the text themselves and think their own thoughts about it and reproduce those as articulately as possible. I tell them not to worry about pleasing me, that they are not going to flatter me by giving back exactly what I think. I'll be all the more interested if they diverge from what they have heard in the lecture, particularly if what they come up with isn't wildly speculative but rather is based on research or intelligent analysis. So yes, I try to break down the barriers of hierarchy.

Ciaran Cosgrove

Ciaran Cosgrove was educated at Queen's University, Belfast, and the University of Essex. He then lived and worked in Spain and Mexico and now teaches Latin American literature at Trinity College, Dublin. His poems have appeared in various magazines in Ireland, and his first collection, *Lassoed Suns,* appeared in 1988.

It's Not There for the Taking, It's There for the Making

STUDENTS HAVE TO understand that they have it all to do, that they have to make the whole thing happen. I'm very much against the supermarket concept of education: that the students are walking round the shelves taking things and filling up their trolley with goods for four years. They should be making the products themselves. Whether or not they know that at the end of the four years will depend on how they're taught, but I think it is utterly fundamental in the whole operation. They are there to learn things, not to be taught things. They must cultivate independence of mind. They must not think they have to regurgitate what has been told to them in class and lectures. Their independence of spirit can put to one side the very real power question which they are obviously caught up in. We as teachers adjudicate and pronounce on their competence and they do not have a reciprocal right to do that to us. So we have to recognize we're in an unequal situation, but that the university can provide a space for freedom, for self development, which has to be capitalized on by them at every turn.

I might not put it that bluntly to a first-year group, but I outline to them the possibilities of the university. I explain to them the function of the library. I talk about how they should structure their time, how they should move away from the notion that the knowledge that they're going to get is going to be got in class time. A lot of them think that if they turn up for class and take notes, then they're learning. It's very important that they know they have to plough certain furrows on their own. It has to be inculcated into them that they have a job of work to do and they have got to do it. No one can do it for them.

Teachers in foreign language departments face a very different situation from teachers in English departments. There may be the problem of language competence. We take in a substantial number of students who have no previous knowledge of Spanish, so they receive intensive language training. We also introduce literature to these students, using dual language texts. We encourage them to start reading in the Spanish at a very early stage, even though they don't comprehend very much. There are several levels of comprehension which a student of English will not have to confront – basic comprehension of the words on the page using dictionaries and so on. This poses real problems of enjoyment.

Students come into university with a very unformed notion of what literature is. Many of them have arrived in our subject area having wanted to do degrees in other subjects.They didn't get enough points so they end up doing Spanish and history and so on. Also the Leaving Certificate syllabus as presently constituted does not provide an adequate basis for entry into third level. The shortness of the second-level cycle, the spread of subjects students have had, the young age at which they enter, mean that that first year is a pre-university year in many respects. Students are also confronting a whole new life and lifestyle. They're in a state of perpetual explosion really. I think these are problems specific to the Irish context which may not occur in other European countries. There is a prevailing assumption that we in Ireland have got one of the best education systems in the world and this is constantly trotted out as though it were a self-evident truth.

When I'm talking to students individually, I do take into account the fact that they're in an excited state in their lives, and aren't very prepared for studying literature and may not want to be there at all. In class, I pitch myself at a level consistent with where I think they ought to be, rather than where they may very well be in reality. Obviously you have to tailor the discourse for the group you're dealing with. Certain vocabulary might be used with the fourth-year group that you just wouldn't use with a first-year group. For example, in fourth year we were talking yesterday about the presence of theory, and there would be a vocabulary attached to theory which one would expect a fourth-year group to recognize immediately. So if we talk about Bahktin and his concept of the dialogic, a word like dialogic would be an awfully big word for a first-year group to handle, whereas a fourth-year group, if exposed to that kind of vocabulary, would understand not only the meaning and usage of that word but also would feel into the theoretical context in which it was used.

Complexity is almost inevitable as you move into difficult areas of intellectual engagement. I think the concept of difficulty in itself is not to be rubbished. There is a very liberating notion attached to difficulty. We live in a culture where ease and consumption are held as the desiderata, and difficulty stands at an angle to that culture of ease. Difficulty doesn't just have to do with difficult words, but the question of using difficult words might have to be addressed at some point along the way. I'm not sure I could deal with difficult questions in very simple language. Certain words would be necessary.

You have to make the distinction between being complex and being complicated. The jargon of literary theory, for example, is not very effective precisely because the jargon takes over. But I'm not referring to jargon at this point; I'm talking about an adequate medium for handling challenging concepts. There is a danger that if you teach concepts through a certain vocabulary, the students can't help aping your view and might lose that essential sense of independence. But I think provided you say often enough to students that you want them to think independently, they will find their own language. They will make use of these concepts and this vocabulary, rather than accepting them as their meaning.

There are certain misconceptions of meaning built into the educational system from a very early age which are pernicious. The notion, for example, that the book already has its meaning which one has to retrieve and, if one is assiduous enough, one will find it. That is very dangerous. Students can easily feel that the teacher has access to the meaning and is withholding it for some perverse reason. This immediately puts them yet again into an inferior position because they look at the author and the teacher as sovereign controllers, possessors of meaning, whereas what needs to be done is to show students that they have the freedom and the responsibility to produce a meaning for every text that they read. These are strong words, freedom and responsibility. Students will begin to think about them even if they can't yet take them on board. Many students, perhaps the weaker ones, are terribly afraid of assuming responsibility. You can see the weaker ones assuming the less dominant positions in class. They tend to hide behind other people and not to be triggered to discussion. I would try to assess who those students are and bring them out a little. I wouldn't be happy just letting them sit in that passive position from the year's beginning to the year's end.

When I look at a text with students, I always emphasize how important it is to have a very close engagement with the text. I encourage most of my students to adopt a first practice of fast reading followed by more careful and considerate second and third readings. They haven't been used to reading fast because the syllabus in Leaving Certificate has probably required a very small number of set texts to be read over a two year period, and now all of a sudden in university they're being asked to read a text a week. This clearly produces a crisis for them. They get very frightened. It's very important to encourage a certain speed of reading so that they can get the bones, the structure, of the text into their heads.

All teachers of literature in a foreign language face the question of students seeking out translations. You can't pretend that translations don't exist. They can have a certain function in helping students towards an understanding of the text, just like dictionaries in many respects, but they should not be used as substitutes for the text. I encourage students to become involved in the original text by reading aloud frequently from it. I try to show them a method of close reading by taking a page of a novel and looking at it in great detail. The more general the picture you give of, say, a novel, the less chance there is of your saying anything strong or interesting, because the more we stand back, the more chances there are that we'll all see the same thing. Whereas the closer up we come, the more closely focused we are on particulars, the more chance there is of eccentric and memorable visions of the text.

I try to develop throughout my teaching the notion that no reading is absolute and no understanding, no experience, of reading a particular novel will ever be replicated. I stress that the reading will always be different from year to year by the same person, so that one never reaches the end of the meaning of a book and that there will always be more to be said. That's exciting, if one can encourage the students to understand that. You never plumb the depths because there are always more depths.

Then there's the question of form and content. Students tend to feel that there is a real, meaningful dichotomy of form and content, that they can spend a lot of time talking about what they think is the content, the meaning of the text, and then at the end if they have time they can come back to what they call the form, the language or whatever, as though the language did not constitute a feature of what they're dealing with. You can't get away from language. Language is it. It's that specific. It's the expressivity which we're dealing with when we're reading that story by Borges or García Márquez. It wouldn't be the same story if it were written by someone else.

One way of helping students to take an interest in language is to talk about the etymology of words. You could argue on the one hand that etymology is terribly abstruse, and that could take from more primary enjoyment. But, on the other hand, etymology is part of my own background, having done Latin and been very much involved with the Latin language at school. I love looking at words, seeing how words developed, and I think that increases understanding. Certain writers enjoy etymologies more than others. Writers like Beckett enjoy etymologies very much. Borges loves using words in a very strange way. One of his most famous stories, 'The Circular Ruins', begins with the words, 'No one saw him disembark in the unanimous night.' You're struck by that adjective 'unanimous', because the word unanimous is a word we all would use. But when you begin to think of *una anima*, one-souled night, the word becomes extremely powerful. Evocative power increases the more one understands how language works, what language means.

I think close reading is a prerequisite for enjoyment. There are some who say that analysis and explication destroy pleasure, but I think that enjoyment is not just instinctive and emotional; it's shot through with experience and understanding. Intellect comes into it. And then you're in the business of trying to make sense of what you've enjoyed and I don't think we can avoid doing that whether it's a book we're reading or a film we're seeing. Making sense of things does seem to me to be a valuable activity, just as we would get together with friends after seeing a film to discuss how we reacted to it. I don't think that destroys enjoyment, and it can enhance it.

Most students find concentration very difficult. I think it's important to make it clear to them that you don't expect them to be working twenty-four hours a day, that you think it's reasonable that they should have a good social life but that they need to construct certain patterns of work. They're a bit shocked when you tell them you expect them to do a bit of reading in the vacation, but they need to understand they're in class for about six months out of the twelve and they can't just let the other six months go. As a teacher, you can either simply advise – like suggesting that you cannot concentrate on a book and hope to become involved in it if the TV is on – or show the example of your own personal involvement with a text. You can help students realize the connection between what they do in the university and what they do outside. Politics comes in when you start to show that nothing exists in and of itself but has connections with things outside. There is the question of power, the question of responsibility, the question of making sense of language and of the different contexts in which language is used. All these have relationships with all the other things. The language of literature has some relationship with the language of television, the language of advertising. To come to terms with the language of literature in a very real sense allows one to understand more comprehensively how language works in all the other daily contacts, so that when a politician speaks one can understand how clichés work, for example, how tired expressions are inserted, and how this contrasts with the language of literature which is a more complex and interesting kind of language.

I would argue very strongly for the precedence of literary discourse precisely because it prepares you to deal with these other discourses, which on the whole are much simpler, but may be extremely destructive.

Students may not be convinced of this argument while they're studying, but I've often had the experience of a student turning up three or four years after graduation saying, I'm beginning now to understand one or two of the things that you said a few years ago; I didn't understand at the time but I remember you saying them and somehow or other they stayed with me and I now do see what you meant. It's what I would call the drip effect of learning. Certain things make their way into the mind but they stay dormant there until they are activated by some external forces perhaps later, perhaps years after leaving college.

In my own area of Latin American literature there are socio-historical matters which need to be gone through before close reading. These are dangerous moments in class because students tend to take a lot of notes and assume that this is the sort of stuff they can learn and give you back. I always notice in those situations that the general excitement of the activity is reduced considerably, that everything becomes somewhat mundane and routine. That information is necessary though, because students have got to understand that the work is being produced in and out of the context. It isn't being produced in a void. There are so many areas you have to take on in order to encourage reading activity in the classroom.

Sometimes I will talk in class about what happened to me when I was living in Latin America. It helps students to realize that there is a connection between the reading of a particular novel and a lived experience, whether mine or anybody's, but that it's not a disembodied kind of thing. You can't plan how you'll introduce your own experiences; it just happens. Those kinds of travellers' tales can also encourage some students to go to Latin America, which is of course extremely helpful to their studies.

Many students go away after the third year, to Spain or Latin America. When they come back, they often give a very good fourth year. They are just doing one subject by then and they can give their full attention to it. I would say that a fourth year is quite distinct from the other three years in every respect. They do have set courses, but independent study is encouraged, so that the writing of a dissertation, in consultation with a supervisor, can constitute the backbone of the year. It's almost a master's year, especially if students can strike up a good working relationship with a supervisor. They may have two days completely free of classes, so there is a good deal of time spent in the library and they can develop quite substantially.

In earlier years I'm happy for students to choose their own essay topics if they're unhappy with what's been set. For example we were talking yesterday about the question of ethnicity in Latin American countries with a very strong indigenous population. The conflict between the indigenous and the Hispanic would be a major issue. So ethnic identity would be one area I'd like students to explore in relation to a couple of novels.

There's a very interesting analogy between Ireland and any Latin American country in the sense that Ireland is using a language, English, which many people might feel is not adequately internalized by Irish people. There is a problematic relation for the Irish speaker of English in a way that there is not for the English speaker of English. A lot of people argue that writers like Joyce and Beckett precisely indulge in linguistic pyrotechnics because it is a language that they're not entirely at home with. Latin Americans make similar comments about Spanish: that it is a relatively recent arrival in the continent just as Roman Catholicism is a recently arrived religion which has never properly grafted. You see this in a lot of texts where writers incorporate, for example in the case of Peruvian writers, the Quechua language into Spanish texts. Similar phenomena can be observed in the Caribbean, where aspects of African dialect are often incorporated into Cuban literature. This makes writers hyperconscious of language. Students often haven't thought about this before, and it can be the stimulus for a lot of independent thinking.

This sort of hyperconsciousness of language is very much the twentieth century phenomenon in literature. When you take writers like Nabokov and Kafka you're very, very conscious of the language as you read page by page. You're conscious of a certain kind of caressing of the words. You can't penetrate those words through to some kind of putative content on the other side of the words. The words are there to be looked at not looked through. People like Susan Sontag were saying this thirty years ago; the essays that she wrote against interpretation were fundamental in pioneering new ways of looking at the text. She talks about the importance of not necessarily excavating the hidden meanings of the text but looking at what is there, on the surface. Maybe that means that we must redefine the word surface, the word superficial or superficiality. Maybe it has got a very pejorative connotation and we should revalue it and give a new definition to the word.

It is important that teachers redefine parameters often. This is also true in what we expect from our students' written work. In the university there is overt lip service paid to freedom of expression, but in reality students feel that freedom of expression is not open to them. Is that a feeling based on some reality or have they just got the wrong end of things? I think we have to credit them with the correct assumption that there are a lot of people who are paying lip service to freedom of expression who do not want the execution of freedom of expression in exams and essays. The evidence is that students who have shown that they can use independence of mind to produce interesting readings are actually marked down when the readings don't conform with the readings given by the lecturer. Some teachers tell students they are not allowed to say 'I think that . . .' That is horrendous. It's a complete negation of everything literature and education stand for.

All one can do is to say to students that they must be brave and courageous and realize that they owe it to themselves to stand on their own two feet and articulate what they believe to be the case, and to try to marshal their arguments as best they can. What makes an essay more interesting, more valuable, than another essay is the compelling way that evidence is marshalled, and the way the student writes.

We also need to question the conventions for the writing of dissertations. The manipulation of sources, references, procedures and so on are rarely challenged or questioned by the world of academia. Then if students don't conform to those conventions they tend to get marked down. It begs the question as to whether the procedures are immutable. There are a lot of questions that we, as teachers, have to ask ourselves which currently we are not asking.

On the other hand, it's not fair to throw students in at the deep end and say, 'I as your supervisor think you're on the right track and to hell with the world of academia.' I think you have to help them through the situation by playing the game to some extent, but playing it with your own rules. That may mean in the case of citation of sources, actually citing from political or historical material or whatever. You don't necessarily have to cite from the most recent critical article. You can also encourage students to read more books by the same author, rather than critics. This is particularly important in the case of a living author, about whom perhaps little or nothing has been written.

There may be a problem which can never be adequately resolved between the so-called creative and the so-called critical. I don't necessarily accept the division, but I think as long as university departments of English or languages exist in the way they do, they will put at a premium critical work on primary literature rather than encouraging students to indulge themselves in the creative writing – and 'indulge' is exactly the word they would use. Perhaps the distrust of creative writing on the part of academics stems from the fact that some people feel they have failed in that they might have been writers themselves. They might even have tried it out a few times and not been successful at it and then turned to criticism. If you write about other people's words as a way of giving yourself prestige in the world, you've got to justify that and say it is a very important thing to do. That means you then have to rubbish the other activity as being beneath your dignity.

To some extent I do think they are different activities. The writing of a poem or novel is not the same as writing about someone else's poem or someone else's novel. I find that, in my own life, I'm constantly dividing my time between what I want to write on my own and what I feel impelled to write about other people's work. The two activities draw on different resources. I would like to see the distinction between the two activities become almost meaningless. I don't see it happening because I think there are vested interests in the world of academia tied in with publishing which would not want that to happen.

The critic's attitude to the text is fundamental. If the critic feels that he or she has a certain proprietorial claim over what the text means, then there are real difficulties. You do get this where a particular critic has made his or her reputation out of writing on one author. That critic sees himself or herself to be almost as important as the author, and having a kind of prior right to pronounce on the work.

One of the main problems students come up against is that they're meeting different teachers who tell them different things. Students soon realize that attitudes towards bibliography differ from lecturer to lecturer. Some lecturers put an extraordinary emphasis on the reading of critic X, so the students would be encouraged and indeed almost compelled to spend a lot of their time reading critic X. Then they might encounter another teacher who says, be sure to work out for yourself first of all how you feel about this primary text. Take on board what the critic has said, but don't feel you have to agree, and in fact challenge it if possible, put it next to what others have written and how you feel, and come up with a balanced overview. That way you put criticism into its proper place.

At the end of the day there is a certain reluctance and fear among students that they should not rock too many boats because it may work to their disadvantage. At the same time I have a feeling that there might be a kind of grudging respect, even from the type of person who does want the regurgitated notes back in the exam, for the student who has been brave enough to stand up and say what he or she believes. If the student is courageous enough, he or she may very well win through.

Edmund White

Jerry Bauer

Edmund White has taught creative writing and literature courses at Yale, Johns Hopkins, New York University, Columbia and Brown. He is the author of several novels, including *A Boy's Own Story* and *The Beautiful Room is Empty*, as well as a biography of Jean Genet.

Ed's Favourite Books

I STARTED TEACHING at Johns Hopkins in the mid-seventies. I was teaching creative writing there with John Barth and I also taught a course in contemporary world fiction which I later taught in various other schools – Yale, Columbia, New York University. And then I ended up being a professor with tenure at Brown. I taught for three semesters there, but had to leave when my French partner, Hubert, became ill with AIDS; we had to return to France since he had no health insurance in the States. I almost always was engaged pri-marily to teach creative writing. Usually at most of these schools you teach one or two courses of creative writing and then one literature course. I would always vary the literature courses as much as possible just to keep myself awake and challenged.

One of my students the other day wrote me a letter saying, 'I remember taking your course, Ed's Favourite Books.' I taught this course several times with different books each time. Actually it was called Contemporary World Fiction. The idea was to read in translation books that had been written everywhere except in the English-speaking world since World War II, to give students an alternative to the English language tradition of social satire, realism, regionalism and first-person confession. Those were the major trends in our fiction and I wanted to show them something different, such as Robbe-Grillet's *nouveau roman*, so we would read *La Jalousie*, then we would read maybe *Notre-Dame-Des-Fleurs* by Genet, then *The Tin Drum*, then something like *A Hundred Years of Solitude*, maybe one of Nabokov's Russian language books like *The Gift*; then we'd read Kawabata's novels. Oddly enough, the students always loved the Japanese books the most and those are the ones they most wanted to imitate.

Most of the students were my writing students and there were others from the English department who were interested in picking up a credit. They were elective courses. In some schools everything is elective; at Brown, for instance, there is no set curriculum. I think it's sad in a way because it means that students know everything about critical theory, which is a big thing at Brown, and they've never read Homer, which seems odd to me, but anyway why not? If you want to be a writer, you make your nest as best you can, you pick and choose wherever you find things that interest you. If you just want to be educated, then it's useful to know about the Western tradition, whatever that is, I mean just broadly speaking, so that you know the references and you can put things in perspective. I myself should not be speaking out on the Western tradition since I majored in Chinese and never, ever, took a single course in English. I was always involved with Oriental literature and art and never studied anything to do with the Greeks or English. I suppose my studies prepared me for the current 'rainbow curriculum' in the States.

I have mostly taught courses in foreign writers, the ones who most influenced me. I taught a course on Genet's novels, because I was finishing my biography, so it was useful for me. I taught a course in Proust and that was very interesting. My idea was to read Proust and to read all the important critics around him. This was with postgraduate students at Columbia. Every week we would read a section of Proust and then we would read, for example, Deleuze's ideas about him. I decided to look at the critics because I thought that Proust has a way of being so yummy when you're reading him that he becomes quickly your best friend and you feel that you too want to live in Saint-Germain and you too want to call on the Duchesse de Guermantes. Proust appeals to snobs, to the kind of people who like Impressionist painting. He's very reassuring to bourgeois values when read superficially, which is the way I think most people read him. It's hard to see how modern Proust is unless you're helped along by something like Deleuze's book. I wanted to break through that reassuring surface tone which is remarkably old-fashioned. When he first started publishing, his contemporaries thought he was terribly *vieillot* and it was hard to get them to see that his novel was in fact a great modernist work because it didn't have a new tone. I think he's still very seductive in that way to middle-class readers. His writing is like a sustained dream that can replace your own life. That is both its great appeal but also its great danger in terms of studying it.

These were always courses about writing technique. For instance, with Proust I would point out the fact that characters are spoken about a long time before they're actually introduced. You can either observe characters from the outside as caricatures the way somebody like Dickens would, in which case they have a very firm bounding line. They're extremely memorable characters, but they're rather far from our notion of actual experience. Or you can be very inner in your exploration of a character, the way Henry James is, and include all the nuances moment by moment, in which case you get something very close to the experience of actually thinking and knowing the world, but it's so nuanced that all the characters are sort of interchangeable and their lines begin to waver. Proust came up with the ideal solution to this problem because he has brilliant social scenes like the Verdurin salon scenes where the characters are perceived pretty much from the outside, in the Dickensian manner – Dickens was a great influence on him – and then he has scenes of great innerness that alternate with that. In the presentation of a character like Charlus, Proust shows him all one way as a very brusque military man, and then as a mad queen, and then finally as King Lear. In other words, you get a composite portrait which, taken globally, is very nuanced, but no given moment is qualified to death in the Henry James way.

That's the kind of technical problem that I would always address with my students. I found that if I acted as if the students were on a much higher level than they actually were, it would shame them into working harder. Recently I gave a seminar in Italy where there was a very hostile man from India who said, 'Oh, so you gays, what are you going to want next? You think that we should put up a monument to you?' It was a very tense moment for everybody in the room. I said, 'Oh, I'm delighted you brought up the subject of monuments. For a long time we were trying to put up a monument to Stonewall to mark the beginning of gay liberation in New York. George Segal did the statues and there was quite a controversy over them and now I'm happy to say they're up.' That kind of technique in teaching leaves students in a state of mental confusion, which is naughty, but I think it's much the best way.

One of the things I do in presenting a new author in a literature course is to give a potted biography. For example, with Proust, I would take some of the more colourful aspects of his life: the fact that he tortured rats and that he gave his mother's furniture to a male bordello and things like that, just to get them all awake and again to undercut that reassuring tone of the comfortable narrative. Or with somebody like Kawabata, I would discuss his relationship with Mishima and how both of them committed suicide at slightly different times. The nature of Kawabata's suicide was as ugly and ghastly as possible – he was found sucking a gas tube – so that it would undercut the aestheticism of his writing and also not inspire another rash of romantic suicides.

I usually will go into a little potted history of the whole literary moment that the writer emerges in. So with Proust I might talk about how there were no important French writers just before him. For the period of about fifteen or twenty years before him, there were Anatole France, Pierre Loti and Paul Bourget, not much really. It was a kind of dull decadent moment in French literature, aside from the poets, who were better. Then I'll talk about his having to self-publish at the beginning, and how he had an overall formal plan for the whole book, which he envisioned as just three volumes. But then two things happened which he couldn't have predicted: World War I and his falling in love with Agostinelli. Then I talk about the 'Albertine strategy', the claim that Proust's women are based on men in real life, and I ask if this theory is legitimate. That would be a debating point to get the students to think about.

When I was a student I was horribly bored in class all the time and I found the teachers were very unprepared. They would sit on their desks and wag their legs and just say general things about anything, not even necessarily about the subject. I hated that and resented it bitterly. When I became a teacher I resolved never to do that. I resolved to be over-prepared and to talk very fast with lots of detail and lots of preparation, lots of readings, lots of jokes, lots of provocative ideas and so on. I wanted to put on a good show for them, but not just to entertain them, also to give them plenty of content. In America people have to pay for these schools. At Brown it costs twenty-five thousand dollars a year, so even a rich family has to take out a major loan. Usually the student's the one taking out the loan, so he or she sits there with burning eyes and resents it if you waste a moment of his or her time because their taxi meter is ticking all the time.

I taught a course on gay and lesbian literature at Brown. I only wanted to teach classics such as Virginia Woolf's *Orlando*, or Gertrude Stein's *The Autobiography of Alice B. Toklas,* Willa Cather's *The Lost Lady*, and so on. I didn't want to just teach contemporary fun books that they might be able to identify with, but that were actually not any good. I wanted to show that there was a major canon of books, such as those by Ronald Firbank or E. M. Forster, which could be read in this context. I was always reminding them that it was a rather peculiar way to read these books from the gay perspective, but that it could be done. My idea was to pretend that we're ground-breakers and pioneers. Nobody else has really ever taken or taught such a course before. We don't even know what a lesbian or gay canon would be. I wanted to give them the feeling of being on to something new, which students always appreciate, instead of a feeling that they're just grinds repeating chores assigned to generations of students. I had written a long article in *The New York Times* about gay and lesbian fiction and I got dozens of letters from teachers saying they couldn't figure out what a curriculum would be, or a canon. So I mentioned that to the students. I said, 'This is something very new. Gay and lesbian studies, gender studies in general, are replacing deconstruction in America as the hot thing, and so maybe if you do want to go on and teach, this is something you might want to specialize in, who knows? But anyway we have to figure out whether it's even worth doing, or is it just a trend? Do we really learn anything about lesbian and gay life by reading these books, and if so what is the relationship? Is there really a very tidy relationship between literature and this kind of minority experience? Can gays and lesbians even be called a minority as though they were Indians or Pakistanis or whatever?'

I would make them give book reports out loud before the class about recent lesbian and gay novels. I'd say things to the students such as, 'Many of you in this room want to be writers and one of the ways you can make a living as a writer is by writing book reviews, so you better learn how to write a book review because there is in fact a standard format for it. You must give a notion of the plot, place the author, place a particular book in his or her oeuvre, give a sample of the style by quoting a paragraph or two and evaluate the book, say whether you liked it or not and why. You have to do this in five hundred words or nine hundred words. Please turn in one next week. Pretend that *Orlando* has just been published, that Virginia Woolf is not all that well known and that you have been asked by the *Times* to write a review of this book in seven hundred and fifty words.'

The most important thing is to figure out ways to make classwork seem fresh, first to yourself and then to the students. When I lecture, I work from very structured notes with lots of detail. I digress a lot; I don't write it out every word. Because my teaching was always oriented towards writers I would always be pointing out technical tricks. For instance, Kawabata has a curious way of repeating descriptions. He'll be talking about a butterfly, then he'll shift to talking about a mountain, then he'll go on to talking about the rain, then he'll come back to talking about the butterfly, then he'll talk again about the mountain and the rain, and then the rain again – and you wonder what is the *system* governing all this. I finally figured out that there's a form of Japanese poetry called *renga.* It's linked verse, a bit like *terza rima*, in which you have not words but subjects that keep coming back in a routine but not entirely predictable way. There's a system but the system isn't totally symmetrical. I might point out to the students how such a poetic scheme might underlie these descriptive passages. I felt that such a technique was something highly interesting for them even to try to do in their own writing.

Or, for instance, with *A Hundred Years of Solitude*, I would show them what I thought was a real contradiction at the heart of the book. The author is himself a Marxist, and Marxists believe in history rather than nature. They believe we don't have a human nature; we only are created by our economic and social circumstances. Yet Márquez chose the most rudimentary kind of biological determinism in his book, so that there are only two kinds of possible personalities for the male characters and they alternate like clockwork. They even get one of two possible names generation after generation. I tried to show this contradiction, and to say that writers are not intellectuals usually, that they oftentimes are inconsistent, and that the contradiction that lies at the heart of a book can be its animating principle. That's what makes it interesting to read. The writer hasn't really worked it all out yet. He's very passionate about it, but he feels of two minds about it.

Teaching creative writing is a very special process. It's almost like being a therapist. The raw material that the students are working with is their own feelings, even if it's not necessarily their own lives, though more and more people do write very close to their own experience. In a creative writing class people feel licensed to give a full response to somebody's story, even an irrational one that would seem insufficiently objective in discussing a classic in a literature class. For instance, a student might say, 'I found that girl very irritating, and when she talked about her abortion for the third time on page sixteen I wanted to strangle her.'

The teacher will also give a very subjective response. It's probably the most democratic kind of teaching situation. A story is written, xeroxed, and distributed to everyone before the class begins. Everyone comes into the class having already read it and made marginal notes, and then there's a discussion in which the teacher will say, 'Jane, what did you think of this story?' People tend to be a little hesitant and diplomatic at the beginning but since usually it will be a two hour class in which only two stories are presented, you have a whole hour sometimes for a ten page story, and so people will finally let down their guard toward the end. What's interesting is that the *moral* dimension of literature comes up more than it does within literature classes because people feel more free to say, for instance, 'I don't know what your intention was but if you think this person's admirable then you're fooling yourself. I think it's despicable what he did to that girl, it's really deplorable, and on page seven you have all these excuses he's offering himself and do you honestly think those are convincing or is this meant to be a satire? What is your intention?' Then another student in the seminar will tell the author of the story under discussion, 'Well, you haven't realized your intentions at all, it's a terrible case of where you don't even seem to know what ordinary human beings feel and maybe you should rethink that because how can you possibly write it if you don't even know what ordinary human moral reactions would be?'

When the students practise this kind of comment in creative writing classes, it carries over to their talking about past literature. It's not a bad thing to combine the two, because somebody who's very keen on writing himself or herself will read the classics in order to ransack them for things they can use and imitate, borrow from, reject, and so on. They're interested in theory that will propose certain technical solutions, so that Robbe-Grillet's *For a New Novel* is a very challenging book for young writers to read because it's so dogmatic. Just as Ezra Pound's *ABC of Reading* is very challenging for young poets to read.

Most contemporary theory doesn't outrage students because it's descriptive rather than prescriptive. Prescriptive writing is irritating in a fruitful way. When somebody like Todorov describes a genre of literature you can't really take exception to it, but it seems mildly dismissive of the genre as well. It's like a taxonomist just telling you that such and such is the case.

Creative writing in combination with literature is very good. It is flattering to the student when the teacher says, for instance, 'I want you to pay very careful attention to the transitions at the ends of these chapters in Tolstoy, because most of you in this class tend to finish a chapter on a rising note. You think you have to beat the drums and that's all very impressive, but the problem is it doesn't lead you naturally into the next chapter. In the old poetics, they used to talk about the end of the line in poetry as a feminine ending, in other words instead of being "ba BOM", it would be "BA bom". The voice falls away. That's called a feminine ending, and you could say by analogy that oftentimes a good writer such as Tolstoy will let his voice fall away at the end of a chapter which will lead the reader into the next one.'

The wonderful thing about literature is that it's a focus for talking about history, philosophy, morality, art and society. I majored in Oriental literature, so I was interested in talking to students about the influence of Buddhism on Kawabata, or Tanazaki, who for instance wrote a story called 'The Bridge of Dreams'. I would say to students that first of all that story is an imitation of a chapter of *The Tale of Genji* which is also called 'The Bridge of Dreams', but secondly it's also a familiar metaphor for earthly life in Buddhist thinking, an insistence on the transitional and transient nature of our experience. In all Japanese writing reincarnation plays an important role, so that, for instance, a man will be in love with a woman who will die when she's very young and he never forgets her, and then when he's a grandfather his grandson will marry a very pretty young girl and he's convinced that she's a reincarnation of that woman he was in love with so long ago. The granddaughter-in-law and the grandfather will enter into a special non-sexual but highly erotic relationship which will be a recapitulation of that earlier experience of his own youth.

I'll point out the delicacy of the eroticism of Japanese literature. For us eroticism is always so grotesque and heavy, whereas for instance in *The Sound of the Mountain* there's a scene in which this daughter-in-law has a nose bleed and the old man helps her and then she goes in the other room and there's still a little bit of her pink blood suffusing the water and he licks it clean. That's as erotic as it gets, but it's very erotic and perverse and beautiful.

America is very different from Ireland, let's say, in that an American would really think he could appropriate a Japanese technique and a Japanese philosophy because we feel as Asian as we do European. I do think that's one of the nice things about America; it's very open to appropriating other cultures.

Three or four writers I've tried to teach haven't worked. One is Firbank, who has such a sophisticated and elusive sense of humour, a very camp sense of humour. Camp has vanished even from gay culture among the young, so that students don't get it at all, and they don't want to know about it; they find it just irritating. Colette doesn't interest people any more. I taught *Chéri* two years ago. It is, I think, a masterpiece and one of my favourite books, but the students didn't like it at all. Then there's an American writer called Glenway Westcott who lived in France for years and years who wrote a short novel called *The Pilgrim Hawk* in the 1930s. This was one of those very Jamesian, very balanced tales of morality that is written with enormous finesse and the students just didn't get it, didn't want to know about it. Another failure in class was Elizabeth Bowen. Again, I think, because of the moral complexities she poses students don't connect with her.

On the other hand, Kawabata certainly works. Raymond Queneau works, they love him; they find him charming, naughty and funny. I remember teaching *Le Dimanche de la Vie* and they liked that, it was perky and funny and cute. They all love *A Hundred Years of Solitude* and that becomes their favourite book, I think. I find it rather heavy going but it's a good book when you're at a certain age. They don't like Tanazaki. They don't like Jane Austen. They don't like writers for whom the social mores are the great focus. They're young; they don't want to know about these things. They're interested in romantic individualism. It doesn't have to be a young man or woman that they're identifying with, the character can be a very old person, but students like books in which individuals are pitted against society, and the assumption is that society is at fault and the individual is right.

One of the strange things about teaching literature is that presumably you're teaching all world literature to these young people in order to pass it down from one generation to the next and to preserve something like a canon, but the truth is that very young people, the age of these students, respond only to *part* of the canon because of the nature of their age, their own particular psychological moment. So in fact you can't be too parnassian in your decisions about which books to teach, you really do have to teach books that will interest them, because otherwise there's no point in the entire fruitless exercise.

Anne Enright

Amelia Stein

Anne Enright was born in Dublin in 1962, where she now lives and works. She went to a convent school in Dublin before getting a scholarship to an international school on Vancouver Island. She went on to Trinity College, Dublin and later to the University of East Anglia to do an MA in Creative Writing. She worked for six years as a producer/director in RTE before going freelance. Her work includes *The Portable Virgin*, a collection of short stories; *Revenge*, a screenplay for RTE; and a forthcoming novel, *The Wig My Father Wore.*

F slits T

When I was a student I thought it was important to study as much as you could and then forget about it as soon as you could afterwards. It's all sinking in whether you're conscious of it or not, and it's all going to be useful when you're writing. But you have to de-academicize yourself, because you leave college so young. So unless you want to write about being young and leaving college, you have to live a bit.

Some of the skills involved in literary criticism can be useful in a professional sense. I went and worked in the media so the links are more obvious – how to tell a story, the difference between showing and telling – but there are other uses. An ability to make psychological interpretations never goes astray, although it can be overused by ardent English students when they hit the workplace and give everything a subtext. But the experience of gathering information, thinking it through, taking it to its natural conclusion, as well as being able to turn a phrase, all of those are useful. Being able to put a full stop where you should put a full stop.

Now that I am writing, I read people to check that I am not copying them by accident. It's very important to know how people have done things before you, even for the technical nitty-gritty of writing. When you come to some of the mechanics of realism, say you need to make a transition and you're wondering whether you need to work through it or whether you can just abandon the whole idea of a transition and go ahead anyway, it's always useful to know which writers did what, you can just open a page of their book and remind yourself, get some moral support.

You tend to think of English literature as some kind of monolith before you go to college. You think it has to do with realism an awful lot of the time, because at the age of seventeen, with a convent education, you have a very moral view of both life and fiction. You have the idea that literature is like, or should be like life, even though at that stage for me life would have been imitating books and not the other way around. It was just a case of reading the right books for life to imitate. If you start experiencing something that isn't reflected in realism or isn't adequately expressed by it, you have to find new models. So the courses in modern fiction and poetry were like opening a window for me, expanding horizons and turning things on their head. They meant a lot.

I was always a reader, until I had to do exams. I was a very voluntary and happy reader all during primary school and up to my Inter Cert. After that the curriculum tends to interfere. But I read very widely and was a desperate snob. My sister was at college so I read all her books. I didn't understand a word of course, but I read happily without understanding. I thought that literature was such a huge project that comprehension wasn't part of it, wasn't necessary to it. I struggled very badly with books that were on the course because it never really occurred to me that you were supposed to do simple things like remember the story or reproduce the plot. I thought you had to write the essay with as large an agenda as the original writer. I would have had no problem, for example, writing an essay on *Huckleberry Finn*, rhapsodizing about the river and about rivers in general, but I wouldn't necessarily have related it properly to *Huckleberry Finn*, or even think that I had to finish reading the book first. I thought it was part of the conversation or something, like listening to adult conversation where you relate to some of it and the rest you ignore. I picked up and liked the rhythms or the intentions or the tone and the mood – without knowing words like tone and mood.

Tone was a revelation and I discovered it very late. I didn't understand for example that writers could be joking. Students often think that books are in some way sacred, that books are intelligent and they are stupid. But I didn't have that when I was young. I didn't feel that the book was far more intelligent than I was in the same way as you don't feel that adults are necessarily cleverer; they just inhabit a different space.

But I do remember how simple it seemed when someone started breaking things down. We had a temporary teacher who came in called Miss Egar, which I thought was a great name, or maybe the fact that she was only temporary and not doing *Hard Times* made me listen. And she wrote 'F slits T' up on the blackboard. She said this is what you write in exams – Form Style Language Imagery Theme Tone. Something like that anyway. So I finally knew what they wanted. She also said that the piece in a poem where you stop understanding is the most important piece, which was a revelation. No one ever says that not understanding is not only fine, but essential. Nobody had said, well, not understanding, that's the important bit, that's what the poem is about, bringing you to a place where you don't understand and where your powers of comprehension are transcended. Which is the whole experience of reading in the beginning. It was the first time that incomprehension was made into a virtue.

So with F slits T, I had a method for doing exams, as opposed to reading *Macbeth* for example and then retelling the story or just floundering in what it all means. What is going on in a Shakespeare play is very important, but hardly the end of the story – and who knows what it means? It isn't the beginning of the line, it's not the end of the line.

I discovered irony in a kind of transitional school in Canada. I was going to do au pair work for a while to improve my German, but a teacher in school saw the ad in the paper and suggested I go for it. In Canada I had a teacher called Theo Dombrowski, who was wonderful. He read out loud all the time, and because he had a great ironic inflection tone was not a problem. Before that, at secondary school, we read out loud, I think, in this kind of leaden way just to prove that we could read, to get over the big words. The first big discovery that I made with Theo was that it was possible to write about sex, which nobody had ever clarified. Part of the sacredness of the text in school was that it was too sacred to talk about something as dirty and quotidian as sexual behaviour or sexual activity, and obviously they weren't going to talk about sex in the context of literature. With thirty six girls in the class floundering in this state of ignorance and precocity it would take a brave teacher to start telling us what it was all about. I don't think there was time.

In Canada we were doing the same kind of books but in an

adult way; people are adults at that stage, or bits of them are. That was one of Theo's greatest qualities, to make you realize that you knew something all along. He would say things like: 'Well, we all know what that means.' And we did, surprisingly enough – and he knew that we knew and that was okay. He was honest, I think. There was a sort of complicity. We had a range of books on the syllabus, from different countries and different times. He just picked books he liked and thought we might like and also books that students might write well about, books that provoke. He presented them as likeable books, good books. They weren't necessarily part of the canon. We did Edward Bond and Pinter, as well as Shakespeare and Joyce. We discussed them all the time, we discussed them out of class. I don't think he taught anything that didn't have jokes in it and the jokes became catchphrases, like, 'Gillian, that's a good name for a whore,' from *The Homecoming*.

We staged *The Homecoming* as well. Acting is very bizarre. I acted in some of the course choices in university later and I found that acting is a very stupid way to learn a play. I remember playing the servant in *Ghosts* and not realizing, after a three week run, that it was about syphilis. You can say, how can you be so stupid, but I was really more worried about the fact that my shoes were too big and I was going to be felt up by this guy in the first act. A director is usually adding things to the text rather than looking at it. He's working with gesture and movement and motivation, and many of these things are a kind of burden. With a good director obviously not, but we're talking about students. So it's not necessarily an advantage to be in a play that you're studying – except it's good when it comes to quotes in exams.

After the two years in Canada I really did enjoy university. I was like a pig in shite. Theo had made me realize that this was an essentially enjoyable and conversational and approachable and interesting thing to do. You read books and then you talk about them. It seemed like great fun to me. It's a confidence thing as well. Enjoyment is ancillary to confidence. If you haven't got the confidence to write or speak then you can't enjoy reading as much and it's all a burden. But once you realize it's something to play with, and that you the reader can use different tones in talking about a book, just as the writer can use different tones in writing it, then it isn't sacred and alienating, it isn't bigger than you. I wouldn't have had that confidence if I had gone on straight from secondary school.

The other great thing about college seemed to me that you didn't have to go to all the classes; you could pick and choose. That was part of the enjoyment as well. I think teachers are very indulgent. Once they twig enthusiasm, they take a lot of foolishness. I remember turning up after an all-night party to a tutorial and I was supposed to give a paper on Shakespeare's history plays, which were never my favourite anyway, and I was waiting for the blame and it didn't arrive. It always seems amazing that teachers aren't your parents; they don't care what you do really. Some of them do think they are parents, more in school than in college. They want you to be a better person. You become part of their ambition and you don't know the rules and it can be very destructive.

I did have a lot of freedom as a student. I managed to do *King Lear* nearly every year because I loved the play so much and there's room for a huge number of different approaches. I wasn't ticked off. There was nobody saying, well, you said something different about it last year. I just managed to tie *King Lear* in with whatever else we were doing at the time. *King Lear* with *Troilus and Cressida* got around doing *Troilus and Cressida* quite nicely, and actually made sense of it in a way. I think I wrote about paradox and contradiction. You had to choose your own topic, which is the only way it makes sense. Students have to be weaned off this dreadful attitude to teachers we had when we were doing the Leaving Cert. 'We want to do everything that's on the syllabus and nothing but what's on the syllabus, and it's your job to do that because we've got exams to do and it's your job to get us through them.' We were outraged by any kind of creative or relaxed approach when our careers were on the line. Age fifteen. If that continues it's very unhealthy. And I hate that kind of whiny, strident reaction to your own lack of self-confidence.

One of a teacher's functions is to make their students confident enough to do things without being told to. Thinking up your own questions is part of that process. Also to narrow the focus can be a very good idea. Just spending a couple of hours on two lines of poetry. You can say extraordinary things about two lines of poetry if the poet is good. That way students don't feel overwhelmed by the bulk of what they have to get through. They don't feel they have to know everything and quote at length. But the teacher does have to show them that it's possible to talk about two lines of poetry for two hours, has to let them know that this is a very respectable approach. Or even that it's an essential approach. What you can say about a paragraph of a novel, you can say about it all, if the writer is good. We did have a practical criticism class in our first term in Trinity which was based on the first pages of books, or sometimes just the first line. The beginning of *Lord Jim,* where it says he's just under six foot, is the key to a lot in the book. Maybe you could do it with endings as well, like the last line of *The Crying of Lot 49* which ends with this hair-trigger ambiguity, leaves you still saying 'Is it all paranoia, or is it real?'

You could choose what courses you were going to take at Trinity. I regret not having worked with some teachers who didn't appeal to me at the time, who would appeal to me now. I didn't ever want to be a teacher myself. I had thought of being an academic, but I didn't like the idea of doing a PhD, which meant writing a book about someone else's work when writing a book of fiction would take the same amount of time and maybe would be more useful. Not that academic books are useless. I think some academic books are wonderful. I felt when I left university that your early creative energy is extremely important. Before life snarls up on you, you have to use that energy. I thought if you don't write your book early, it might be difficult to write it later, and if you use that first flush on an academic book you're wasting it. I liked academic life; I think it's a good life to have, but I just wanted to do things, I wanted to make things. Or at least something concrete, tangible.

After my book was translated into French, I was invited to a short story conference in St Quentin, north-east of Paris. The local high school had put one of my stories on the Baccalauréat course and I was invited to talk to the students about it. I was confronted with 150 very worried French teenagers who wanted to know what it was all about. Their anger was very obvious, the fact that they didn't understand and needed to pin things down for an exam. I think they hated me for putting them through all this.

Apart from the fact that I couldn't remember the thing properly – I tend to blank out the ones I grow out of, or don't like – so I really wanted to say the unsayable to them, 'Maybe it isn't your fault; maybe it's just not very well written.' And when they wanted things clarified I had to say, well, it's this, but it's also that, it's supposed to be ambiguous, which sounds like a cop out, but which was in fact true. Students of that age dislike ambiguity intensely because they're not reared for it. Their lives are full of it, but nobody has told them that you can say in an exam, 'this is ambiguous,' as an advanced thing to say. They're told to nail it down. So ambiguity was not their favourite word, and the fact that it meant two things at once was not their favourite response. Part of the difficulty was that it was written with two languages in mind – one old-fashioned pedantic Irish, full of ironies and self-referential, civil service language, and the other the language of the fifteen-year-old girl in the story, who didn't know what to say most of the time. How do you explain Flann O'Brien to a French class? They just put the story on the course because it was about a fifteen-year-old girl.

For me it was a great experience talking to them. I don't think the students enjoyed it. It has made me more careful about implicit and explicit references in work. I think if you're writing about fifteen-year-old girls and you fail to make it relevant to fifteen-year-olds then you're doing something wrong. Though I remember reading *The Awkward Age* by Henry James at an awkward age and it didn't make any sense. Or I tried reading *Lolita* when I was Lolita's age, so I could find out how you had sex from it and then gave up halfway through because it was too vague, but I do remember not being shocked she was so young.

It had never crossed my mind that my own writing might be taught, though when I was thinking of being a writer when I was about fourteen, I thought that being on the Leaving Cert. course was about as high as you could get. But that was before I started writing and realized that to be on the Leaving Cert. course was the worst thing that could happen to you – well, not the worst, I don't want to do anybody down who's on the Leaving Cert.

course. But it was not appropriate to what I wanted to do. I don't mind the books I write being part of a conversation. I would like them to be part of a conversation. I would even like them to be part of the national conversation if they were relevant to it, but the idea of people writing exams on them as a way of getting ahead is really very unpleasant. It makes you think in a peculiar way about what you're writing. The kind of confidence I had as a student is not mirrored in my confidence as a writer at all. The idea of a text settling into a course takes all the fluidity out of it, takes away all the possibility for change as the world around it changes. It makes it set in stone or something. I wouldn't have the confidence that it would survive that. I don't like the idea that when you become part of the monolith nobody can say, well, this is badly written, which I would love to have been able to say about, for example, some of Shakespeare's history plays.

I am very conservative as far as the canon is concerned. I really believe that people have to read Shakespeare and love Shakespeare. I don't think you necessarily have to love the Romantic poets and I don't think that you necessarily have to love Tolstoy, but I think a teacher has to communicate enthusiasm about these great works, about some of them anyway. Some of them are pretty glorious. Some of them are there because they're extremely good. I'm always amazed, particularly in the old library in Trinity where they have millions and millions and millions of books from the dawn of copyright, at how many books were written which were abandoned and totally forgotten and often extremely bad. So the canon has survived partly because some of those works are extremely good. I think there are geniuses around and it's foolhardy to ignore them. Geniuses aren't that sacred. A good genius isn't sacred. A good genius doesn't make you feel stupid. A good genius might make slips.

Guy Davenport

Guy Davenport was born in South Carolina in 1927. He was educated at Duke, Oxford and Harvard. He has published collections of fiction, essays, poetry and translation. He taught for many years at the University of Kentucky.

Interview by Mail

3 Nov 1993

Dear Judy Kravis:

I have had such bad luck recently with interviews that I've sworn off. *Paris Review* tried three times, ending in failure. I avoid newspaper interviewers, who never quite get anything right. Your request, however, sits in a different light and category.

Could we possibly do this by mail? I'm not antisocial or shy, but since your end result is to be 'a sense of one person talking', why not start there? You might also tell me who I am to be: a writer of fiction (my 7th collection of stories has just been pub'd), a professor of lit (I taught for 37 years, and am now retired on a MacArthur Fellowship), a translator, a critic (7 books here), or all of the above in the one machine?

I have no ideas at all about my fiction, though it is studied in at least three seminars in France, and turns up (I hear) in courses around the USA.

I think I may have been a poor teacher, in that though I had some very good, responsive students, for the most part I simply confused the general run of Education Majors and cultural shoppers who wandered into my classes. Higher education over here is a tragedy, a sorry mess, and something of an elaborate farce.

My standard course was Comp Lit IV (Flaubert to Beckett), together with seminars in Joyce, Pound, and others. As a Distinguished Prof, I was free to give courses in Monet, Ruskin, Marianne Moore, Wallace Stevens, a seminar in Zukofsky's 'A' (against all likelihood, a great success), Johnson's *Ark*, Olson, in literature-in-context (such as Christopher Smart in his time, place, diction, culture).

I've done tutorials in Greek, in iconography, in literary and artistic epochs (a course in the year 1922, for instance).

I suggest you make a list of questions, to which I can reply, obviating a journey to remotest Kentucky in winter. I think we can both control matters much better than with a tape recorder.

7th February 1994

Dear Guy,

Sabbatical term has begun, along with Spring (the Irish optimistically start Spring on Feb 1st!). I'm coming to the US in a couple of weeks, and thought I'd begin by setting up the interview by correspondence with you.

I'd like to take my start for your contribution to *Teaching Literature* from your letter of last November. Here are some points you made and my initial responses to them.

You asked were you to respond as writer/professor/translator/critic or all these in the one machine? (The last, yes please, but also a bit about having these different perspectives and how they affect your teaching or your writing.)

More on the tragedy/sorry mess/elaborate farce of higher education in USA? (The broad picture and some ghastly close-ups?)

Comp. lit. IV (What did you teach? How did you choose your books? Why do you like comp. lit.?)

More on your course in the year 1922, which books? pictures? music? (How did you encourage a sense of epoch?)

Any thoughts yet on how you would like/could envisage your fiction being taught?

Why do you think, as you said, that you may have been a poor teacher who had some very good, responsive students? I think I am a good teacher who has some very good responsive students but far more who find it difficult or impossible to understand what literature has to do with them.These are the ones who concern me most. But also the good ones who may go on to talk to others about literature.

Could you respond to these points, and any others that may occur to you along the way, so that we can start putting something together?

I like the idea of interview by correspondence. It seems like some sort of lost art!

Looking forward to the next stage,

all good wishes,

Judy

17 Feb 1994

Dear Judy Kravis:

The Seminar on the Year 1922 (autumn 1989, 10 graduate students) involved reports (by one student, with discussion from the whole seminar) on works (books, poems, buildings, paintings) by Eliot, Vladimir Tatlin, Georg Grosz, Wyndham Lewis, Duchamp, Cummings, Thomas Mann, Picasso, F. Scott Fitzgerald, Brecht, Janusz Korczak, Rilke, DW Griffith, Kafka, Le Corbusier, Braque, Pirandello, Pound, Pasternak, TE Lawrence, Joyce, Anna Akhmatova, Edith Sitwell, Mies van der Rohe, Virginia Woolf, Willa Cather, Sinclair Lewis, DH Lawrence, Edith Wharton, Gertrude Stein, Vachel Lindsay, Wittgenstein, Tutankamen (the discovery), Arnold Bennett, Stravinski, Osip Mandelstam, HL Mencken, Mayakovsky, William Carlos Williams, Eugene O'Neill, and Somerset Maugham.

Lord knows what the students learned; some history of the arts, I hope. The reports ranged from very good to very bad. The students chose their own subjects from a long list.

It might be useful to list my other seminars over the years, working backward from the last, which was The Poem as a Field of Force (poems from all periods, analyzed iconographically and in cultural context – Jonson's 'Triumph of Charis', Smart's 'Hymn to David', Pound's 'Mauberley', and so on).

The Joyce Seminar (repeated many times, reading everything except the Wake, on which we had some lessons).

The Pound Seminar (repeated several times, reading *The Cantos*). Symbolism.

David Jones and Stanley Spencer (5 students).

Charles Olson and Ronald Johnson.

Monet: Iconography of the Impressionists.

Zukovsky's 'A' (grand success! two faculty sitting in. For the last week I had T-shirts made for us all, with a big *A* and in a circle around it, 'A round of fiddles playing Bach'). An outside class project was a transcription of LZ's marginal notes and underlinings in about 70 of his books which were available to us.

Art + Writing in the First Machine Age.

Iconography applied to Poetry.

Satire in Modern Verse.

Projectivist Poetry (given three times).

Ruskin.

Practically every year I gave the lecture course Comp Lit IV, always beginning with Flaubert's *Three Tales*, proceeding to Mandelstam's prose, Mann (various books, changing with the years), Rilke, Beckett, Bulgakov, Kafka, Proust, and so on: the reading list, usually six substantial books, changed from year to year. My method was to give lectures on the historical context of each writer as well as a survey of all of each writer's works.

This should give you an idea of what and how I taught (there were many more courses. My very last year I chose to teach freshman composition, having noted that all the sections were taught by graduate students). My very last course was in American comic prose, from O. Henry to *archy & mehitabel*, with Booth Tarkington, Wodehouse, and Milt Gross along the way.

Now back to your queries:

I'm aware that my fiction *is* taught (lectured on, whatever) around the USA and in France (by Pierre Gault, Marc Chénetier, and Laurence Zachar). This has nothing to do with me, and I don't give it a thought.

I've tried not to allow activities to get in with each other. That I wrote fiction was almost completely unknown to my students, or that I wrote for magazines (scholarly and journalistic). I taught as if that were the only thing I did.

I feel out of higher education. I am incompetent to comment on what's going on. In broadest terms, it looks awfully as if traditional matter has been abandoned. Fairly early in teaching I formulated Dr Davenport's Law of Infinite Regression. That is, a poem of Louis MacNeice turns up in the anthology we're using for Modern British Poetry (one of my courses). Well, it's an eclogue ('The Six-Barred Gate'). No student knows what an eclogue is. So I sink past the Renaissance back to Vergil and Theokritos. Then we go back to Christian things, sheep and shepherds, and Hebraic traditions. And so on.

I once found myself lecturing on color reproduction when I'd set out to show a class around in Botticelli's Primavera. I'd given everyone a color print of the painting. One student wanted to know how I got all of them the same. It turned out that very few knew what printing is, or how you get from a canvas in the Uffizi to a piece of paper in Kentucky.

I evolved potted histories of God knows how many things – the Revolution of 1688 for Defoe, the Russian Revolution, bibliography for tiny tots, the discovery of the New World, the architecture and fixtures of the Bloom household.

Another course I've just remembered: the city of Paris, its geography, history, and 20th-century doings.

I was a poor teacher in that I never really learned how to deal with ignorant indifferent tell-me-exactly-what-to-memorize-to-pass-this-course students.

The American university is little more than an extension of high school. Most. At Harvard one still in my day (1950s) had to assure the professor that one had read ALL of Melville to get into a Melville seminar. At Kentucky I had students signing up for the Joyce seminar who had never before seen the name and couldn't find Ireland on a map.

You must be aware that the American university is a social event for the students: one 'goes to college' to drink, fornicate, drive a fast car, belong to a fraternity or sorority. 90 per cent of them have the intellectual passion of an armadillo.

19th Feb A warm day! Crocusses up. The only traces of the blizzard and Great Freeze are mounds of snow along the sides of parking lots and in shaded places. I gather from your remark about students not understanding what literature has to do with them that you teach some species of lit. English?

Some read, some don't. Reading is an imaginative act, a completing of the what the author has provided. I wish I knew HOW one learns to read. I had a hard time of it: years of working at it. And I still try to extend it as a skill.

It is a falsehood that the text comes off the page into the mind like a sausage forked from the plate. When I got my students, they were deep into bad habits (of reading), and I don't think I *ever* had one who knew what style might be, certainly not how to talk about it.

I'll send this along, as you're packing for the USA. March is usually the worst of our winter, so bring your woollies. You'll be exchanging Gulf Stream weather for The Canadian Air Mass.

bon voyage!

22nd March 1994

Dear Guy,

Thank you for your survey of courses you have taught, and responses to my queries, plus Dr Davenport's Law of Infinite Regression and the flowering of crocusses. I'm back from New York a week now and pleased to be in Spring in Ireland: soft light and endless burgeoning, which barely stops in the winter here. New York was freezing but strangely peaceful and civilized. (I was in Cairo at Christmas. 14 million people in constant perturbation, honking their horns whenever possible. This is why New York seemed civilized.)

I interviewed more than twice as many people as I'd planned, some of them on the phone, which was surprisingly cosy even with strangers, and came back with a head full of thoughts about how, what and why to teach, and why not. Fortunately none of this thinking has yet had to face the reality of the university, since I returned from sabbatical into holiday. (This is why my postman representing many others can't understand what sort of job I do.)

Some general thoughts arose out of my trip, about America and Europe. I grew up in England, of Central European background, and came to Ireland in 1974. I teach French literature to students for whom Europe is a mythical entity that might bestow a job one day. Although physically close to, and technically part of the Europe from which their literature comes (English departments teach some but not much American literature), they mostly cannot manage a vision of it. It's as if vision-making were confined to personal gain and strapped by TV.

Your writing has always seemed European to me, or a blend of European and American which suited my transcontinental psyche. How are you aware of Europe? Do you visit? How are students aware of Europe? (You mention a student of Joyce who couldn't find Ireland on the map.)

How are they aware of history? Or of the arts? Many of your courses have a strong sense of history: literature and art as a presence in society for thousands of years. I only discovered a sense of history when in about 1980 I talked to students about Paris '68, at which I was a bemused witness, and heard their curiosity about what for them was vaguely alluring history.

How did you convey to students your sense of European or American cultural context? How did you introduce a new course? Was there much difference between graduate and undergraduate teaching?

Did you ever have large classes – 100 and up? We do here, as many as two or three hundred in first year. I wonder how it would be to issue them all with T-shirts with a big A or a big X.

You fear that 'traditional matter' in universities has been abandoned.

Did you teach traditional matter?

What is contemporary matter?

What was your main concern as a teacher?

How do you think your students perceived you?

Did you have any memorable teachers?

What you say about American universities could also be said about European ones, except that in Ireland no student can afford the insurance on fast cars – or any car at all. I wonder if a teacher can expect students to arrive equipped with intellectual passion. The few who will become writers or teachers or artists, perhaps, but not the rest. Although you claim to have had no patience with indifferent ignorant students, it seems to me that your approach and the words you choose to describe it, the strong combination of the abstract and the concrete, might well draw some students out of indifference and ignorance.

You say you taught as if that were the only thing you did. Is this an observation recollected in tranquillity? Did you decide to exclude your other modes – writer, essayist, guardian of crocusses?

Did you enjoy teaching? In general or in particular?

Could you say some more about your learning to read?

What did you learn from teaching?

Enough questions for now.

So far this is the only interview by letter. I was reading recently about an interview with Bill Gates the computer software wizard, which happened through E mail, or email, as Bill Gates called it. The different time scale but lack of telephone immediacy made for a funny style: two men plugged into the information highway, reading each other maybe fifteen minutes after writing, dispensing with all greetings, getting into the business straight away.

28 March 1994

Dear Judy!

Your address seems improbable and insufficient.

On our way by train to Auvers-sur-Oise once, Bonnie Jean and I were trying to figure out the ticket-punch device. An Irishman in a black suit, somebody out of Seán O'Casey, showed us how. 'The Frinch are a very particular people,' he said. 'You would not want to get on the wrong side of them.'

Years ago I met an Irish young man in Paris who was wanted by the police, I didn't ask why. And then there was Beckett, mustn't forget him. We sent him a pneu, with no hope of his answering, and went off to spend the day in St-Germain-en-Laye. Back at the hotel M. Papierny (out of Balzac) was in a dither. M. Bequette, gagnant of the Prix Nobel, had left his telephone number. So we found ourselves at the Closerie des Lilas talking about Proust and Joyce, Montherlant and Shakespeare.

How am I aware of Europe? (My Europe is imaginary, though with physical inspection for support.) I was at Oxford from 1948 to 1950, doing a B. Litt. In these years I nipped off to Paris and Menton as often as I could, and spent a summer in northern Italy. Then, years later, Bonnie Jean and I began having summer vacations in France, England, and Denmark (the latter most recently). In 1964 (before meeting Bonnie Jean) I spent a summer in England, France, Italy, Greece, and the Netherlands. I correspond with French and Danish friends.

'Students' (that is, the young in college) go off to Europe with NO information whatsoever. They think that what it has to offer will be evident.

It has been observed that the American middle class has no history, no past. History as the road travelled does not exist for them.

When I taught, I tried to tell stories about an historical event, in lurid colors. The *Avrora* steaming into St Petersburg with its red flag. Lee crossing the Mason–Dixon Line, standing in his stirrups while the band played 'Dixie'. Gumilev before the firing squad. On a student evaluation: 'Professor Davenport knows everything, and what he doesn't know he makes up, which is even better.' This (if I recognized the handwriting) was from a very good student.

My classes at Kentucky were small. Lecture courses are limited to 25. My seminars ranged from a dozen to 3.

You make a good point in asking if I taught traditional matter. I did and I didn't. As a modernist I gave the first courses ever, anywhere, in Olson, Zukovsky, and Johnson.

But I would like to have had the sense that I was adding to the students' knowledge of a tradition. Contemporary writers have a way of standing on the past, especially Pound, Eliot, and Joyce.

My main concern as a teacher was to get students to read for themselves. To show them that reading is in some ways as important as writing. A reader is NOT an audience, is not passive.

Did I have any memorable teachers? O yes.

In high school, JACK SPANN, the first intellectual I'd ever seen. He taught history, French, and Spanish. He had been on a bicycle tour of France. He changed completely my idea of a teacher. My grade-school teachers were all nice middle-aged women, friends of my mother and my aunts. I discovered books around age 10, and *knew* (accurately) that Miss Anna Brown knew nothing of Leonardo da Vinci or Tarzan of the Apes or Sherlock Holmes. So not until I got to Jack Spann's classes did I find someone who *did* know about cinquecento Florence and Picasso.

At Duke I had some very good language teachers, a Dr Rogers for Latin (who was willing to meet in the evenings for sight reading *ex togam*), and James Nardin Truesdale for Greek. The teacher who influenced me most was Katherine Gilbert, philosopher and aesthetician. And her friend Clare Leighton, of the art department (I became her printer and model). She had known David Jones, Eric Gill, Augustus John, had painted Gandhi's portrait, and was, I suppose, my first European.

At Oxford, HUGO DYSON (Henry Victoria George Dyson Dyson, called 'Hugo' by his troops in WW I because of his fluent French). I hated his friend C.S. 'Jack' Lewis as the biggest fraud I'd ever seen, and had no way of appreciating his other close friend Ronald Tolkien.

At Harvard, HARRY LEVIN (my hero) – I now see him as a man meticulously repeating Georg Brandes, a subject Proust could have analyzed subtly. Also CEDRIC WHITMAN, the Greek scholar. ('Don't mind Davenport, he's probably translating from the Laurentian manuscript' – to the class when I had, through poverty, not the Jebb edition of the Antigone but the Loeb text).

Alas, for every good teacher I suffered under the dullest and most ignorant lecturers of the century. I had a demented psychology prof at Duke whose schema was that 'grass iss oll-vase grinner on the other side' (he was Swedish). And a philosophy prof who talked to the blackboard. I've spent lots of time undoing much miseducation. My course in Romantic Eng Lit was entirely anecdotes about the poets, with some hint that Wordsworth wrote about daffodils and Shelley about Intellectual Beauty.

I tried to model my lectures on those of Hugo Dyson and my preparation on Levin.

In *Every Force* there's the material for a class in the iconography of poems. This gives an idea of how I worked.

I'm still learning to read!

I don't know if there *is* a psychology of reading, but the act (the event) interests me. There's a chemistry of two imaginations. You address a text both passively and actively. There is a personal response in with the critical and the aesthetic.

Jules Verne, for instance, and Michel Tournier. I am aware in JV that he's writing for children (and my command of French is about that of a child). Tournier is writing for God knows who, and his vocabulary taxes my French (there's a word in *Les météores* that I've never tracked down, something to do with garbage dumps).

The resistance of a language not one's own is beguiling and satisfying. At the moment I'm having to read Zolla's *Lo stupore infantile*, as he sent it to me and will be expecting a response. I can read the words but the tone escapes me.

To answer What did I learn from teaching. Everything. My advice to beginning teachers is to know ten times more than the students.

★

I read the Bill Gates article. BJ (who uses it all the time) notes that e-mail is terser and more aggressive than conversation or writing. Nor have they got the kinks out. BJ was inviting some local Women Studies faculty to lunch (there's a key that will reach them) but she mistakenly pushed the key for a list of WS faculties at every university from Hawaii to Maine, and invited about 2000 people for lunch the next day. Regrets came in all afternoon.

To clarify a point. I taught as if I were only a teacher. I never mentioned being a writer, certainly not a painter. Tolkien never alluded to hobbits in his lectures on Anglo-Saxon. That I wrote fiction was apparently a great secret for the faculty also. Once, to oblige a fund-raising reading for the student literary magazine, I agreed to read a story. A colleague in the English dept came to this reading.

Afterwards, he said he was surprised that I would read somebody else's story as mine. I tried to fathom his remark. 'You read from a book.' I handed him the book (*Da V's Bike*). He was upset that I hadn't told him that I had a book of fiction published. I told him there were six, with more in the press.

Distance may be our difference. (Your Irish students and France.) I remember gathering from our hôtelier in Bordeaux that Parisians are an uncivilized bunch without manners or morals. The Danes talk about the Swedes as if they were Martians.

Your vita shows you to be in the thick of things, even film. Do you have your students memorize verse? That's something I wish I'd done.

9th May

Dear Guy,

I'm delighted that my vita shows me to be in the thick of things! As I was delighted to hear from the publisher of this book when I suggested the subject to her, that I'd popped up in the middle of a hot debate! It's true I have done a great variety of things in the last ten years. I think it was my way of de-scholarizing myself. All those other things – film, opera, collaborations – to say nothing of growing veg on a hill in Ireland – have everything to do with teaching. Like a common style, rhythm, a common diversity. I like the phrase I heard from Gayatri Spivak about her knowledge being a mile wide and an inch deep. Most approaches to education in the arts lack breadth, and with it an attendant wisdom.

Many people's accounts of being taught suggest that a teacher is not necessarily memorable and influential because of what students understand of his or her words, but because of some habit or manner or passion that distracts them. I'm sure when your students listened to you they heard a painter, they saw a story writer, they absorbed a critic, they remembered a human being.

What habit or manner or passion might your students have noticed in your teaching? (You mentioned one student who enjoyed the bits you made up!)

Do you think you were a subversive teacher?

Did you like your students?

Do you have children?

You write about adolescence a lot in your essays and stories. Is the kind of learning that goes on at that age, in boxcars and pine trees, in lavender fields, comparable with the kind of learning that goes on in universities?

Were you able to teach as a wise and exploratory 12 year old?

What governed your choice of books?

Can you say more about Hugo Dyson's lectures and Harry Levin's preparation?

How much did these teachers actively involve you as student?

Did they ask questions? Tell stories? Sit still?

Let me add to the world store of awful teachers: my French teacher in grammar school (who perversely wooed me or shooed me to the heights of Mallarmé years later) told us one day that she never took books out of the library because often you found people's hairs in them.

An artist/detective friend of mine told me about a class he gave once at art school. He told the students that they should stay very quiet because something important was about to happen. Then he made his way over to the window, which was high in the wall, clambered up to it with some difficulty, opened the window and climbed out.

You ask do I get my students to memorize verse. No, I don't, though I've thought of it. The huge classes are a deterrent. When I was about nine we had to memorize Keats's *Meg Merilees*. I carried it out of the schoolroom, I inhabited it. It had the open road and a fresh breeze blowing through. That feeling of inhabiting is a good model for reading. Many students talk about finding it hard to concentrate, to focus for long enough on the page. Older people in Ireland were often educated to memorize. One of my students told me once that her Granny knew *Macbeth* by heart. The complete works of Shakespeare are probably in armchairs by the fire all across County Cork.

14th May 1994

Dear Judy!

Dan Seltzer, the actor, used to do a wicked mimesis of Harry Levin. First he smoothed his Adolph Menjou moustache. Then, looking at each of us around the seminar table in turn, '"C'est une grande habilité que de savoir cacher son habilité", to pile Pelion on Ossa, as Virgil says in The Georgics, "l'éloquence se moque de l'éloquence", to quixotize Quijote, following Nietzsche in an unpublished Zettel at Heidelberg, comedy transcends its exigencies by mirroring itself, so to speak . . .'

The seminars unrolled like film in a projector, flawlessly, quotation by quotation. One sat in paralyzed awe.

Hugo Dyson began lecturing in the hallway outside the lecture room, continuing up the aisle. He may have begun in the High as far as we knew. I think his friend Tolkien must have based the hobbit Meriadoc on him: chipper, smiling, bright-eyed, and hopping about, gesturing.

This was a series of lectures about moonlight and fierce sunlight in Shakespeare, and about nonrecognition because of disguises or because of tragic blindness. 'I thought you that cunning whore of Venice!' – disappearing from view as he plunged to the floor to strangle Desdemona.

I never said a word to Harry outside class except to give him my advice (which he asked for, moments before my doctoral viva voce) on a damaged Picasso that had just arrived. I said he should send it back. I gathered Pablo had himself packed it, and made a mess of it.

⋆

Your questions. Over 37 years of lecturing I evolved, I hope for the better. My very first lecture – I was just out of the army and a week late (St Louis, Washington Univ) for the semester. I was told that a sophomore class was reading the *Odyssey*, and that the class began in ten minutes. So I went over to the classroom and gave an extempore account of the hypothetical Phoenician periplus posited by Victor Bérard, filling the blackboard with Greek and proto-Hebrew and a map of the Mediterranean, quoting from the Odyssey in Greek. Apparently I might as well have given the whole lecture in Greek. Over the next few days I discovered that they were all functionally illiterate, totally ignorant of any history, and as unconversant with Greek (or any other culture) as a horse.

Thus began, first crack out of the box, the Law of Infinite Regression. By the time of retirement, I had various techniques for laying down historical contexts, narrative and dramatic. I had a letter from a student of a decade back just last week. She remembered a whole lecture on a single sentence of Mandelstam (the opening of 'Theodosia') 'about wheat' as she recalled – actually about the adjective white, and starch, and the Red and White armies, and so on.

A subversive teacher? In what sense? There's very little to subvert in the USA. A course I gave in the modernist movement in Paris delighted a Jewish student, who came to the office to ask if I were deliberately giving a course in Jewish creativity.

Kentuckians are a primitive lot, but they are also, at their best, an honest, frank people who like to have their backwardness challenged and changed. The only courses in religion are in the English department, disguised as Biblical Studies. These are in the manner of the German higher criticism, and frequently draw Fundamentalists, surprisingly open-minded and respectful of critical perspectives.

The univ of Ky has The Donovan Scholars program: anybody over 55 can take all courses free. This is a wonderful leaven of experienced, mature souls. I made many friends among them – Mollie Seletsky, originally of Odessa, a NYC grammar school teacher, retired, who came here to take my Joyce seminar (bringing a 1922 *Ulysses* she'd bought in Paris). We corresponded until her death, for some ten years, and I got her to write her autobiography, now on deposit at the Jewish Archives in Cincinnati.

Yes, I liked my students, when they were likeable. I have many colleagues who were once students. At one time the editor and chief editorial writer on the local paper were students of mine.

[This is an anecdotal subject that could fill a book.]

No children.

Adolescence in my ravings. I'm convinced that we're at our intellectual and imaginative best around age 12. I've worked with the young all those years, and became aware that I was teaching students who ought to have been educated five-to-ten years earlier. European students (English, French, Danish) have the equivalent of an American university education by age 15.

Hence my (probably sentimental) interest in precocity and in Fourier's scheme to shape personality very early in a utopian society. Every child a Mozart, a Picasso, a Piaget.

I hold with Agassiz that man is as metamorphic as frog or butterfly. The child is a different animal than the adolescent. Zygote, foetus, infant, child, adolescent, *juventus* (in Roman law a person under age 35), grown-up (I have a psychiatrist friend who says the mind is mature at 60), *senex* and end of the line. 'Second childhood' is quite real.

Choice of books? You mean that I lectured on? Mine, and I didn't use 'text-books' or anthologies (except for poetry surveys). *I* was the text-book.

Biographical, the bare bones. Born 23 Nov 1927, Anderson, South Carolina. S. of Guy Davenport Sr and Marie Fant Davenport. Daddy was the Southeastern (later Railway) Express agent.

Kennedy Street Grammar School (2 blocks away). High school, four blocks away. Art classes at Anderson College.

Duke University, BA 1948, English and Classics.

Oxford (Merton College) as Rhodes Scholar, B. Litt. 1950, with first thesis at Oxford on Joyce (Symbolism in *Ulysses*).

1950–1952: XVIIIth Airborne Corps, at Fort Bragg, NC.

1952–54: taught English at Washington University, St Louis.

1954–61: PhD, Harvard, English tutor at Eliot House.

1961–63: Haverford College, Philadelphia.

1963–90: Univ of Kentucky, retiring as Distinguished Alumni Professor of English, on being given a MacArthur Fellowship.

Books and articles. Drawings and paintings. Surely you're not putting bibliographies into this book?

Meanwhile,
Guy

Andrei Codrescu

S. F. Tabachnikoff

Andrei Codrescu writes poetry, essays, memoirs and fiction. He has translated the work of Lucian Blaga from the Romanian, and has edited the magazine *Exquisite Corpse* since it began in 1983. He is a frequent commentator on National Public Radio's *All Things Considered*, and a frequent contributor to ABC News's *Nightline*. He has written and starred in *Road Scholar*, a documentary film directed by Roger Weisberg, which has won many prizes. He lives in New Orleans and teaches at Louisiana State University in Baton Rouge.

Passion and Possibility

I'M IN A PROGRAMME called Creative Writing, but really secretly I teach reading, because I figure that the more books they read the less they write. I have a policy, like the government's policy of paying people not to farm. I'm trying to prevent them from graphomania. There are too many writing students and they produce the same thing, which is, nothing. Most of these writing programmes have become mandarin factories. They produce essays for the Emperor in the hope of obtaining Civil Service jobs. These schools may not exist much in Europe yet – where you still have a good conservative sense that certain arts should get plenty of slack – but they're coming.

I teach both graduate and undergraduate courses in poetry and non-fiction, though I have occasionally taught fiction workshops. I give them a reading list that is composed of about three to four hundred dollars worth of books which makes them groan with horror, but I tell them that this is the beginning of their great library so they need to have these books. I have some anthologies and then some collected, selected poems by poets that they should not be able to live without, and some volumes by contemporaries.

I assume that they've been through the *Norton Anthology of American Literature* or *English Poetry*, but that is not always the case. I've had undergraduate classes that I've asked if they knew who Coleridge was and they had no idea. They've heard of Blake but they thought it was Robert Blake, the guy in *Baretta* on television. I was so infuriated once by the undergraduates that I divided the last four hundred years of English poetry by fifteen – there were thirty of them in class – and I gave everyone a chunk of time they had to become expert in and then I had them present all these various chunks, some of which were overlapping, and so we had four hundred years of poetry in one semester in tiny pieces in which everybody held only one piece of the puzzle. These are the people you might take to the woods like in *Fahrenheit 451* and reconstruct, if not literature, then, at least, the world according to Norton.

This time around they just read the poetry without looking much at what life was like when it was written, but I think next time I'm going to ask them to dress appropriately and bring their opium and their port wine to school. They should have a sense of the time the literature comes from. But how exactly you do that, I don't know. It would be ideal if the university itself wasn't designed the way it is but rather more monastically and had small locked cells where we could just keep them for fifteen days at a time and make them translate the complete works of someone or other. But failing that, I think they get more from it if they themselves are going out to get the information and imagine the period rather than being lectured at, which they can dispose of very quickly.

I do occasionally lecture. I taught the twentieth-century novel and that was a series of lectures and I really didn't pay any attention to anything but the most interesting questions, like, What are the 'tricks'? What is live and what is dead? Is it generative? I taught Conrad, Ford Madox Ford, Wyndham Lewis, Nabokov. I taught books I knew were not being taught in other literature classes in the university. The canon is fairly conventional and I don't think it means anything. I base my choices on the fact that I think that literary history, the way it's crystallized in the canon, is wrong, simply wrong, that other choices could have been made just as easily and in fact they have been made but remain outside. This has partly to do with the whole business of criticism and literary history.

So I make my own canon. But it's not just my own, it's really a writers' canon; it's writers I've found useful to me as a writer. And the phenomenon of writers coming to English as a second language is an important one, maybe the most important in the twentieth century. One of the good books about this is Terry Eagleton's book on exile, though it's somewhat simplified by his Marxism.

I do encourage students to read some books about books. There are certain texts that I would like to teach as literature. I haven't done it yet because in this country we are flooded by a great wave of theory. We have one of everything in the department. We have our Marxist and our post-Marxist and our feminist Marxist etc. I think I'm an ultra-realist if anything. I read theory the way I read literature. I read Derrida and I found him very funny. Actually one of my favourite texts which I would love to teach if anybody could read it the way I read it, is a book called *Anti-Oedipus, Capitalism and Schizophrenia* by Gilles Deleuze and Félix Guattari, which is a poetic work. The problem is that the English academic school, well the American anyway, has taken these books and made a deadly business out of them. If you leave out the humour, that's what happens. They offer the opportunity of a specialized language to people who are groping wildly for another ghetto with high walls. So creating specialties and subdivisions of specialties is the business.

These books make students throw up mostly, unless they get caught up in it and then of course they become clones. Putting the theory in front of the literature is a disaster and students don't like it either. The only purpose for the language of theory is to amplify literature, or that was the idea in the beginning. If there was a beginning. I think it was the critics' desire to dispense with literature altogether and write their own. I understand that because it's too difficult to apply yourself well to something written by somebody else. Impressionist criticism is pretty bad.

So I haven't really taught critics, but I wouldn't mind reading them alongside works of literature. I would have them read Foucault, for instance, because he's a writer and he's a good one, or Gilles Deleuze, who's a poet. It's a different genre really, you could call it the philosophical poetic essay. The form of our time may very well be the poetic essay or the essay novel – like Kundera's novels, for instance, which are essays with characters. I think that's an attractive literature.

As for what the students like to read – a few of them like to read stories with sex in them. They like to identify with characters, they like wish fulfilment, daydreaming. I suspect that a few of them who are readers probably read a lot of bad books that they don't talk about. And why not? I haven't taught any of these so-called bad books, but I would love to teach a course in romance novels, for instance, or cowboy novels. My good friend Ted Berrigan who was a great poet, was addicted to cowboy books and he read all the two hundred and fifty books that Louis Lamour wrote. Actually Ted wrote a terrific pastiche cut up cowboy novel called *Clear the Range*. On the back of it the blurb says, 'In front of him were men, behind him were men, he was a man among men.'

I let the students hang out because I live in New Orleans and teach in Baton Rouge and I have a little apartment there where I stay two nights a week. So I hang out with them and what often happens is that people will read poems part of the night and we write a few collaborations. It's the best way to teach. In the *agora* of my flat. Some of my best students in writing have gone to New York or to San Francisco where the action is, although that may not be quite true today so much. But they left and they are doing things, they're still in it. Most of them do other things but some of them, the bright ones, get further institutionalized and go on to do PhDs in teaching and they really never leave the institution. The ones who become bankers write splendid memos in iambic pentameters.

It was just an accident that I got into an institution in the first place. I came out from Europe after a year, went to California, then left because things weren't too good there; I didn't have any money. I came back through Baltimore where I had a friend. I went to a party and met John Barth, the novelist, and he said we have this visiting writer gig here at Hopkins for a year. I ended up staying two years and then I thought well, this might be the way to do things. I had always been teaching on street corners and in cafés, so why not get paid for it?

The teaching I had myself was informal really. One of my great teachers was Ted Berrigan, who taught at the corner of Second Avenue and St Mark's Place in New York standing up with his morning coffee and sometimes at 2 a.m. It really was simply that kind of thing. So I'm really anti-institutional. And I am in one, it's a paradox. I was born in Romania, I live in America. That's another paradox.

The teaching that I got in school in Romania almost destroyed my love for literature. It was dull, it was uninspired, it was done by bored people. The only thing that saved me through my schooling was in high school I had a window to look out of and daydream and a notebook filled with scribbles. I never heard a word those people said for all those years.

I'm sure many of my students would say the same thing. I think the ones that read may get something from interesting professors. If they read, they may also conceive the idea that it's possible to be a writer or an educated person without actually having to write the type of papers and answer the type of questions that are put to you in school with all the assignments and grades.

I do give grades and I make assignments but I do not bore myself; I invent problems. I've taught non-fiction undergraduate classes and I sometimes tell them to write letters to the dead and some of them do very well. Most of them are not quite sure who died in history, they mostly write letters to dead people they knew. I have a large file of wacky assignments. Cut up the tabloids with Shakespeare. Translate by sound from languages you don't know. Write reviews of non-existent books. Invent ancient poets. I teach collaboration as well. I've taught a class in *Exquisite Corpse*-making. Those are a lot of fun because they are a kind of x-ray of the class mind. Students also like to do that on their own because when they leave class it's one way to communicate with people and get close to them under the pretext of creating literature. They collaborate furiously. They like to because it seems like a more high-minded way of learning.

I started the magazine (*Exquisite Corpse*) because I was completely disgusted by the low quality of discussion in American literary magazines – particularly the university quarterlies which are dismal – and by the fact that there is a very enfeebled buddy system in literature. I know it gets interrupted now and then by us nomad-beatnik-warriors. I started it because I found that everybody lied all the time when they put pen to paper, especially in magazines, and I thought if I could create something that had a degree of frankness, not as high as actually talking in a bar and telling the truth, but at least approximating that, then it would be a new thing and it was and is.

It's timidity, it's fear that make people lie when they write, it's a kind of modest professionalism that American writers admire, a lot of it having to do with the appearance of this new type of being called the professor-poet rather than the poet-professor which is an earlier version. Also there is only a small pie around and people get various kinds of rewards from it. That makes them careful and timid but also mediocre because people who are truly great don't really give a fuck.

There's also the problem that many of the certainties of the modern are completely dissolved now. We are in a time when almost anything goes and the idea of making something new or appealing, or something that incorporates an *esprit de temps* is very tenuous. Of course the *temps* have to have an *esprit*. The eighties didn't have one, besides making money. The nineties does.

The *Corpse* provides some fresh air space in America. We were sued twice almost immediately after we started, so that was a great honour and we continue to be polemical and it's made a difference. I see now that the tone we set is coming out of a number of things being published but mainly from young folks. It's amazing we've lasted this long. It's a miracle, particularly since we haven't taken any government money and it's not a university magazine. It just barely makes the printer's bill every month.

I like my students and I like talking to them and I like turning them on when I can. I don't like the frantic business of the university with its army-like rankings. I'm not too thrilled either about the quality of discussion that goes on about the curriculum and debates about what to teach and I'm not crazy about the political correctness fever that's sweeping the campuses and I don't like the people who are against it either because the whole debate seems to be really irrelevant.

What matters is passion and possibility. The extraordinary thing about being nineteen or twenty-something years old and being in school is that you're absolutely open to anything. There is a mind in an absolutely wonderful potential state and if it doesn't get shut down in the many ways that we know how to shut it down, anything could happen. So I have the sort of awe for the genius of adolescence or near-adolescence and the fact that if the right thing sparks them there's no telling what they will do. They could be lit up for a long time.

If they do remember very clearly things that happen to them, they are not the things that we usually think or suspect are our main teaching. It's the remarks of their fellow students, or occasionally something addressed to them, but I don't think much else makes a difference. If teaching happens in a real way, it happens in the interstices or the margins or in an oblique way. I had a student, a fiction writer at Hopkins, who told me that he was haunted for years by a remark somebody made in one of his workshops, or something I said afterwards, and it stuck with him. Being a rather psychotic type, he ended up doing some time in the loony bin and he based the reasons for his neurosis on this moment. Of course that's an exaggerated example, but I have a feeling that to some extent that's what happens to everybody.

The teacher has tremendous power, even the most informal teachers – and I think I'm probably one of those, although I can be a horrendous dictator as well – even the most informal people are in fact surrounded by an aura of authority that they might not realize. Even if you undermine authority, in fact you're still an authority figure, just a peculiar one.

Louisiana is a Catholic state, but I think the way they take it to mean here is that they have licence to do everything and then they go to confession and it's cool. One of the things that distinguishes Louisiana from other places is that there are bigger families here and they still hold together in a way that they don't in the rest of America. One of the things that does is really make them fairly gifted at language because they do hear stories from all kinds of people of all ages.

But the television and pop culture business is probably a lot worse in America than in Europe because we've done it for longer. I think this is the land of the digest, what do you call those things? They tell you a book in five pages of pictures. It's true that in writing classes students come because they want to, but in the undergraduate classes there are some who come because they have a requirement in English and they heard that poetry is easy. They may have heard this about other people because they get scared when they come to my class and realize they have to read so much. I also occasionally make them memorize poetry which they can do quite well. It's good just to hear it out loud, hear how pretty it is and make them get up and say it. I read to them also. I have certain poems I have memorized too, so there are occasions when I burst spontaneously into song.

When I start teaching a poet, if I have known them personally I will tell salacious stories about things that happened in my presence. If I don't know them I still try to tell them stories that these were interesting people. I don't place the text above the story. In fact everything is relevant and it's possible that what's not in the poem is what's relevant.

For instance, you can read a poem by Frank O'Hara called 'On Rachmaninov's Birthday', which he wrote during the third movement, and bring in the piece. The reason Frank wrote it was because somebody asked him to, or challenged him to write it, dared him to write it while the music was playing, and he did. So the circumstance is very interesting. The poem and the circumstance are two parallel worlds. So in this case I play them music because he wrote the poem during that third movement. The poem is the music, you can hear both of them at the same time very well.

I show them pictures if I'm teaching a poet who was very good friends with painters. One of the things that really makes sense about their way of composition is to talk about how their friends work in another medium. Like the New York school of poets. Or someone like Max Jacob; if you're teaching Jacob it's natural to talk about Cubism.

I teach some poetry in translation and how to read it in the original and hear the sound. I use the very good Random House *Anthology of Twentieth-Century French Poetry* edited by Paul Auster, which has the original alongside the translations which are done by a number of very good poets. The foreign literature departments here don't teach much modern literature.

I hope I create readers. I know that students say later that they had a good time in my classes. I don't know what that means because publishing poetry is not a business proposition in this country and if we were successful in creating readers then poetry books would sell more than they do.

I try to create an illicit aura around books as well, to make them feel that they're very lucky to have this book assigned and to be able to read this because in fact it should be forbidden. I think that the best readers of Joyce are those people who read him when there were passages underlined in it, in the era before pornography. I like to convey the sense that there are certain books that will do that. To make them read Bataille is to immediately give them an unbelievable shock. Then it gives them the feeling that it's permissible to go ahead and read and find out strange things.

I use my authority to link what would seem on the surface to be shocking and forbidden and perhaps pornographic, with some profound sense of thought and the deeper activities involved in it. The forbidden and the sacred are connected. It's the sense of awe and trespass and mystery that comes with reading something one should not be reading.

Schools should be built more like caves than crash pads, they should be like honeycomb mountains with places that you need to find, secret doors that say Do Not Enter.

There is an erotic component to all teaching. You have there a group of people who are thinking very intensely about sex and death. The atmosphere that you create, or the kind of tolerance or space that you allow for that to play itself out, the theatre of sexual drama, is really very important as well in determining whether they're going to be bored or attentive. Teaching is a form of seduction, as is writing. You play with a whole class of young bodies with minds attached perhaps. It's a marvellous minefield. Some reporter asked Allen Ginsberg, 'What is your teaching method?' and Allen said, 'Well you must sleep with your students,' and she laughed. She thought he was joking and he was deadly serious. It's not something I would recommend particularly – you'd lose your job – but Allen just articulated that. He brought it back to Socratic teaching, which is probably the oldest way of doing things – older men to instruct younger boys – in every way.

What Allen Ginsberg says is that the only thing he has done was to continue Walt Whitman's project of complete candour. Whitman said the poets of the future will be candid. This is something that remains desirable and hasn't happened. I think there should be no difference between the teachers and the poets. Candour and passion. Teachers have to feel vulnerable because vulnerability is our condition. Cloaking yourself in the trappings of authority is a dangerous illusion. It cuts off the ways in which the students can articulate their own truths and it makes them into terrible people, the kind that learn how to hide and exploit and manipulate and not kill – because that's an honest thing – but hide and perpetuate it. What you learn is what you pass on.

David Matlin

Anne O'Neill

David Matlin is a novelist and poet, who has been teaching in a prison education programme for the last ten years. His novel *How the Night is Divided* has recently been published. He lives in New York with the painter and ceramicist Gail Schneider and their son Clay.

Macbeth as Serial Killer

I NEVER REALLY DID teach in a regular situation. I didn't have any formal degree. I had gone to did college but not a great deal, just as a kid in California and then some in Detroit. I took my work to the poet Robert Creeley about twenty-five years ago. He liked it very much and asked me if I'd like to do something with it. I said yes and plus I'd like to read. He got me a fellowship and I got into a PhD program with no Bachelor's or anything like that. So I didn't have a teaching fellowship.

Then when I did start to teach I taught EFB – English for the Foreign-Born. That was very interesting for me because I literally had to teach people how to speak English and I had to make up everything. So when I began teaching on a more formal basis, as an adjunct, that sense of literally how to make up everything from a new beginning each time you walked into a class was very important to me.

Since I've never taught in a so-called normal situation, I feel very strongly about it. I feel it's a very high calling. Where I do teach (in the prison) it's so significant, not only for the people that I work with, but for myself. Literally, people's lives are at stake here. There aren't all of the usual assumptions: that it won't get you a job or get you this or get you that once you receive your bachelor's, or put you into a situation where if you want to become a writer, you can start networking from that point onward. It's not like that. For these guys it's their first and last chance to realize something about themselves and their own minds that has never happened before. It's for very high stakes. So I have to be completely prepared every time I go in.

They're much older, even though some of the prisoners might be of college age. They're just so different. There is such a completely different approach and the difference in expectations really doesn't have any comparison with anything I know on the outside. Every man I work with for the most part is either Black or Hispanic and then there are sadly, and surprisingly in some ways, a number of Irish in the prison. There's a large amount still of poor Irish-Americans who are in prison and I would suppose that the problems of poverty that they began their migrations with, that feeling of who they are with the problem of the Irish background still, even that still haunts – the presence of an American history. So I see a lot of those men too and they are tough and as dangerous as everybody else in the prison.

They are in prison and so the end is a much greater jeopardy for them: can they get a job? What kind of crimes have been committed? If they are crimes of specific kinds of violence then they are shut out no matter whether they have paid their price to society or not. If they are sexual crimes, they can't teach; then the possibilities are really limited. I don't know for the most part which crimes have been committed because it's not my job to know that. I don't have, nor do I want access to files, even though I know in many instances – because I have become close to these people – what crimes have been committed. I don't want to know who's a rapist. It's not my position, it's not my business, because the nature of the program is that everybody gets a chance to get this education, if they want it, if they qualify for it. And the judgement about which crimes have been committed has nothing to do with it. Most of the men I work with are junkies, or have come into the prison system on the basis of what it means to live in the inner cities at this point in America's history. Or Vietnam veterans at the beginning, who were in for armed robbery or various forms of violence that overwhelmed them when they fought the war. If mixed in with this are criminals whose crimes are personally repugnant to me, I don't want to know it and it's not my job to know it. And everybody else who teaches in the programme also lives under the same shadow. So there's a lot of questions you ask yourself.

Teaching people how to read and write puts you in a position to know people in this very strange way. It's essential. You see individuals who start to realize that they can at least in part overcome the shape of the backgrounds that they're from. I don't know if they can ever overwhelm the problems of racism in this society. Individually they might, but as a group of people it still seems very difficult. But once you see the beginnings of a recognition of another kind of mind emerging – because even though they're criminals it doesn't mean they are not smart, they're very smart – and how important that can become in that person's life, then you see at the same time a completely different kind of imagination taking shape.

Many of the men I work with are very gifted. Many of them have already been writing plays, poetry, short stories. They have been deeply involved in the nature of a personal reading for a long time. They come in with this extraordinary hunger. When I teach creative writing, I try not to impose upon it unnecessarily but to attach to it a series of readings of poetry, novels or plays so that what is being attempted as first or second expression also has some bearing upon a deep reading of something else.

There was one man in a class who had been in the Americal Division, you know, the My Lai massacre in the late sixties in Vietnam with the platoon that was headed by this young kid named Lieutenant William Calley and they went in and killed children, women and old men, killed about, I don't know how many hundreds of people. It was an instance of the wrongness of the war and what had taken place. So this particular man was Black and he was in the Americal Division, but he did not take place in the massacre, he got sick of the killing and ended up in a tiger cage in-country and basically was in prison there for refusing to take part in any more violence. When I met him he was in for a second bid, I mean he was in for a second return to prison for armed robbery and I had him in this creative writing course and started him reading William Carlos Williams and H.D., Hilda Doolittle. And Jane Harrison, one of the really great mythographers of the early twentieth century, who along with Pound and a group of others made some of the first inroads into a new recognition of myth.

So I gave out these reading assignments along with what they felt they might want to do in terms of their first exploration of a deep writing. He ended up going through this material, he just ate it like it was the first piece of cake he ever had, and ended up writing the most extraordinary first poems I ever read. I got him published in a national magazine on the basis of those poetries and they were really the most startling, expertly composed pieces of music of their kind that I have ever seen. He completely grasped, understood and mastered Pound, Williams and Rimbaud within a semester. It's not unusual to see that first awakening into real genius.

One of the things that you see in teaching in prison is what the price of racism is historically – as a historical crime. You see that it could be a different world. So that's the way I spend my time, as a teacher or as a so-called teacher within that kind of atmosphere. So it is very different.

I contract as an adjunct for an English department at a local state college. I'm the only one who teaches English in the prison programme. I'm the only one who teaches literature. The rest of the faculty won't come in, because they are either scared or they think they are too goddamned good or whatever it is. They won't come in and belittle themselves trying to teach in this program. I think it shows a terrible lack of courage, and also the fact that this group of students – not in opposition to the students on campus because they are all students – but this group of students has one of the greatest potentials for national recognition of any group of students I've ever seen. They're on par, once they get their basics down, with fellow students at Harvard or Princeton or any of the so-called best schools. The faculty that's supposed to service them or that might want to service them won't even come in. So that's a kind of ugly detail. But there are other programmes in New York State where a majority of the professors from the various departments do go in and have significant impact. I meet people from other programmes who have made a very strong commitment to the prisoners who might be adjuncted to their particular departments. For instance SUNY at Buffalo. That program became an extension of Black Mountain in 1963. Robert Creeley and a whole bunch of other people have a very strong programme up there for students on campus and those coming out of prison education programmes in New York State. If a student studied, got a bachelor's degree and wanted to go into a really strong programme, Buffalo offers that student the possibility of coming in and getting a PhD or even a Masters. So there are instances where there is great care.

There's no degree in literature right now where I teach. I have been lobbying the English department at SUNY at New Paltz to consider instituting a bachelor's degree in literature and perhaps even at some point a master's degree which would be the first instance, I think, in any program either in New York State or in the country in which an art major might be possible. Many of these guys are very interested in play writing, in writing novels, short stories. And they get PEN awards. So I'm hoping that at some point they might consider this. Right now it's not possible because these programmes are under attack on a nationwide basis. There's a great hatred now for these programmes. They're still considered experimental. The men and women who go through them experience an eighty-seven per cent reduction in return rates. In other words eighty-seven per cent of these people will never come back to prison again once they get out, which is remarkable, given the fact that prison is the number one growth industry in the United States.

So the hidden intents that lie behind all of this really are – I hate to use a word like evil – but the viciousness of these shadows of intent that lie behind all of these statistics and all of these revelations are very, very difficult to comprehend. And I think if it's this way in Europe – and it's certainly this way in America – that we are all in for some ugly surprises.

I feel that the only place to begin to do something beyond words is to start at the most difficult of all places, which is prison, to begin to establish counter-statistics and counter-realities that go against the tradition of segregation, racism and superstition. That's the strongest place that one might start, rather than putting words before yourself. Just do it, you know, just for those people. It's very important for me to do this.

Two years ago I did a literature course. There were eight or nine texts that had to be done in one semester including: William Carlos Williams's *In the American Grain*, Joan Didion's *Play it as it Lays*, Claude Brown's *Manchild in the Promised Land*. Claude Brown is a Black writer who wrote this extraordinary autobiography. He was a young boy truly headed for a life sentence in prison and somehow he got himself out of it and it still is a profoundly moving document. As a piece of experimental literature it's not so great, but as a piece of profoundly honest, moving personal content it's marvellous and these guys really loved it. I introduced them to Chester Himes. He's a Black writer who's very long in getting recognition and actually had to end up living in Europe like James Baldwin and Richard Wright and others. I use James Baldwin. The piece of Chester Himes I used was called *If He Hollers Let Him Go*, which is about a Black steelworker in shipyards in Los Angeles during the Second World War. It's one of the most difficult, nervous and angry pieces about racism that's ever been written by an American author. The other ones included were *Last Exit to Brooklyn* by Hubert Selby Jr, and two or three other ones that I can't remember right now. And these guys went through it.

I chose books not only because of who the students were, but also because of the maturity that they could bring to it. These are very difficult and in some ways violent novels. I used also John Rechy's *City of Night*. It's one of the most moving pieces of work of its kind that I've ever read. It's very difficult for me to present them with simple, undetailed works because of their maturity and because of the immensity of their experience even though they might not be as skilled as they – quote – should be. At the beginning I present them with such a difficult demand in reading that they do get good. They have to read it. If there are seven to nine texts that have to be read within a fifteen-week period, they have to really get it on.

The classes are seminar-like, sometimes as many as thirty students. I don't discuss themes or any of that stuff; I just go right into the book. I do my preparation, I do my reading and I certainly do my thinking and imagining about the materials and where they fit into an imagination of not only history but also literature. I try to make the tone of my teaching as tight as I can, poise myself and my students over a new abyss every time. And then I go into it right there. I don't have an approach where I talk to them about characterization, theme, narrative form. I try to recreate it in the classroom as a living thing rather than as a thing that can be analyzed or a thing that can be determined as a literary object that does not necessarily touch the deepest parts of you.

If I'm teaching a lower division course, say a freshman or sophomore course, a lot of my time is spent just teaching them how to write. What's a sentence, what's a paragraph, what's a subject-verb agreement? How do you begin to formalize the contents of the English language that are going to be the demands, not only for the university system here, but when you get outside? Where I am it's being watched so closely politically that if there is any question that these guys can't read and write, then the programmes are over. There have to be no questions, so these guys have to be good and they want to be good. Their pride in it is overwhelming.

When I'm sitting next to a Black man who's twenty-two or twenty-three years old and is in on a drug charge or in for a gun fight or whatever the kinds of violence there are that exist in the inner cities right now, and that kid has been in for three or four or five years and it's finally settling in what's happened here, you know, the grotesque horror of what prison really is and the equally grotesque horror of how that individual's life is going right down a shit tube, then to realize that the one thing that's going to save his ass is to come into contact with how smart he is, then it becomes a matter of life and death. So it is up for high stakes.

These guys that I work with are the most dangerous psychologists I've ever known, because they're, well to be honest, they're predators. They live in a predatory world, and living in a predatory world, they become predators and the kinds of psychology that they are masters of is a predatory psychology that is superb and the most dangerous of all psychologies I've ever seen. To tell you the truth, had I been younger, I don't know if I'd have been able to do this.

I get essays on Macbeth and Lady Macbeth as serial killers that are unlike any essays I have ever seen. I mean they really know what this is and they go right in. When it comes to the secret contents of these kinds of sicknesses, they know what they are and frankly some of the essays contain such quality of penetration, it scares the hell out of me. Do I really, really want to know this about Lady Macbeth and Macbeth? And is it new? Yes it is. They're not just cute academic analyses that propose one more inch of the pile; they're really different.

So they know they're smart. There's no doubt that they're smart. The way that they exercise their minds is within the framework of a specific kind of a predatory criminality. Their language is incredibly slick. These people are conmen; they're artists of their language on a very, very high level indeed. To begin to care about the tradition of thinking, of being a writer, or being active in the community as a businessman or a banker, which is all possible to them within what the fate of these programmes might bring them to on the outside. If you're a kid who has been making thirty-five thousand dollars a week running crack and cocaine and suddenly you're in prison and you're making twelve cents an hour licking up floors with yourself. But you're alive. That's certainly one comprehension.

I can't speak for these people because I have no right to. I can only speak for my side of it, but once they realize that they've got the one accomplishment, the other accomplishment is as hard to come by and it's a matter of whether they care about that accomplishment, whether they come to terms with the fact that it can give them a lasting pride. And it does. I end up knowing not only the people that I work with in the prison but knowing their families too, and there is great pride in it. These guys have a chance to go to college – they should have had a chance when they were young. The institutions that might have nurtured myself or my wife or my kids, if it had equally nurtured these people, probably eighty-five to ninety per cent of those people in prison right now would not be in prison. There is nobody to say that these guys couldn't have come up with a cure for cancer or new musics or anything. That one should see this happening, and at a late age, not at an early age, you know the contents of loss are so huge that there's almost no words for it. So that's the tragedy you know, another part of the tragedy is that.

They read secondary texts, if we can get a hold of them, on microfiches and through the inter-library loan network. But it takes time. They're so scared when they first hit Shakespeare, you know, that it takes about two weeks for them to get over the shock and then they realize that they can read it like the newspaper. Oh man, beautifully. I mean that's the way I approach it. I don't approach it as a difficulty, I tell them just to read it. Don't worry about whether you understand it, just read the goddamned thing. Then after you read it, sound it out, because you're really looking at a new art form. You're looking at a new object and it takes a long time. It takes your mind's eye maybe two weeks to find a focus for what it is. If you're looking at a new corporeal object, it takes time to focus on that too. What is it I'm looking at?

You know, and maybe there's a fossil there you've never seen, or whatever it is. So I try to approach it in that way, rather than just overwhelming them with, you know – we're going to read Shakespeare now man!

I try to tell them that the one way that you can really find an entrance into any of these kinds of readings, no matter what it is, is to get over your embarrassment and act it out. And if you can start acting it out, then you can start feeling it and if you can feel it first, even if you're feeling it blindly or groping at it blindly, you're going to feel something. And it doesn't have this awful analytical distance that so often is contained in other styles and forms of teaching.

Right now what are we reading? We started out with *Richard III* and my approach to it was: what in our more recent history matches this personality? Can you think of Nixon, Margaret Thatcher, Jimmy Carter, Ronald Reagan, Franklin Roosevelt, Abraham Lincoln, Frederick Douglass? Where can we begin to point out who Richard III is? What is this personality? And by the time they come to me they know Machiavelli – and if they don't, I try to make them aware of Machiavelli. Plus when I try to make them aware of Machiavelli, they care.

I taught about thirteen or fourteen years ago at a private expensive college, with relatively wealthy kids, mostly white, and we were reading Martin Luther King Junior's 'Letter from a Birmingham Jail', which he wrote in the early 1960s. So I had them read this document and we weren't that far away in 1981 from 1968 when Martin Luther King was assassinated. And I started asking them questions about the thing and I was looking out and I thought, you know, what the hell's going on here? I kept thinking, how can I approach this, what kind of questions can I ask and finally I said, 'Does anybody in this class know who Martin Luther King Junior was?' And none of them knew. Or one said wasn't he some sort of civil rights person? So that's what you're dealing with here. There's a deprivation of living knowledge that is really discouraging. But rather than getting discouraged, which I don't do very easily, I just got mad. I let them know it.

It's a different deprivation when these guys in prison are so hungry for it that when I start to talk about it, even though they might not have the working knowledge that I have, only because I'm more experienced and have done the reading, they will do it, they're interested. They don't have any expectations about the future because they're Black or Hispanic, because of the racism. What they will have is the possibility of this great accomplishment which will give them a quality of self-confidence as they get out to survive that they would never have had otherwise. And it represents for them this thing that they did not let their minds die, that they have great pride in their minds and great pride in what they feel they can accomplish.

I have a number of students who have gotten out and have started clinics for advisory and counselling with families whose children may be on the way to prison, with families and the kids. Many of them are getting masters and some as far as I know are on to PhDs. So there is a sense that these guys carry when they go back into their home communities, that what they've got is very important for the life of their community, since their communities are dying at this point.

These guys are very aware, as Black and Hispanic men, that up until 1960 or '65, that a large mass of their histories were censored. So they're very interested in history, and the political nature of that censorship, over hundreds of years, matters to them. They know what it is. So when you start talking about history to them, they want to know. They do not want to be lied to.

Dermot Healy

Dermot Healy was born in 1947 in County Westmeath, Ireland. He is the author of *Banished Misfortune* (short stories), *The Ballyconnell Colours* (poetry), *Fighting with Shadows* and *A Goat's Song* (novels), *On Broken Wings* and *The Long Swim* (plays), and *Our Boys* (film script). He is editor of *Force 10*, a community arts magazine, a member of Aosdana, and writer-in-residence in north-west Ireland. He lives in Sligo.

Stories from the Beginning of the Word

OVER THE PAST few years I've acted as writer-in-residence in various places like Mayo, Sligo, Clare. One of the more difficult duties is to attend schools for informal talks. These are more draining than adult workshops. Some writers have the knack of storytelling and this works fine for a once-off visit, but if you're trying to instill a confidence in literature, you have to get beyond mere performance. One of the things I learned was that you'd better return to the same school, a few times if possible, because the students are only getting a vague idea of what you're on about. They're very insecure, as you are, at the beginning. On your first visit you're not going to see what work they're capable of. You'll be the star attraction. You have to go back a second time to find them. You ask them to send on texts. You have to have time to read it on the page. And each school you go to, you hope you'll find kids that are writing. But a few are. They'll try to shock you. Often they copy out an Emily Dickinson poem and send it on in an effort to please you. They use all a writer's tricks to win your admiration. What happens is that literature is as undignified as everything else.

When I first meet a class, I know that they're seeing the next hour or so as free time. So the first thing is to enter their world immediately. To get them talking is a strain. You're an outsider. I ask them do they ever write. They shout out a name, a hand goes up. I ask them what they read. I ask them things about their life. They ask me about mine. They want to know the usual things – when did you start writing? Same age as you, I say. Why don't you try? Send me something on. A few years ago a girl in Mayo sent me an amazing story which I felt was quite forthcoming. It described a pregnant schoolgirl going off to have her baby and returning to school the following week. And she was actually able to do this in spite of her parents or what her peers might say. Is this possible? I asked her. And she said to me, well it would be a much worse thing to fail the Leaving than to have a child. I asked the class was that true. They said it was. That taught me something.

A girl like that, if she read books she'd probably be reading *The Diary of Anne Frank*. The boys read a lot of fantastic literature, like Tolkien, science fiction, Celtic mythology. These would be fifteen-, sixteen-, seventeen-year-olds. These would be books that they found for themselves – on their parents' shelves, in films, in video magazines, from their friends. In their reading two elements were constantly at odds with each other: the real historical world of concentration camps and the escapist half-world of fantasy. World War II stories are read by the boys, but they have a greater hunger to escape into wild fiction than the girls. The girls are more practical, yet see themselves as locked-away victims, as people who are going to escape at some stage when the thing, the bad thing, is over. Hence Anne Frank. I wrote down the reading habits of perhaps two hundred children and Anne Frank topped the list. Maybe forty per cent of the class would read outside school. And they might only read half-a-dozen books a year. The rest abandon reading when they enter secondary school. What's on the curriculum is all they attend to. They read up till about eleven or twelve, then stop. Reading is seen as another form of doing lessons. They lose the knack of being alone, except when there is homework to be done. Once they're in secondary school, they select particular things that turn up on the menu. From then on storytelling is a visual medium, and has little to do with the language of the alphabet.

There are actually teachers that pull a book in for you out of the random world of literature. This happened to me in St Patrick's College in Cavan. The English teacher, a Mr Barry Cullen, introduced us to *A Tale of Two Cities* by Charles Dickens when I was fourteen to fifteen. The book was not on the exam course, he just set aside an hour each week, and we'd read a chapter. He'd read a bit and someone else would read a little bit and then someone else and so on, till over the year we finished the novel. We had conquered a huge tract of language, and through discussion, knew what it meant. It was great, even for those who didn't particularly want to write. In the long run it was a great escape from the humdrum. There was no exam question coming. You were free to explore the story. I really loved that book. It opened a whole world to me. You could suddenly grasp the scope of a novel. I owe Barry Cullen a lot. I'd like to have the chance in my turn to hand on a particular book to a child. One of the things about enjoying reading is that you don't know it's happening at the time. It's only long afterwards that you realize what shaped you. A story you've read only begins to make sense somewhere well down the line. The same with poetry. That's why I've nothing against learning things off by heart. I'm glad some of the poems were hammered into me.

I encourage them to write as close as they can to their own lives. And you can get some rare gems about drinking, going to discos, being let down by boyfriends, being sarcastic and scurrilous about lovers, showing up braggarts, mourning lost ones. But there's also a blur in someone's imagination, a hazy space, an indistinct area. The opposite of competitiveness and plot. I tell them to look at the blurry thing that you're not too sure about, to write about the indistinct areas, not the thing that's loaded down with concrete details. They often come up with that inconceivable thing – their own perspective. When you're making up things that you think are unbelievable, you run for cover behind the familiar. You subdue the wild thought structures inside your head. You think you have to comply with the norm. I ask them to trust their jealousies, the half-seen things, their fears, their sexuality. In other words, don't be afraid of appearing psychologically unfit. I ask them, well, what is the thing that's hidden behind? And if you can't see it, well, say so, don't worry if the image is blurred. Sometimes they come out with very concrete facts like, 'I like very much the stained floor to the left and behind the lamp in my little bedroom.'

I never correct the spellings of the way they hear words, not at least when they're young. What they see is their actions, they're racing forward unselfconsciously; it's lovely to see the pace of their minds. I leave it as it is. But I might suggest cutting. I love teachers who send me kids' writing exactly as it was written. Once you start correcting grammar, you're sealing off the imagination. A teacher who trusts that the writer judging a competition will not be put off by exact dialect is to be praised. Often it's the other way round. I get loads of stuff sent to me by teachers that's been changed into proper English, as if misspelling will be a poor mark against them. One of the loveliest and funniest stories I received was written by a nine-year-old, Paula Majella O'Meara. I published it in *Force 10* magazine. Here's a part of it.

> Night came quicty. And the wind was blosing around pot town. There was not a persson in sight. It was like an abbanden town. In the morning the storm was over and the sun came up. The town was a mess the Mayor said that he would give some money to who ever pick up the most paper. One little boy went down to the beach. And saw a gaint. It was a gril.

'Gaint' here is exactly how 'giant' is pronounced in East Cavan. 'Gril' is a mystery. But we all know the wind when it's 'blosing'. These sleights of hand with words tuned to the ear are the ingredients of books as far removed from each other as *Huckleberry Finn* and *The Butcher Boy*. I like a nice English sentence, but it can only contain certain human experiences. How the mind thinks or the voice speaks needs other devices. In secondary school when they start telling you to put in the full stops, that wildness comes to an end. I think there is room for proper paragraphing and sentence construction in set pieces, but storytelling should not be constrained by good manners or rigid rules. If this were the norm then how the Irish write English would be declared illiterate. So I try to teach them basics – reserve proper English for paragraphs, in dialogue range freely, and if an I-person is telling the story then let the tenor and rhythm of their voice dominate.

I don't think older kids read with 'pleasure and understanding'. I think they read with restricted vision, like we all do. Only at odd moments in your life will you find certain books that open on to another world. When they read Anne Frank, they identify with this girl who is hidden away while war rages outside. They feel this is a story of tension in which they can bury themselves. It's nothing to do with that wise, literary, liberal business of pleasure and understanding. These pupils are struggling with hormones, world catastrophes and fear of failure. They also have a cruel sense of humour. They identify with victims. They love the outrageous. They go off into scientific fairy lands. They both love and detest authority. The pleasure they get is not pleasure at all. That comes later. Meanwhile they're questioning, they're experiencing something that imitates their needs and wants. They love romanticism. And they love frightening themselves. They live out the life of the character without knowing it's an illusion. They want to believe the story is true, but I think it comforts them that the violence is happening elsewhere. And at the same time they want the worst to happen.

If you listen to what kids are telling you when they talk and when they write, they're often describing their immediate problems, one of which is the loss of innocence. With younger children you are dealing with a very clear conscience, but they write with an immoral haste. Nine-, ten-, eleven-, twelve-year-olds do not make judgements. They wander at will. If they do make judgements they put them in an adult's mouth. Later when they cross the threshold of adolescence they begin to make judgements, the moralization and the test mentality come in. Of course it must start sometime, but it's strange how it affects story-telling in particular. Everyone is going to get their just reward. No one questions this phenomenon, as if moralizing in essays was somehow a good thing. But to moralize in a story may in fact be a means of avoiding grave decisions that the psyche must make. It's a way of appearing to conform, and is often totally at odds with what the pupil really feels. Once judgement comes in, and the overall moral issue rears its head, the storytelling is over. At fifteen or sixteen they've reached this wall. To break it down you have to use tricks. I say things like, No, I won't accept that. You're avoiding the issue. Fine. But.

The older ones are fighting you. The slagging starts. What you do is you challenge the person, you challenge the preconceptions, you point out the clichés, you say, no, I don't agree with you, and they fight back. If they bring in *The Diary of Anne Frank* and say, this is what we want to talk about, then I say, well, I don't like that part there, and they say, why? I answer, it's sentimental. But it's a true story, they reply. They have a desperate need for true stories. What 'really' happened cannot be criticized in their eyes. And when you say, but it's only based on words, and words themselves are there to create an illusion of reality, words can be wrong, they can lead you astray – when you say these things they panic, no more than adults do in literature workshops. The true story is taken for granted. The fictional is seen as a lie. You try to explain that in fiction there is another truth which does not declare to the world 'this really happened!' but is assembling in words a story from the imagination, which works if it is believed. We have to go over and over this difference between true stories and fiction. You have to pitch yourself between their want for a story to be true and their need to enter the world of the imagination. I might say I don't believe a fucking word of it and have them tell me why they do. When things are going like this, you're well away. And often you lose the argument because even you tell lies and they find you out. They like to be challenged, not patronized. And you have to remember they're vulnerable.

One of the key questions students ask when you get them going is, why is all this language on paper? How did it arrive there? So you tell them stories about memory, how language is an aid to memory, how communication comes into being. They ask you why some poems rhyme and some don't. You say, when we had no books, rhyme was an aid to memory. Poems could be easier learned. Now that we have poems in print, they need no longer be memorized. You tell them the difference between oral history and written history. They're very interested in the technical details. I think that's the sort of thing I would have loved to have heard at school, the real basic stuff that you only learn years later. It helps you with mythology. That's where pleasure comes from. In science, you're told when you mix oxygen with hydrogen you get something else, one and one makes two. In literature, grammar becomes the crux of the thing. But grammar will look after itself in the long run; it's inherent. It's the history of words that needs to be learned. Stories must be told. Etymology turns the learning process made into a crossword puzzle. It's a science kids love. They love the stories of how writing in various cultures came into being.

I tell a story about a man called Ceann Faelad – head full of wonder – who got hit on the head during a war in Armagh. He was the warrior son of the High King of Ireland. It happened in a time before writing had started. The blow left part of his brain exposed. He was brought for an operation to a university in West Cavan where there were important branches of learning – law, surgery and barditry. And barditry was the most important of the three because the knowledge of the doctors and lawyers was turned by the bards into rhyming verse so that both of the disciplines could easily remember their laws and traditions. Ceann Faelad came and the surgeons operated on his head. In doing so, they cut off a part of the brain with which you forget things – that was the part that was exposed. Now Ceann Faelad was condemned to remember everything. At last he went out and wrote down his knowledge on white stones, and that's how writing came to Ireland.

They love that story. It tells them something that makes sense. We move on to religion and its role in literature, and finally computers which store memory in these times. They're very interested in why languages differ. How does the word change as it crosses frontiers? Is the word a picture or a sound? Is painting a language? Why did we put language to that? They like to know how does the word change in different languages. They love all that and I think that's the key. It opens up a mirage. It opens up the whole magical underground behind the words you use every day and they're enthralled by that.

I was a student at University College Dublin but I left at the end of the first year. I thought the teaching was quite good – it's where I first read T. S. Eliot – but I'd enough of college. After being locked up in boarding school for years, you went crazy when you found yourself free in Dublin. I couldn't learn within the university. I wanted to return and work on the buildings in London as I'd been doing every summer since I was fifteen. I needed physical labour. I wanted my own income. There was plenty of work in London. It's the opposite these days. The pupils I deal with now have already projected at what age they'll get married, they know the degree they're going for, they're talking of what country they'll end up in if things go well, and what will happen if they don't get so many honours in the Leaving Cert. Sometimes I'm amazed by their rational approach. They have a very logical structure ready for their future, which would have been anathema to us in the sixties. The threat of unemployment makes them very wary. We were spoiled. In fact we were probably more conservative than they are, because they in general are not fazed by what lies ahead of them. But their weakness is for PR speak, they see themselves as products and are tutored in the many ways of selling themselves. This can lead to straightforward, no holds barred, market-researched consciousness, which, albeit better than the soft, hippy, transcendental, instinctive flabbiness of the sixties, strips language away from meaning into psycho-babble and sales talk. If you no longer mean what you say, you feel disorientated. Of the six or seven stories you may receive from a class, thirty per cent of them end in suicide. And unfortunately, despite your delicate prodding to make the story end otherwise, the student's version is the most authentic. This emerges when you talk about competitiveness in exams. 'No,' they say, 'it's not the teachers who pressurize us into getting good results. It's not the system. It's ourselves. It's we who want to do well. There's no one else to blame.' Whether they will think like this in a few years remains to be seen, but, as it stands, this is a formidable burden to carry, and in their best stories of contemporary life, this is what they write about.

But, despite everything, people read. It comes to you. You'll find books. A good teacher will start you reading earlier. They can introduce you to books they love. That's how it starts – through someone else's enthusiasm and through your own curiosity. One of the hardships kids have now is: can they switch off the TV, switch off the radio, and sit down and read in silence? Maybe the constant bombardment will drive people back to reading. Some say they can switch off and sit down and read in silence. I think we can underestimate the spiritual needs of fourteen- or fifteen-year olds. They will search for silence. Sometimes writing classes turn into just that – discussions on silence. Half the time you are trying to reassure them: don't be afraid of the thoughts going through your head. They're in everybody's head. In the long run, they'll check it out for themselves. Like adults, children love to hear stories of the beginning of the world.

Mike Hayhoe

Mike Hayhoe is Senior Lecturer and Senior Fellow in the School of Education at the University of East Anglia. He has published articles and books on a wide range of aspects of the English curriculum, in England, Australia, Canada and the US, and has lectured and run workshops in the United Kingdom, Austria, Bermuda, Canada, France, Germany, the Netherlands and the US. Teaching in local high schools and having a wife and daughter who also teach English prove invaluable in helping to keep his feet on the ground.

Jostling with the Text

THE FIRST QUESTIONS we should ask are, 'Why *should* kids read literature?' and 'Are we trying to keep some sort of obsolescent creature alive?' I was quite struck by a book I read recently by Paul Theroux (*The Happy Isles of Oceania*). He was travelling around the South Sea Islands and at one point the remark is made that anybody there who goes off on his own reading must be pathological in some way – there's something terribly wrong with the poor idiot. Why isn't he enjoying himself with the rest of the gang? He must be suffering from *musu*, the deepest form of depression, which will lead to suicide or murder.

It's important to remember that what we mean by literature started as a sociable, aural thing. People came together and there was a storyteller. It could be a mum telling stories to the kids or a professional or semi-professional one in a pub in Ireland, for example. People *told* stories – shared them – and because they were shared, the storyteller adjusted the tale according to the response of the audience. Everyone was involved. And you can still see that. You watch mothers or poets nowadays. We had the poet Carol Ann Duffy here a couple of weeks ago and she adjusted as she began to read to her audience; she read according to her living context, if you like. In a sense, we're back to the aural world of literature nowadays. There are interactive fictions available through technology which, in their own ways, are going to be a bit like taking us back to such people as Charles Dickens who used to read to his audience and then sort of say, I'm going to scrap this and tell it to you this way.

So maybe the fixity of the literary text and the imposed privacy of the text are now starting to be seen as penalties. Compare reading on your own with what happens when people watch a television fiction – they chat to each other. Okay, they can't adjust the teller much, the medium, in any electronic way, but they do adjust it constantly by co-texting with it and among themselves. I think that, in a sad way, three things have happened to the printed text. One is it's being seen as being fixed because it's in print. Secondly, it's seen as having some sort of authority because it's seen as fixed. And thirdly, in our educational world, it's used as a means of calling students to account. That isn't where fiction began and that isn't where fiction necessarily is nowadays. Kids who chat as they watch TV and replay bits of video are not treating these fictions as fixed: they're there for them to be active with. Maybe they're picking up some of the age-old talents of the group, processing and affecting the fiction.

That's been my preoccupation in my own work: how to help young people get together in groups and 'work' on a text together. There's a wonderful paper by Gabriel Josipovici called 'The Lessons of Modernism', in his book of the same name, in which he talks about the two principal tactics in handling any text as being 'silence' and 'game'. I think those are the two things that we as teachers have to start from. Everyone has a right to remain silent, the right to interact with the text on their own and on their own terms, if they wish. Alas, in schools and universities, that right is often denied – denied to the teacher and lecturer as well, by the way. Just as warders are also prisoners, so teachers and lecturers are prisoners of a protocol which demands that they articulate in particular ways, ways which perhaps diminish what they're about since those forms of articulation don't always result in expansion. I still recall one occasion when we were doing some work in film study, way back in my days as a lecturer in a teacher training college. We took in the film of *Culloden*. We had heard it was brilliant and about its exceptional use of cinema vérité, and it sounded ideal for our work on cinematic techniques. So we went into this room with these very intelligent and pleasant young women and men, our future teachers, and we shut the curtains, and the shutters and put the film on the projector. At the end of the film somebody got up and opened one shutter in this Georgian mansion, with this block of sunlight cubing in. Then somebody got up and opened the door at the back of the room and everybody went out in absolute silence, including the lecturers. We were all bereft. Nobody knew what to do, and to have said, 'Let's now discuss this film' would have been something that none of us could have done. And we never talked about it again. That right to silence I think is something which the processes of education should respect.

As for the notion of 'game' as one of the key aims of education, I'm always reminded of D. H. Lawrence when he said about work that if it doesn't absorb you 'like an absorbing game', then you shouldn't do it. I once got my students to work out what they meant by the word 'game' and we came up with 'a self-justifying, rule-governed activity', which includes elements of risk as well as pleasure – it's an alloy. That's an important thing to grasp, when it comes to reading literature. If I said to you that your partner's lost in Norwich or you said that you'd got lost in a wood in Italy, those would be negative. 'Lost' in a book? It's interesting that we use a negative metaphor for what we assume is a simple, uncomplicatedly positive activity. It isn't. It's bloody scary, reading. Because what you're reading reads you. There's a paper by George Craig where he describes the impossible point where the author who is no longer herself and you who are no longer your original self meet 'out there somewhere' at the point where the text becomes fiction, and that is a desperately bold (and sometimes wonderful) thing. There's that lovely poem by Ferlinghetti called 'Desperately Risking Absurdity' about the poet always wobbling and being ridiculous, trying to find this amazing, astonishing thing he wants to share with his public in some way. He's a clown, a buffoon, a Charlie Chaplin figure. So, authors are at risk; but so are readers. I think we tend to forget that certainly adolescents are at *negative* risk when so many of their encounters with literature occur in contexts which a) call them to account and b) call them to account as isolates. There are adolescents who enjoy being voluntary soloists, but none of them enjoys being an involuntary isolate. So we have to think about approaches which help naive readers – and that can often include university students, to my mind – to collaborate as and when, in ways which preserve their right to be individuals. And that's quite a balancing act.

How to get that balance? I'm known by my trainee teacher students as the T T T and P I P man – the two notions that they need to pass on to their students in school. T T T stands for Time, Team and Task – how much space and how many personal resources a group has to work with and what they ought to seek to achieve. P I P stands for Privacy, Intimacy and Plenary – and I'll come back to that. I'm particularly interested in group work when it comes to literature, because that's how you can shift the political structure of the classroom or lecture room. There are various power bases and vulnerabilities: there's the individual student, there are the students as collectives, and there's the teacher, who's also vulnerable because by and large the pupils will try to push the teacher to give 'the' answers or at least give enough questions to point to what 'the' answers ought to be!

There is the curious and perennial phenomenon of some teachers going away to read and prepare a text in the spirit of what I call the hide and seek approach. The teacher assumes that the poet has been breathed into by some amazing force and his or her job is to seek out what the poet has hidden and then to come down from the mountain and say to his students, 'Okay, turn to page thirty-three,' and the poor students turn to page thirty-three. The teacher has probably spent the whole summer vacation on the task – or at least part of the previous night – but for the students, there's this sudden unseen thing confronting them and they're expected to answer *his* agenda of questions and interpret *his* clues as to whether they're 'getting the poem right' or not. You know the sort of thing I mean. The drawn out 'Yes', which is a polite way of saying a partial 'No'; the 'Um, interesting' with a stress on the 'in', which equals 'Foolish answer'; 'the 'Ah, yes, yes indeed, very interesting' which means you're getting really warm. And the kids aren't interested in *their* understanding of the poem at all. They're interested in getting hold of the poem which they believe *the teacher* has defined. Forgive the vulgarism, but this method can lead to the puke curriculum. The teacher has digested the poem; the students eat what he has digested and have to regurgitate it. If their regurgitation is the same as *the teacher's*, then everything is fine; high marks and it's all done. You can see that attitude in extreme forms of the heritage model which implies that teacher and student are there to respect what has been bestowed upon them, without question. That's no way to work.

Hence PIP. Privacy is the first stage, where pupils have time as opportunity and obligation – time to sort out *their* initial ideas and feelings about the text in front of them – to establish a beach-head, if you like. Intimacy is where they share what they have found within a trusted circle – a pair or three or four, so that they can sort out and extend themselves in relative safety. Plenary is where everybody is involved, in some way. I've found that the provision of that initial Privacy is important, to prevent tyranny at both the other stages. In most classrooms you find that there are adolescents who shoot from the lip, and then there are the silent ones – the shy ones, the lazy ones, the complex ones, the highly intelligent ones, the slow ones, who get blocked out. Privacy gives them that vital chance and obligation to establish their own property, and then they're much stronger, much better equipped to go into the sharing phase of Intimacy before going into the wider, more public sharing of Plenary.

Bill Corcoran wrote a very elegant paper on this topic – about the journey from seeing reading literature as an obedient 'heritage' process through to the collaborative role of response reading through to what he called a resistance model. Now I don't like the label 'resistance' in resistance theories, because it has overtones of a negative relationship. I prefer to talk about 'questioning' or, better still, 'questing'. What Corcoran argues is that the heritage model can all too easily become a political tyranny, potential cultural fascism. The response model is very much about gaming. It's to do with reworking text into other forms – newspaper accounts of Duncan's death, for example – but what comes through the so-called 'resistance' model is the recognition that that particular poem or play or novel has been made by somebody who did or didn't clean his or her teeth, who maybe fell in love, who got cold and died or is going to die. It was made by a human being in a time and a place – by a human being who is or was a 'construct'. That's an awful word, but no other will do. Somebody who was made by his or her culture made this particular thing, this literary text – and similarly, when we come to read it, male/female, young/old, we come to it as human beings constructed by our time and culture. So you have two individual histories meeting at this impossible point, at what I like to call the *act* of fiction. That seems to me tremendously powerful. The problem is that it can also be potentially very destructive. Adolescents seek certainties and if you look at most work in school, the thing that the students do, especially in examination forms, is to try to force the teacher to give them 'the right answer'. And that applies to university level as well, where they often want to know what will get them to fit that assessment slot on the big day. If it's a round hole then they want to know that they can give a round hole answer; if it's a square hole, then a square one. They know the politics of assessment in schools and in universities and they're tough-minded enough – quite rightly – to want to go through those holes because, let's face it, if they don't, they're dead.

What Corcoran and people like him believe and I believe it as well, is that the moment of meeting is a time for 'mutual reflection': you read the text and the text reads you. There's a wonderful Canadian poem called 'An Exchange of Gifts' by Alden Nowlan and it begins 'As long as you read this poem / I will be writing it.' It is about the non-fixity of the text – that it is *not* 'fixed and solid'. The words are printed and fixed, but the text is not the words; it's what comes out of that when the text becomes a fiction because of what the reader also puts into it. So anything at all which will get kids to examine 'the nature of the fictive moment' – gobbledygook! – is important because in that state they are examining themselves.

I took part in an international research project looking at how thirteen-year-olds crack poetry and I think there are some clues there as to why many adolescents have problems with the stuff, some of which aren't necessarily to do with school. A lot of the pupils saw poetry as an attempt to say something important in an important way. A lot of them said, 'Well, there must be a story in this somewhere', so they went through the poem and said, 'Well, what's happening here is so and so.' They simply told you a prose version of it, if necessary filling bits in which weren't there, to make a story – and once they'd told you the story, goodnight, that was it; they'd solved it and why the heck couldn't the poet have given you a simple story in the first place! There were others who clearly saw that poetry is important because it has 'important' features such as rhyme and rhythm and is in little blocks and it doesn't come to the edges of the page, and so on, and these tended to presume that the poem had messages and so they'd spot a word and say, 'Ah, there's the word "tree" – this is a poem about Nature' and they would just push the poem until it fitted their 'Nature' theme. A lot saw poetry in terms of an important message about how to live, and so they started finding moral significances, an allegory.

But the important ones, the ones I called 'the questers' saw a collection of words written by somebody else and they were constantly adjusting what they saw. They knew that they were changed from what they were a second ago and they were picking up bits from the beginning, bits from the end and going outside the text to things in their lives, things they'd seen on television, things they'd heard about. There was this lovely sense of restlessness about them as they wove all this into the rest of the living tapestry of their experiences. Most of them enjoyed this sense of reflective adventure – but a lot were quite often low in self-image, which was very sad. I wonder how far the pressure to be called to account by exams and tests might have had something to do with that. It's interesting that my colleague called these students 'problem solvers'. I wonder just how often school and university set up literature as a problem.

What interests me is finding devices to get students to claim their individual ownership of a text first of all and then as far as possible to encourage them to share their ownership with others. There's a technique that a teacher called Penny Blackie devised called Asking Questions, where she gives the pupils ten minutes or quarter of an hour at the end of a lesson or as part of their homework to look at a poem, to think about it, so that it didn't come out of the blue at them the next day. She says to the class, 'I want you to write down half a dozen things about it. Anything that strikes you about it, anything at all – something you like or dislike – a word you don't understand – a line or phrase which worries or annoys or delights you – something that reminds you of something in your own life or of something elsewhere in your reading', and so on. The important thing was that every item had to be written down as a question.

Now remember that usually it's the teacher who asks the questions. Here were the kids being given the teacher's role. It was an amazing shift of power. It was also important that the questions were in writing. It's a brave kid in the classroom who dares to say, 'Please, Miss, I don't understand what's a bombardier', or, 'What's a grate?' or, 'What's a bus conductor?' Since they could write down things to which they knew the answer as well, nobody could tell which were the embarrassingly real questions. And the other thing about this simple technique is that everything becomes provisional. A question mark is like a '. . .'. It says, 'We haven't finished yet.' And where kids could have been negative with the statements, 'This poem is stupid. This poem is boring,' the slamming of the door becomes its interrogative opening – '*Why* is this poem boring? *Why* is this poem stupid? *Why* don't I like this poem?' '*Why* is this the worst thing since sliced bread?' Suddenly, the door is burst open.

Penny Blackie's technique was to collect her pupils' questions and produce the lesson's agenda from them – a move from Privacy direct into Plenary. My way of working with this technique is to get the pupils to move from this Privacy stage into Intimacy, meeting in twos to look at one another's questions, to see if they can answer them, then decide on the most important three and go into foursomes, to identify the top two items they've found which they feel the class ought to discuss and to star the most important one of them all. Then the teacher can say, 'Okay, what does your group want us to discuss?' So the teacher is a manager, but a manager of these adolescents as the agenda-makers. It's totally unlike the traditional system of teaching where the teacher says, 'Turn to page twenty-two. Why is there a metaphor in line one?' with all the classroom worries that if you get it right you're seen as a creep and if you get it wrong you're a twit. Under the Penny Blackie system, first you use what arises from the students, and then the groups build on each other, so that by the end of the session you get the most amazing range of insights and depths, many of which you yourself would not have thought of.

That technique can be used at all levels, it's not age-related. Bruner said that you can do anything at your own level of sophistication and this technique is a nice example of how you can achieve differentiation by outcome instead of by task. Another technique I've used with pupils as young as eleven, as well as with my masters students, is to get them to slow down their reading. Most reading is efferent, if we accept Rosenblatt's term, and in most of our daily reading we tend to read quickly to get the gist. So this is a technique to get children to slow down – to become what I call slow and backward readers, readers who are able to read 'backwards' (and sideways) as well as forwards. One of the the techniques I use is to unroll a poem, one line at a time, and to say, 'Okay, with your partner, what do you know so far? What don't you know? How come you know that much? Where did you get the information from?' And of course it's in the text and it's in the texts of their lives. Then I say, 'Now, with your partner, if I say to you that you can have only one word as the keystone of that line, what would it be?' That second task is artificial and they need to know this, but it works because it produces debate within the pair and then within the class as we see who voted for which word and why. *Their* choice of words and *their* reasons are being valued – and they're on their way to being persistent readers. I'm very fond of a poem by Henry Treece called 'Conquerors'. It begins, 'By sundown we came to a hidden village / Where all the air was still / and no sound met our tired ears, save / for the sorry drip of rain from blackened trees.' In that first line, pairs choose such words as 'sundown', 'hidden' and 'village' and I've known a class to spend half an hour debating the first eight words. I join in late, if at all. I may say, 'Well, the word I would choose for my keystone is 'a' because they must be strangers – it's not 'our' or 'their'. In conventional teaching I'd have got in first by making the class look at my choice of word and making them answer my questions on it: 'Look at "a" in line one. Why did the poet use that word?'

My older students are often terrified of these techniques; they're not used to them! But I take them back to the notion that being a bit afraid is part of the wonder of reading. Another approach that I use which is not one of my own but one that my daughter gave me is Ante-pastiche. You say to the class, 'You're going to cook a poem. I'm going to give you the ingredients and the instructions and I want you then, working in twos, to cook me that poem.' So you take a poem such as Thomas Hardy's 'In Time of "The Breaking of Nations"' about the narrator seeing the old man and horse harrowing, then the couch grass burning in those little drizzling heaps and how the man then sees the boy and girl walking past in love and he thinks about how cleansing the soil and falling in love will continue no matter what happens by way of power and politics and what happens in war – the original scene struck Hardy at the time of the Franco-Prussian War. You tell the class to make notes as you perform the poem for them in an evocative prose version.

'There you are: it's late November, December, perhaps very early January or February. It's winter time, a dead time of the year and this old man and this equally old horse are there, way back when – and they are stumbling along, almost asleep, dragging the harrow through the ground, breaking up the frosty ground, tugging out this weed, this noxious couch grass which can strangle the crops and they're tired but it's got to be done, and there are these heaps of couch grass they're trying to burn, but it's too damp, and they're exhausted. Then you see a boy and a girl coming past, a young courting couple, talking quietly, probably even whispering to each other, and the thought strikes you how these scenes you see here will continue, come kings and queens, come war or wars – these will continue. Okay. The man and the horse are verse one. The burning of the couch grass and your thoughts about kings and queens come in verse two. The courting couple and your thoughts about war come in verse three. Four lines to a verse, ababa, cdcd, efef. Have a go.' If students say that that's too difficult, I say, 'Don't worry about the abab, cdcd bit.' So you get their versions of the poem and those are printed up – and there are your literary texts for next week which they can discuss – and *then* they meet the original poem and can compare what they wrote with what Hardy set down.

Another technique was given to me by a Canadian college teacher called Tom McHendry. It's called the Cryptic Triptych and I've used this with great success with university students and sixth-formers. You take a poem and you give them the first two or three verses – but the original last verse has two very, very faithful, 'respectful' versions of it which you have written – and the students' task is to work out which of those three they think is the original and which two are the faithful frauds, if you like. This is a wonderful thing to do, because the debate becomes quite ferocious, especially when the students are encouraged to write the triptychs instead and the teacher is as vulnerable as everyone else, everybody collaborating in trying to work out which might be the original version and what makes them think so – where the echo-soundings are strongest – tremendous technique.

All of these, of course, involve mutual vulnerability, which many teachers find very hard. But in the case of university lecturers, in particular, we have all the space in the world to be vulnerable, because for a start there is the university library where students can go and read up what they ought to be thinking for the examinations, if they want to play safe. And these techniques are also excellent research devices. If a lecturer is looking for an idea for a paper, here's a set of papers waiting to be written on how he or she and the students feel about using such devices within a university climate.

All these techniques – and there are plenty more – are about creating what I call positive dispute, positive disagreement. It's interesting that if you look at the Northern Ireland National Curriculum for English, it actually enshrines statements about the text being the object of debate; the text is to be recognized in this positive and optimistic way as something produced and interpreted by dynamic people. That means that the text is 'unstable', just as a gyro is, – if it wasn't spinning, it couldn't remain stable – and that's why we also have to spin. Anything which tries to fix literature kills it. I think more and more places have picked up notions of destabilizing the text and destabilizing the reader as a means of generating a new excitement. I don't go overboard with all the continental theorists, but I think there has been a sort of pragmatic application of some of the ideas that they have propounded about readers being co-authors, and so on. These have become respectable which raises another issue: that over the course of years, what may have been a liberation can become in fact a liberation into another prison. For example, there were the awful comprehension passages which I had to suffer when I was a secondary school student, a chunk of prose and questions like, 'What is the meaning of . . .? Give examples of . . . Why is there this metaphor in line 6?' In the 1920s this sort of task was the great breakthrough into hosanna land. Before then, it was just grammar exercises and suddenly students were being given real pieces of writing by real people. All I'm saying is that what we set up as pioneers can become in due course a vogue and then it just gets picked up in some form; people tend to pick up Chinese Whisper versions of things and they become caricaturized and deformed – and deforming.

I think you can reconcile the teaching of literature with the teaching of grammar – though I'm not sure which grammar you should teach pupils anyway, because grammars keep on changing! One technique I have used, especially with poetry – I've used it with pupils as young as fifteen but with university students as well – is to get them to sponsor a poem: 'Your group is in charge of nouns, yours of verbs, yours of adjectives and yours of adverbs', for example. Their task is to read the text and see how much use the author makes of their particular grammar feature and how he or she uses it and what effect those uses have on them as readers. Then they reassemble into new groups, so that each group has a noun sponsor, an adjective sponsor, and so on. Suddenly around the room there are six, seven, eight teaching groups in which everybody is an expert. Now that may sound very crude, but it means that they're slowing down as readers again – become reflective, debative, provisional. And it's amazing what *they'll* find in a Hemingway passage, those exhausted verbs for example – or in a Dylan Thomas poem, those hyper-charged, polysyllabic adjective strings.

You can use the same 'jigsaw' technique with the senses. I'll split up 'sight' into groups for colour, shape, size, movement, texture; then there'll be sound touch – which I occasionally split up into texture, pressure and temperature – and smell. The groups' task is to go through the poem and see where these are present or absent, stated or implied, and decide why, in their opinion. Then the groups reassemble, with an expert from each sense or sub-sense, and the quest continues.

All these techniques depend upon groups which can be given instructions on how to manage themselves and they depend on a safe environment in which to do them – a classroom in which you can get small groups together in semi-privacy. A lecture theatre which is raked isn't easy! The biggest group you can get there is three – you can't get bigger groups unless you start using the stairs down the side, but they're not often big enough. Possibly you might be able to do a 'goldfish bowl' which takes students a bit of time to get used to, but it can work very powerfully. This is where you ask some students to carry out a task and you ask the others to observe how it's going on. Those on the outside become observers who try to understand the problems the insiders are facing and how they overcome them; they seek to outline what the insiders achieve. The rules are that they never go on about where the working group went wrong, where the fault lay. You have to set this up very carefully, but on that basis, you can have a smaller half of the class doing a task and a larger half observing it. You're probably talking about classes of about thirty people here.

With very large classes, it is possible perhaps to persuade some of them to engage in certain tasks before the 'lecture' session begins, such as Penny Blackie's technique. They won't all do it, but some of them will. Or you could use such techniques as unrolling the poem. Or how about this? I was lecturing in Montreal some time back and I was very homesick and I wrote a very miserable poem called 'City Blues'. I came across it in my rough notes and all the places where in fact I'd squiggled words out and squiggled words in. I give this to the students and say: 'Okay, now which word do you think is superior wherever there's a choice – and, if you don't like the ones that the writer thought of, what would you want instead?' Now on the basis of that, we've had some tremendous times because it signals again the fact that a text is unstable and a text is a possible solution to an impossible problem. There are plenty of poems like that around in manuscript – Lawrence, Eliot, for instance. You give them to your students and ask them, 'What's going on? What would you do? Why would you do it that way?' There's a poem by Thomas Blackburn, I think, where he quotes Yeats. 'Poems arise from quarrels in the mind.' I wrote a little verse once when somebody pestered me to write a poem for them. She pestered me so much I wrote, 'Poems to order / just aren't on / they come from disorder / wherever that's from.' That's it – that's where the energy comes from.

Our students do have to write essays during the year, but we must bear in mind that the word 'essay' means to try and that therefore there should be all sorts of ways 'making attempts', of essaying. There could well be more than the conventional literary essay. There's the conventional book review but there could also be all the potential of audio and video tapes. The conventional essay is a critical device which is of value, and some people can work at their best using that medium, but what are we after? We're trying to find means of helping our students to be at *their* best, I assume, and there will be those who can do their best by other ways. We have to make legitimate a spectrum of devices. One of the purposes of assessment is a formative one, to tell you how well you are teaching, as well as to help the students realize how well they are learning. Therefore there must be, to my mind, an assessment spectrum going all the way through the course which allows adjustment of yourself as much as of them. Anything which doesn't allow for that results in rigidity, which is death. It is, isn't it? There are some super teachers, I'm sure, who in fact have 'taught the same tape-recording' for the last thirty years, a highly polished performance, and they haven't really learned a thing themselves in the process. They're brain-dead.

I began by questioning whether or not we should be teaching literature. I think we should. I went to a private secondary school where I had virtually no maths, and only one term of science teaching in my entire school life. It means that there's a whole menu of human curiosity which I'm frightened of and it seems to me that life is about being a nosy parker, and therefore anything which helps us to become wide-ranging nosy parkers is super as far as I'm concerned. And literature is one of those devices.

Now some students will find that literature is not for them. They're going to find their sense of wonder through sport or motor mechanics or music or whatever, but at least they've been through the menu and found something they like. We develop taste through tasting and I want them to at least have a taste of literature – this curious phenomenon of taking the everyday business of making squawks and decoding squawks, oral and visual ones, and making them much more than everyday, in a poem or a story or a play. It's a shame if children and young people haven't at least had a go at this. If they don't want to continue with it, well that's fine. I think that a lot of them do want to have a go but it has to be in a carefully phrased system which gives them rights and responsibilities in an intensely serious (not solemn) and *active* activity – which is what a game is. You don't play games for 'fun' – it's sad how that's become such a weak word, as in 'a "fun" thing', with its slightly specious and facetious connotations. The true fun – the serious, absorbing fun – lies in *enjoying* being unstable, enjoying being in a dynamic and arguing with people, jostling with the text. Adolescents already do this when they read comics and magazines, when they watch television, crack jokes, go out and play – they enjoy being unstable, they enjoy being dynamic, they enjoy the jostle. And yet for some unknown reason, within the school ethos and the university ethos, it's still occasionally assumed that there is a fixed and narrow path and gate which you must go along and through. It's back to politics again.

Katha Pollitt

Joyce Ravid

Katha Pollitt's writing appears regularly in *The Nation*, *The New Yorker* and *The New Republic*. Her book of poems, *Antartic Travellers*, won the National Book Critics Circle Award. She lives in New York City.

This article first appeared in *The Nation* and is reprinted here courtesy of the author, care of Rogers, Coleridge & White in association with the Melanie Jackson Agency.

Canon to the Right of Me . . .

FOR THE PAST couple of years we've all been witness to a furious debate about the literary canon. What books should be assigned to students? What books should critics discuss? What books should the rest of us read, and who are 'we' anyway? Like everyone else, I've given these questions some thought, and when an invitation came my way, I leaped to produce my own manifesto. But to my surprise, when I sat down to write – in order to discover, as E. M. Forster once said, what I really think – I found that I agreed with all sides in the debate at once.

Take the conservatives. Now, this rather dour collection of scholars and diatribists – Allan Bloom, Hilton Kramer, John Silber and so on – are not a particularly appealing group of people. They are arrogant, they are rude, they are gloomy, they do not suffer fools gladly, and everywhere they look, fools are what they see. But what is so terrible, really, about what they are saying? I too believe that some books are more profound, more complex, more essential to an understanding of our culture than others; I too am appalled to think of students graduating from college not having read Homer, Plato, Virgil, Milton, Tolstoy – all writers, dead white Western men though they be, whose works have meant a great deal to me. As a teacher of literature and of writing, I too have seen at first hand how ill-educated many students are, and how little aware they are of this important fact about themselves. Last year I taught a graduate seminar in the writing of poetry. None of my students had read more than a smattering of poems by anyone, male or female, published more than ten years ago. Robert Lowell was as far outside their frame of reference as Alexander Pope. When I gently suggested to one student that it might benefit her to read some poetry if she planned to spend her life writing it, she told me that yes, she knew she should read more but when she encountered a really good poem it only made her depressed. That contemporary writing has a history which it profits us to know in some depth, that we ourselves were not born yesterday, seems too obvious even to argue.

But ah, say the liberals, the canon exalted by the conservatives is itself an artefact of history. Sure, some books are more rewarding than others, but why can't we change our minds about which books those are? The canon itself was not always as we know it today: Until the 1920s, *Moby Dick* was shelved with the boys' adventure stories. If T. S. Eliot could single-handedly dethrone the Romantic poets in favor of the neglected Metaphysicals and place John Webster alongside Shakespeare, why can't we dip into the sea of stories and fish out Edith Wharton or Virginia Woolf? And this position too makes a great deal of sense to me. After all, alongside the many good reasons for a book to end up on the required-reading shelf are some rather suspect reasons for its exclusion: because it was written by a woman and therefore presumed to be too slight; because it was written by a Black person and therefore presumed to be too unsophisticated or to reflect too special a case. By all means, say the liberals, let's have great books and a shared culture. But let's make sure that all the different kinds of greatness are represented and that the culture we share reflects the true range of human experience.

If we leave the broadening of the canon up to the conservatives, this will never happen, because to them change only means defeat. Look at the recent fuss over the latest edition of the Great Books series published by Encyclopedia Britannica, headed by that old snake-oil salesman Mortimer Adler. Four women have now been added to the series: Virginia Woolf, Willa Cather, Jane Austen and George Eliot. That's nice, I suppose, but really! Jane Austen has been a certified Great Writer for a hundred years! Lionel Trilling said so! There's something truly absurd about the conservatives earnestly sitting in judgement on the illustrious dead, as though up in Writers' Heaven Jane and George and Willa and Virginia were breathlessly waiting to hear if they'd finally made it into the club, while Henry Fielding, newly dropped from the list, howls in outer darkness and the Brontës, presumably, stamp their feet in frustration and hope for better luck in twenty years, when *Jane Eyre* and *Wuthering Heights* will suddenly turn out to have qualities of greatness never before detected in their pages. It's like Poets' Corner at Manhattan's Cathedral of St John the Divine, where mortal men – and a woman or two – of letters actually vote on which immortals to honour with a plaque, a process no doubt complete with electoral campaigns, compromise candidates and all the rest of the underside of the literary life. 'No, I'm sorry, I just can't vote for Whitman. I'm a Washington Irving man myself.'

Well, a liberal is not a very exciting thing to be, and so we have the radicals, who attack the concepts of 'greatness', 'shared', 'culture' and 'lists'. (I'm overlooking here the ultraradicals, who attack the 'privileging' of 'texts', as they insist on calling books, and think one might as well spend one's college years deconstructing *Leave it to Beaver*.) Who is to say, ask the radicals, what is a great book? What's so terrific about complexity, ambiguity, historical centrality and high seriousness? If *The Colour Purple*, say, gets students thinking about their own experience, maybe they ought to read it and forget about — and here you can fill in the name of whatever classic work you yourself found dry and tedious and never got around to finishing. For the radicals the notion of a shared culture is a lie, because it means presenting as universally meaningful and politically neutral books that reflect the interests and experiences and values of privileged white men at the expense of those of others – women, blacks, Latinos, Asians, the working class, whoever. Why not scrap the one-list-for-everyone idea and let people connect with books that are written by people like themselves about people like themselves? It will be a more accurate reflection of a multifaceted and conflict-ridden society, and will do wonders for everyone's self-esteem, except, of course, living white men – but they have too much self-esteem already.

Now, I have to say that I dislike the radicals' vision intensely. How foolish to argue that Chekhov has nothing to say to a black woman – or, for that matter, myself – merely because he is Russian, long dead, a man. The notion that one reads to increase one's self-esteem sounds to me like more snake oil. Literature is not an aerobics class or a session at the therapist's. But then I think of myself as a child, leafing through anthologies of poetry for the names of women. I never would have admitted that I needed a role model, even if that awful term had existed back in the prehistory of which I speak, but why was I so excited to find a female name, even when, as was often the case, it was attached to a poem of no interest to me whatsoever? Anna Laetitia Barbauld, author of 'Life! I know not what thou art / But know that thou and I must part!'; Lady Anne Lindsay, writer of languid ballads in incomprehensible Scots dialect; and the other minor female poets included by chivalrous Sir Arthur Quiller-Couch in the old *Oxford Book of English Verse*: I have to admit it, just by their presence in that august volume they did something for me. And although it had nothing to do with reading or writing, it was an important thing they did.

Now, what are we to make of this spluttering debate, in which charges of imperialism are met by equally passionate accusations of vandalism, in which each side hates the others, and yet each one seems to have its share of reason? Perhaps what we have here is one of those debates in which the opposing sides, unbeknownst to themselves, share a myopia that will turn out to be the most telling feature of the whole discussion: a debate, for instance, like that of our Founding Fathers over the nature of the franchise. Think of all the energy and passion spent pondering the question of property qualifications or direct versus legislative elections while all along, unmentioned and unimagined, was the fact – to us so central – that women and slaves were never considered for any kind of vote.

Something is being overlooked: the state of reading, and books, and literature in our country at this time. Why, ask yourself, is everyone so hot under the collar about what to put on the required-reading shelf? It is because while we have been arguing so fiercely about which books make the best medicine, the patient has been slipping deeper and deeper into a coma.

Let us imagine a country in which reading is a popular voluntary activity. There, parents read books for their own edification and pleasure, and are seen by their children at this silent and mysterious pastime. These parents also read to their children, give them books for presents, talk to them about books and underwrite, with their taxes, a public library system that is open all day, every day. In school – where an attractive library is invariably to be found – the children study certain books together but also have an active reading life of their own. Years later it may even be hard for them to remember if they read *Jane Eyre* at home and Judy Blume in class, or the other way around. In college young people continue to be assigned certain books, but far more important are the books they discover for themselves – browsing in the library, in bookstores, on the shelves of friends, one book leading to another, back and forth in history and across languages and cultures. After graduation they continue to read, and in the fullness of time produce a new generation of readers. Oh happy land! I wish we all lived there.

In that other country of real readers – voluntary, active, self-determined readers – a debate like the current one over the canon would not be taking place. Or if it did, it would be as kind of parlour game: What books would *you* take to a desert island? Everyone would know that the top-ten list was merely a tiny fraction of the books one would read in a life-time. It would not seem racist or sexist or hopelessly hidebound to put Hawthorne on the syllabus and not Toni Morrison. It would be more like putting oatmeal and not noodles on the breakfast menu – a choice part arbitrary, part a nod to the national past, part, dare one say it, a kind of reverse affirmative action: school might frankly be the place where one read the books that are a little off-putting, that have gone a little cold, that you might pass over because they do not address in reader-friendly contemporary fashion, the issues most immediately at stake in modern life, but that, with a little study, turn out to have a great deal to say. Being on the list wouldn't mean so much. It might even add to a writer's cachet *not* to be on the list, to be in one way or another too heady, too daring, too exciting to be ground up into institutional fodder for teenagers. Generations of high school kids have been turned off to George Eliot by being forced to read *Silas Marner* at a tender age. One can imagine a whole new readership for her if grown-ups were left to approach *Middlemarch* and *Daniel Deronda* with open minds, at their leisure.

Of course, they rarely do. In America today the assumption underlying the canon debate is that the books on the list are the only books that are going to be read, and if the list is dropped no books are going to be read. Becoming a textbook is a book's only chance; all sides take that for granted. And so all agree not to mention certain things that they themselves, as highly educated people and, one assumes, devoted readers, know perfectly well. For example, that if you read only twenty-five, or fifty, or a hundred books, you can't understand them, however well chosen they are. And that if you don't have an independent reading life – and very few students do – you won't *like* reading the books on the list and will forget them the minute you finish them. And that books have, or should have, lives beyond the syllabus – thus, the totally misguided attempt to put current literature in the classroom. How strange to think that people need professorial help to read John Updike or Alice Walker, writers people actually do read for fun. But all sides agree, if it isn't taught, it doesn't count.

Let's look at the canon question from another angle. Instead of asking what books we want others to read, let's ask why we read books ourselves. I think the canon debaters are being a little disingenuous here, are suppressing, in the interest of their own agendas, their personal experience of reading. Sure, we read to understand our American culture and history, and we also read to recover neglected masterpieces, and to learn more about the accomplishments of our subgroup and thereby, as I've admitted about myself, increase our self-esteem. But what about reading for the aesthetic pleasures of language, form, image? What about reading to learn something new, to have a vicarious adventure, to follow the workings of an interesting, if possibly skewed, narrow and ill-tempered mind? What about reading for the story? For an expanded sense of sheer human variety? There are a thousand reasons why a book might have a claim on our time and attention other than its canonization. I once infuriated an acquaintance by asserting that Trollope, although in many ways a lesser writer than Dickens, possessed some wonderful qualities Dickens lacked: a more realistic view of women, a more sceptical view of good intentions, a subtler sense of humour, a drier vision of life which I myself found congenial. You'd think I'd advocated throwing Dickens out and replacing him with a toaster. Because Dickens is a certified Great Writer, and Trollope is not.

Am I saying anything different from what Randall Jarrell said in his great 1953 essay 'The Age of Criticism'? Not really, so I'll quote him. Speaking of the literary gatherings of the era, Jarrell wrote:

> If, at such parties, you wanted to talk about *Ulysses* or *The Castle* or *The Brothers Karamazov* or *The Great Gatsby* or Graham Greene's last novel – Important books – you were at the right place. (Though you weren't so well off if you wanted to talk about *Remembrance of Things Past*. Important, but too long.) But if you wanted to talk about Turgenev's novelettes, or *The House of the Dead*, or *Lavengro*, or *Life on the Mississippi*, or *The Old Wives' Tale*, or *The Golovlyov Family*, or Cunningham-Grahame's stories, or Saint-Simon's memoirs, or *Lost Illusions*, or *The Beggar's Opera*, or *Eugen Onegin*, or *Little Dorrit*, or the *Burnt Njal Saga*, or *Persuasion*, or *The Inspector-General*, *Oblomov*, or *Peer Gynt*, or *Far from the Madding Crowd*, or *Out of Africa*, or the *Parallel Lives*, or *A Dreary Story*, or *Debits and Credits*, or *Arabia Deserta*, or *Elective Affinities*, *Schweik*, or – any of a thousand good or interesting but Unimportant books, you couldn't expect a very ready knowledge or sympathy from most of the readers there. They had looked at the big sights, the current sights, hard, with guides and glasses; and those walks in the country, over unfrequented or thrice-familiar territory, all alone – those walks from which most of the joy and good of reading come – were walks that they hadn't gone on very often.

I suspect that most canon debaters have taken those solitary rambles, if only out of boredom – how many times, after all, can you reread the *Aeneid*, *Mrs Dalloway*, *Cotton Comes to Harlem* (to pick one book from each column)? But those walks don't count, because of another assumption all sides hold in common, which is that the purpose of reading is none of the many varied and delicious satisfactions I've mentioned; it's medicinal. The chief end of reading is to produce a desirable kind of person and a desirable kind of society. A respectful, high-minded citizen of a unified society for the conservatives, and up-to-date and flexible sort for the liberals, a subgroup-identified, robustly confident one for the radicals. How pragmatic, how moralistic, how American! The culture debaters turn out to share a secret suspicion of culture itself, as well as the anti-pornographer's belief that there is a simple, one-to-one correlation between books and behaviour. Read the conservatives' list and produce a nation of sexists and racists – or a nation of philosopher kings. Read the liberals' list and produce a nation of spineless relativists – or a nation of open-minded world citizens. Read the radicals' list and produce a nation of psychobabblers and ancestor-worshippers – or a nation of stalwart proud-to-be-me pluralists.

But is there any list of a few dozen books that can have such a magical effect, for good or for ill? Of course not. It's like arguing that a perfectly nutritional breakfast cereal is enough food for the whole day. And so the canon debate is really an argument about what books to cram down the resistant throats of a resentful captive populace of students; and the trick is never to mention the fact that, in such circumstances, one book is as good, or as bad, as another. Because, as the debaters know from their own experience as readers, books are not pills that produce health when ingested in measured doses. Books do not shape character in any simple way – if, indeed, they do so at all – or the most literate would be the most virtuous instead of just the ordinary run of humanity with larger vocabularies. Books cannot mould a common national purpose when, in fact, people are honestly divided about what kind of country they want – and are divided, moreover, for very good and practical reasons, as they always have been.

For these burly and energetic purposes, books are all but useless. The way books affect us is an altogether more subtle, delicate, wayward and individual, not to say private, affair. And that reading is being made to bear such an inappropriate and simplistic burden speaks to the poverty both of culture and of frank political discussion in our time.

On his deathbed, Dr Johnson – once canonical, now more admired than read – is supposed to have said to a friend who was energetically rearranging his bedclothes, 'Thank you, this will do all that a pillow can do.' One might say that the canon debaters are all asking of their handful of chosen books that they do a great deal more than any handful of books can do.

Elizabeth Macklin

Anne Hall

Elizabeth Macklin was born in 1952 in Poughkeepsie, New York. In 1974, after studying at the SUNY College at Potsdam and in Spain, she moved to New York City, where she now makes her living as a copy-editor and proofreader for *The New Yorker*. Her work – poems, translations, and essays – has been printed in *The New Yorker*, *The Nation*, *The Threepenny Review*, *Lyra*, *Paris Review*, and elsewhere. She has received an Ingram Merrill Foundation award and, in 1994, a Guggenheim Fellowship. Her first collection of poems, *A Woman Kneeling in the Big City*, was published in 1992.

The Dark Tower of Criticism

LET'S START WITH the word 'reading', instead of 'literature'. I had a mother who read to me. And I read to myself. I was an only child and I spent a lot of time doing that and loving it, being inside it. You know that scene in Frances Hodgson Burnett's *The Little Princess*, where Sara the drudge is in the window seat, reading, and the parlour boarders interrupt her and she flies at them? That thing of being inside a book is something I had before I went to school, through being read to, and all the way through on the outside, not in school. Though I *was* turned on to it by a teacher in second grade who read these extraordinary books to us – stories that had been written for grownups too, like *The Devil and Daniel Webster.*

But in school I mostly developed, maybe through some perversity, a bad attitude: I could never read anything that was assigned. A lot of times I had already read what was assigned and that was lucky. Mostly I was furious with teachers for the ways they would talk about books: about 'theme' – whatever that is. That's an exaggeration, maybe I do understand what theme is. And it's done – theme talk – for certain reasons, it's done to teach critical thinking, more than to teach a love of reading. And if you don't have someone who loves reading to begin with you could have a lifetime problem. They had stopped teaching grammar by the time I was in school. Luckily, in a way. I learned grammar in Spanish, I didn't learn grammar in English. I learned a language for poetic structure in Spanish and French, and resisted learning it in English.

I remember after I had started writing and publishing and was going through a difficult time, I threw myself on the mercy of a co-worker who was a poet, and said, 'Read this poem, why is it being so incessantly rejected?' and as she explained her reading of it, she used one of those words like 'alliteration' or some very simple word and it felt like an insult, as if I had done something underhanded. To make her like that part. Too intentional. Part of the problem is the intentionality in 'literature'. I found this wonderful anthology, *The Rattle Bag* and read 'The Eagle' by Tennyson – which is a *beautiful* poem. But when it was being used to illustrate a critical category – 'clasps the crag': 'Now, children *alliteration*' – it was not a poem. I've been having conversations with a friend of mine about that vocabulary of poetry. In effect it's the musical notation for poetry, to determine what's going on there, and it's highly inaccurate – it's just so broad. It's as if you had a blank staff – no dotted notes – and it's not indicative of the impulse behind the poem. You have to go inside a piece of music to understand what the relations between the notes on the page are. You have to spend a lot of time playing the thing very accurately, before you can go back in your mind and determine what the composer heard that he or she was trying to approximate in written music. There are no emotional connotations in the language that's used to talk about poetry, because it's an abstract language, with interchangeable parts. And that's why they invented it, so they could talk about a number of different things through this esperanto.

To play and make poems was something I did in junior high and high school with a friend of mine, and only once did we use it to academic advantage. That was when we had a teacher we scorned because she was so sentimental; we knew we could just do any damned thing. The assignment was to do a 'poetry project' – maybe illustrating those devices of rhetoric – and we leaped in and made these thrilling booklets, mixing up our own poems and Paul Simon lyrics and 'real' poems just as we pleased. The 'A's we got were ludicrous, because we were just goofing on her and pleasing ourselves. There was not a sense of ourselves in a world as Writers; we were just doing something totally different from what was being taught.

Earlier there was a teacher who, I learned later from my mother, had taken pity on me for social reasons and said, 'Why don't you join the literary magazine?' I can't remember what my social reading of that situation was. I do remember that years after at a high school reunion, I found out that I had terrified my classmates who were regarding me in quite another way than I was regarding myself.

There were poems that I liked, and I was happy they were being published in this little school magazine. I *was* thrilled when I wrote a nasty story using the name of some girl who had been teasing me and beating me with her umbrella, and there she was being a villain in my public story. But aside from that, because I never gave any legitimacy to what I was doing, I couldn't understand my classmates' reaction as related to my writing; I read it as some kind of shunning. Nevertheless, there were three or four of us who played together and we played all the way through high school: making new and sassy or funny words to pop songs, constructing what was actually sort of a long-term novel in illicit classroom notes to one another, writing in these characters that we'd given ourselves. And then writing those poems, which had to do with real things and not just language. The only purpose of the language we dressed them in – and it was very elaborate sometimes – was to make the unspeakable speakable, something we could love knowing. And we liked each other, even though we accepted the 'pariah' valuation from the sorority-girl crowd.

When I was in tenth grade, which would be about fifteen or sixteen, it must have been 1968, we had a student teacher for biology, who on our final exam had put a paper with a cover sheet with artwork on it, mandalas, borders written in Elvish out of Tolkien, and quotations from various things including T. S. Eliot's '*The Hollow Men*'. Because he was – off, you know, he got a lot of flak from the football boys, but I went out and bought Eliot. In twelfth grade we had an essay to do a year-long project where the teacher would walk you through all the stages of preparing a term paper, and mine was on '*The Hollow Men*'. I faked the various stages we were supposed to have gone through in our research, wrote the paper at three o'clock in the morning the day it was due, but apparently I put a lot of thought into it because I loved this thing, this poem. It had been handed on to me in an unlegitimate way. I think the teacher said, 'This is the most analytical paper of all of them.' It was forty or fifty pages long, on a five page poem. And got a very high mark. She took points off, though, because I'd used a letter from this young biology teacher as one of my sources.

That was the first time I went inside a piece of writing. It was surrounded by these trappings of criticism. We were required to have fifteen sources, to read the critics, which would have stood me in good stead in later life, except that I went to a college where, all told, I had to write one paper. There were exams, of course, but the teachers were totally demoralized. This college is about twenty miles from the Canadian border. It's about thirty degrees below zero from October to May. It had been a teachers' college, what they called a normal school, and then it became part of the New York State university system. I think the professors considered themselves to be in exile. It was a big drinking college, and in the poorest county in New York state, and that includes the Bronx. Very depressed area. Montreal is the nearest city with a theatre. And mostly the students were there not out of a passionate involvement with their subject; they were there to get a degree, and a teaching certificate, so they could get employed.

I don't have strong memories of the way I was taught there, except in French classes I did learn *explication de texte* and I loved that manner, just the demandingness of it. It was as if meaning was coming through, meaning that mattered. And the woman who taught it clearly read to be informed, read to be enlightened, even, and conveyed that. It was she who – for an extracurricular reason, or out of kindness, really – sent me to one of the most important writers I've ever read, important for my well-being, I mean. I was silly and insanely falling in love with this guy, and she gave me – in French, so it had a tinge of assignment, instead of seeming like buttinski advice – a letter that Simone Weil had written to a student. In it was a sentence or two about not seeking out love for the sake of the sensation, about the dreadful responsibility involved in making yourself beloved. I don't know that it helped at the time, with the situation, but I did go on to read more Weil, and reread her.

Where also I had a wonderful teacher was in Madrid, when I was studying in Spain for my junior year. It was aesthetics class given by a poet who had written a two-volume work on his theory of poetry and he taught us his language. I still think it's legitimate. It's based on the similarity of poetry and jokes, what he called the rupture of the system, the system of expectations. He'd quote from Lorca's 'Ballad of the Civil Guard', which was not something most people would quote from at that time, at least not as loudly as he did, because Franco was still alive. He was just using it to demonstrate the effect of hearing *uuu* sounds and how creepy they were – the inherent effect they had. Maybe it was because it was in Spanish and was odd, or maybe because he was cranky and passionate, clearly speaking with real feeling, much as he may have been sceptical of this crowd of foreigners, but he had a way of talking about poetry that I could be open to. Maybe it was just that, because it was in Spanish, it wasn't language I'd already been turned off to. Maybe I'd just got past my little pissy perversity.

I have this split view of my school years, because at the time my mother was suffering along through my education and not divulging it, but she did tell me afterwards. She knew I loved to read, and here I was having a 'problem with school'. She hadn't gone to college herself – her family was poor during the Depression, she had to work instead – and she wanted desperately for me to go, to have that kind of, oh, romantically literary possibility maybe, but she was not allowed to say this or convey it in any way. My father, who *had* gone to college, for engineering, on GI Bill, did not want me 'pressured' in that direction, whatever his reasons. She told me all this much later. At any rate she had read the *Jungle Books*, fairy tales, story-stories, and then when time came to teach reading, they were using the Dick and Jane books – 'See Dick run. Run, Dick, run! See Spot. See Jane trip!' – and she told me afterwards that I'd been very disappointed that there weren't any *stories* to be read. Students coming from a household where reading wasn't done, would get a bad impression right off the bat. The essential human reasons for reading at all had got left out.

Books come into your life in strange ways. That Simone Weil experience. And then the professor who was overseeing our junior year in Spain came back – from Paradise to Potsdam – and I did an independent study with him. I'd wanted to do it on Borges and he wouldn't let me: he told me I had to read the rest of Latin-American literature to do a paper on Borges – if I still wanted to by that time. And I'm very glad he did that, because it was the first time I read García Márquez. And that was a blessing.

The first time I ever thought of writing as possible work, as a job that human beings do and I could do, was via journalism: in

Spain I met a couple of people who were working journalists. Since Franco was still alive, it was working journalists who had all the real dope on what was going on, though they weren't allowed to publish it. And here were these guys who were writing for a living and were just *normal people* – that was the first time I'd ever encountered that, a writer just being a human in front of me. So I came back, took journalism courses, got married and moved to New York, and tried to get a job in publishing. Of course that's when I realized I knew no grammar in English, only in Spanish.

When I came to New York and started working, I had a desire for the academic year and for structured reading, and I started graduate courses at NYU. There I realized I didn't like academia itself all that much. Potsdam may have been 'unserious', but parts of NYU were serious in an unfortunate way. I like the Spanish writer Unamuno very much and was thrilled to see there was a course on him, but the professor started, in the very first class, talking about 'publish or perish' and how 'you doctoral candidates have to get yourselves attuned to the realities of academia.' He was a cynic, and a cynic teaching Unamuno is not great for the nation.

But not everyone was as bad as that. There was a professor down there who taught a two-part course on Calderón de la Barca. He had a manner that was as wonderful as that aesthetics teacher in Spain. Rectitude and scorn and passion. 'Read the plays,' he said, 'Read the plays.' There was this Calderón critic called Valbuena Prat and this professor said, 'Don't go reading Valbuena. Crap. Read the plays.' This man had all the knowledge about how the plays were staged, what they looked like to people when they were first performed, what the commonplaces were that the playwright was taking off from.

And there was a woman there who is still there, Haydée Vitali, who was teaching a short-story course and she was a friend to writers. She understood writers as human beings who write for human reasons that have nothing to do with criticism, and she didn't teach criticism. She let me do a paper for that course about Simone Weil and a Chilean writer called Baldomero Lillo.

But I decided academia wasn't for me. It was during that Unamuno course when I was getting a blast of cynicism from someone who was supposed to be serving that author. I just thought, I don't need to be inside this atmosphere; I really can do it on my own if I want to do it: read these things, find out about them myself. I didn't need a degree to do copy work. I was getting a skill that would pay my rent. I thought I would rather be involved in that and spend my time in Spanish literature outside my work day, and not get myself involved in cynical people like this. You do expect someone who's teaching a book to have some kind of affinity with that writer.

I prefer it when someone says, 'You must read this. Here, sit, read.' Just, 'Sit, read.' I love that. There are some book reviews too, that occasionally make me rush out and buy a hardcover copy. And after reading the galleys of a volume of Elizabeth Bishop's letters, I've been looking ever since for a book she mentions: by Stravinsky, about the poetics of music. When it's clear that the writer of a review is passionate about the book, then I want to buy the book. That's a kind of criticism *The New Yorker* used to have a lot more of, when the writer had fallen in love with a book – like Howard Moss's review of Rilke's letters on Cézanne. I think I've single-handedly kept that publisher in business. But nowadays it usually happens in speech – 'Oh, I just read this wonderful book.' Or somebody gives you a book.

I like the 'What did you take away from that?' discussion of a book more than talking about how the author did it. The conversations that I tend to enjoy are content conversations, more than style or structure – though sometimes they merge. In *A Woman's Life* by Annie Ernaux, her way of containing the story of her mother is part of the story.

When I was a student, I tended to stay away from critical books. It was not until I came to *The New Yorker* that I read Edmund Wilson, or a critic of that kind. I had got the impression that the authoritative way in which critics spoke – as disembodied critics – was intended to coerce, and I'm not good with coercion.

I had a good experience in the early '80s. There was this group of people that ran an alternative school, Marxist-based, and they had a woman teacher who was in her eighties and one of those old-time Communists. She led literature study groups, and she was a tremendous quoter. She was really passionate and sceptical and critical all at the same time. She'd written a two-volume work called *The Great Tradition of English Literature*. Her manner of addressing not only writers but critics was very – I don't know where it falls in a lefty or Marxist tradition, but because of the enthusiasm it was very persuasive. It was reading something in one of those study groups that for me broke the Sartre barrier for the first time. He was one writer I could barely touch because he was so coercive, but somehow seeing him in a context, whether temporal or biographical – 'Why would he *need* to write this way?' allowed me to follow his train without being put off by his tone. Same thing with Marx, another coercive writer, angry writer, and hard to read for that reason.

Are most critics resentful, or angry? I don't know. Friends of mine and I have been discussing a piece in the *New York Times Book Review* a couple of weeks ago, a review of a book by a writer we admire, who often writes about working-class issues. It was a mean-spirited review. In the book under review – a memoir – the writer had been straightforward enough to say that he was working-class only by virtue of the Depression, that his family had originally been a middle-class family. The reviewer is someone who speaks often of his working-class roots but as far as his manner of proceeding is concerned, and his subject matter, he has distanced himself from these roots completely. Maybe he's jealous, my friend suggested, jealous of the other writer for having taken his subject matter, and angry that he'd missed his boat.

We were being catty, speculating on this man's motives for writing the kind of review he did, and that was fine, but it's always dangerous to theorize beyond the facts. Edmund Wilson was a very unpleasant man to live with, or marry, and he was certainly decided in his critical opinions. But he managed to avoid the kind of temper that I'm thinking of simply because of his love for his subject matter. His love or his curiosity, or whatever it was, was totally engaged in his writing voice. There's not a whole slew of critics like him, I think. One woman, Wendy Lesser, wrote a book called *His Other Half*, about men looking at women in art: Dickens, Cecil Beaton, Hitchcock, Degas – men who have been accused of misogyny. These are artists she loves and she is trying to clear their names. She is an Edmund Wilson kind of critic. I don't find her coercive, or arbitrary, or having a hidden agenda.

When it comes to teaching the literature of the past, of course, there are problems of simple ignorance. For the last couple of years, some friends and I have been studying Latin, which I had not studied in school, and I keep being continually blown away by the fact of a dead language. When I was studying early and medieval Spanish, the professor had us learn 'vulgar Latin', 'soldier Latin', and I understood that thing of a language changing – so that the knowledge of parts of it is simply lost, or lost to everyone but lawyers and Catholics, and then lost to everyone but lawyers, and then just lost.

Over the weekend, I came out of a long brain-dead spell and got out an anthology of the Metaphysical poets and was reading George Herbert, moving back into that syntax and those spellings and the uncertainty of what might have been meant. At a poetry seminar a while back, someone who knows poetry shocked me by pointing out this one phrase, 'the passing bell', and saying that it meant a transitory bell, the passing sound of a bell, rather than the dead bell. I happened to know that the passing bell is the dead bell from reading a Dorothy Sayers mystery, *The Nine Tailors*, so by chance I had that little piece of knowledge though I didn't have many other knowledges surrounding that poem.

I think there are other ways of going into earlier literature, even if you don't have much knowledge, or any knowledge about it. Not all those poems are totally mysterious. I think that if someone is clear about the legitimacy of lying back and enjoying the music, not demanding sense immediately. If I were teaching my own work, or if my own work were taught, I would hope it was in context of nonsense verse. 'They went to sea in a sieve!' And then move into something different. I have a couple of poems that are very near nonsense. When I've read them aloud, I've had good luck in introducing them as nonsense verse, and once I've done that they turn out not to be nonsense.

Maybe it would be interesting to see how students would respond to Keats's drafts. That sense of a thing coming into being. Up at Vassar they have all eighteen drafts of Elizabeth Bishop's 'One

Art' – 'The art of losing isn't hard to master' – and it started out as a mess! She was just writing it, and it didn't have a form – and it's such a formal poem – and to see her move through that is such a comfort, because at first it had no rhythm; it had three words in the first draft that indicated the direction she then fixed on.

Criticism and teaching are two different things. The problem seems to me a matter of insecurity – 'publish or perish'. There's a young woman who works in *The New Yorker*'s poetry department, reading and doing opinion sheets on poems that are being bought. She has to say, 'Do I like this? What do I like about it? What don't I like about it?' Ultimately she has to say yes or no to the poem. She's also studying at NYU, going for a graduate degree, and she was talking to me about this problem she has of wanting to integrate these two sides of herself, find the kind of freedom she finds in expressing an editorial opinion and move it into her papers for academia, where each thing has to be backed up by a source, and you have to prove your opinion, but do you have the authority to prove it out of the text and the biography? Or the text and the notebook? Or do you have to turn around and prove it by calling on the jury in the background? The critics. That's a caricature of the needs of academia, but it didn't grow up out of people wanting to manufacture insecure people; it grew up out of people wanting to have documentation and proof, wanting to know and be certain about the past, while all the time feeling more and more uncertain, even about the pronunciation of those dead languages. It grew up for a good reason, the dark tower of criticism. But then it's as if the people in it lost hold of their wherewithal to make their own judgements – to feel safe in making a judgement, as if it were not possible to know a writer as a fellow-creature. And so it's as if they speak from a position of weakness, go on the offensive, the literally offensive offensive, when they don't have to.

Becoming a writer made me angry, whether angry at myself for not 'getting it', or angry at its not being taught: the fact that writers who had written what we were reading were human beings.

Luke Gibbons

The Irish Times

Luke Gibbons is a lecturer in communications at Dublin City University, and director of the MA programme in film and television studies. He is the co-author of *Cinema and Ireland* (1987) and was a contributing editor to *The Field Day Anthology of Irish Writing* (1991). His collection of essays, *Transformations in Irish Culture* will be published in 1995, and he is working on a study of aesthetics and the formation of Irish Romanticism.

Ventriloquism and its Voices

HERE ON THE communications degree at Dublin City University I mainly teach film studies, including a course in Irish cinema and the question of national cinema. I also teach a course entitled Cultural and Historical Perspectives on Irish Society, which takes in history, literature and visual culture in a way that allows me to deal with both text and context. I have also taught the history of journalism, which covers writing in a wider sense than just literature. I came to it from two backgrounds: for a number of years I taught philosophy and aesthetics in the National College of Art and Design, and political philosophy in Trinity College. The two were totally dissociated. Part of what attracted me to the area of media, mass communications and film was the prospect of bringing politics and art together through questions of power and influence – questions that are seldom raised in relation to art and literature, but are clearly central to the media.

My training was in philosophy and English in University College, Galway, and my main interest was aesthetics. In one sense aesthetics was a framing device for responding to English. The difficulty I found was somehow treating texts as hermetically sealed objects. The dominant form of criticism when I was doing English was the American 'New Criticism', which gives people admirable forensic critical skills but they do tend to be forensic. It was a bit like analytical philosophy in that it provided very good intellectual training in close reading and close thinking, but it tends to take literature away from, to use Kenneth Burke's phrase, 'equipment for living'. What I was more interested in was language and communication as precisely equipment for living, as one of the ways in which people organize their experience at intense moments of stress or loss or pleasure, or whatever. As

Doris Lessing says, Art helps to break up the paving stones of habit, which is a way of revitalizing and transforming the 'normality' of everyday life. The difficulty is when these disruptions are imposed unilaterally from above, without any acknowledgement of the complexity or the specificity of one's own experience.

One of the more off-putting aspects of my own education in literature in an Irish context was an attempt to inculcate the 'Great Tradition' in a culture that really had difficulties with not only the canon as it was presented, but with the very idea of a canon. It came as quite a shock to me to realize that there were actually debates about the way we were taught literature in school; for example, the way the Romantic poets were presented, as if it was a normal or universal experience to respond to daffodils the way Wordsworth does. John McGahern points out that one of the most remarkable things about Tomás Ó Criomthain's *An t-Oileánach* as an example of an Irish response to nature is that there was no compulsion to name things, or to reduce nature to botanizing, whereas in English Romantic poetry we were taught, even from primary school, that you were somehow deficient if you didn't respond to nature in the sensitive way the Romantics did, naming the names. That's what I mean by culture and literature being equipment for living. To me, growing up in the Irish countryside, English Romantic poems were a bit stilted and cut off from the life around me. You can see in Seamus Heaney's early poetry where he's struggling with Hardy, Wordsworth, Ted Hughes and Edward Thomas. One part of him feels that all this English tradition is within him – and indeed it probably is within him to the extent that he's part of the primary school system in Northern Ireland – but another part of him is pulling against it. He knows that to find a voice he has to accommodate himself to the canon and yet parts of his experience aren't mapped out by the poems, which are presented as universal, simply part of what we are.

One of the conclusions to be drawn from the Irish response to English literature is that it's not simply inclusion in the canon that's required, but a questioning of the canon itself. Very interesting work has been done by Irish critics like David Lloyd, questioning whether greatness or universality on the part of certain marginal literatures requires admission to the canon at all. Maybe what these literatures are doing is standing outside, while engaging in a critical interplay with the official version. Lloyd uses Deleuze and Guattari's notion of minor literature to describe a kind of writing that knows it's peripheral and could not exist were it not for the power of the centre; hence it engages in a parodic or distanced relationship with the canon without wanting to become part of it. There is a danger that if literature is subsumed into the mainstream, the way Joyce is treated as 'our first European', it is systematically divested of a lot of the cultural specificity that made it great in the first place.

When I teach literature now I'm trying to see how texts becomes stylistically, formally, and, indeed, textually dense and rich, not because of their distance from what's going on around them but because of their exposure to it. Literature is at its best when it negotiates those areas of experience that are very difficult to articulate in literal or everyday discourse, areas bound up with what Soviet cultural critics of the 1920s called 'inner speech'. This is still a form of language but is intensified, compressed and condensed because the experiences it's trying to deal with are elusive, inaccessible, or simply repressed, even if they seem to be out there in the open as part of everyone's lives.

I am greatly attracted to writers who are devalued, who are not seen as part of the literary firmament. I try to show it wasn't at all clear when certain literary greats were first writing that they had manifest destiny on their side. No doubt some were assured of their own genius, but a lot of people are assured of their own genius and haven't been heard of since. I would say that one of the first times I saw the limitations of formalism was in that bible of New Criticism, *Understanding Poetry* by Cleanth Brooks and Robert Penn Warren. There was an analysis of 'The Bells of Shandon' a well-known poem by the Irish poet Francis Sylvester Mahony, alias Father Prout. Brooks and Warren proceeded to ridicule this poem for its ineptitude. They used all the forensic skills of the new critics to show how the feminine rhymes, the mixed metaphors and the faltering metre and rhythm demonstrate the poet's incompetence, singling out this hapless performance as an example of how poetry should not be written. They then admit at the very end of their analysis that the poem is a parody, but only by going outside the terms of their own formal analysis, and invoking its wider Irish cultural context – the fact that is was written as a send-up of Moore's *Irish Melodies*. Without this 'external' or historical knowledge, it is almost impossible to account at a purely textual level for the tone of the poem. They argue as if it couldn't but be taken as meretricious, but in fact many Irish people have taken it to heart as a wonderful effusive tribute to Mahony's native Cork, notwithstanding its tongue-in-cheek elements. Again, this is because of another 'external' cultural element: the fact that many such topographical ditties in Ireland have this ambivalent tone that depends entirely on who performs it, and in what setting. Reappraising Prout's poem would be an example of taking a debased piece of literature, so called, and trying to show how rich it is, precisely because there's something slightly off-key about it.

Teaching this is admittedly a problem because minor figures like O'Mahony/Prout mean nothing to students at one level: in fact they would see him as almost the same as Tom Moore because Irish official nationalism tried to make 'The Bells of Shandon' part of the homespun Irish tradition. But if you relate the eccentric Father Prout to someone like Flann O'Brien, students get more animated because O'Brien is a cult figure for them. Students read Flann O'Brien when they think they're not doing literature. They can get a handle on what has been done a hundred years earlier by making analogies to writing that they themselves value. I would do the same in relation to rock music or indeed the kind of films that students like. It is a matter of making analogies and establishing cross-overs, but letting the students follow through these leads themselves. Some of the best essays and responses in seminars are from those who complete the analogies from their own perspectives.

For example one could at a stretch compare the benighted James Clarence Mangan to someone like Sinéad O'Connor. There's a sense of cultural kamikaze in both personalities, though admittedly one sings and the other doesn't. One is, no doubt, more of a celebrity than the other, but in terms of the sense of danger in their personalities, they can easily be related. Mangan was no romantic celebrity; he was a doomed figure. The wonder is he managed to write at all. He was a forlorn personality and a damaged angel, like his modern counterpart. One can make links like that without necessarily following it through point for point in the writing. It's a matter of giving students maps for the terrain but warning them that the map is not the territory. There may be many different maps for the same landscape, depending on what you want to get out of it, as Brian Friel reminds us so forcefully in *Translations*.

One of the advantages of teaching popular culture is that responses are contested from the very outset. There is no one way to read a film like *The Quiet Man*, or a proper way to read films which are circulating in the mainstream. But it doesn't follow that, because of the possibility of multiple interpretations, anything goes. Certain responses are appropriate from certain positions, or points of time, but other responses might overtake them. You have to look at actual and imagined audiences. How did different audiences respond to *The Quiet Man* when it was first shown? Most of my students heap scorn on these films now and that itself becomes a point of discussion in class. Did Americans belittle it when it was first shown? Did they laugh in the same way? How come it is revered by filmmakers like Scorsese and Spielberg? These questions should bring about a greater awareness of the conditions of reception, and the cultural templates that people bring to bear even when they think their response is totally spontaneous.

The same approach works well with literature. The way I use literature, I try to build on, but yet defamiliarize, the experiences students have brought with them from the Leaving Certificate. An example would be a comparison of the various film versions with Emily Brontë's *Wuthering Heights*. This novel becomes almost a touchstone for students, and when I try to show the variety of interpretations that are involved in adaptation, it's rewarding to see the students both drawing on, and yet thoroughly reappraising, a novel in which many have an intense personal investment.

Whereas with other figures like Peig Sayers, I've only to mention her in a first-year class and a groan comes from all and sundry. It's not due to the nature of the original book, but in their own preconceptions towards Irish. But then in a third-year class when I refer to it again in the context of, say, arranged marriages in *The Quiet Man* or *The Ballroom of Romance* – the tradition of matchmaking in our society in the light a feminist history students have said, 'I can't believe that was in it when I read it in secondary school.' It's the same text, but framed by a different horizon. Indeed, one of the most heartening things in recent years is the re-framing of the Irish language itself within a new set of cultural horizons.

Though my academic background was philosophy and English, one of the most rewarding experiences for me was secondary school teaching. I taught for a short time in the mid-1970s in a vocational school in Tullamore. I began to realize that the conventional third-level idea of teaching as simply the transfer of information and interpretations, the handing down of responses from authority to the untutored, just wasn't on for young kids. The most important thing I could bring into the classroom, given that discipline itself was a problem, was motivation and interest. That's how I began teaching the media. I began using the kind of material that they looked at outside school, establishing links between that and what was already on the course. The idea was not to have one eclipse the other or to value one at the expense of the other, but somehow to use the interests and orientations they already had to enhance their response to literature and history.

Teaching at secondary level completely changed my approach to teaching. Questions of motivation and interest and encouraging enthusiasm are so rarely considered in third level teaching. Academics are too deadpan for such trivialities. Even when academics are obsessed with something, as specialist scholars frequently are, somehow the enthusiasm that impels them does not always come across to students. On the other hand, 'The Dead Poets' Society' kind of charismatic teacher presents even more difficulties because then the teaching becomes too bound up with a single personality, which doesn't open up new perspectives at all. I think the courses I teach have best succeeded when the students weren't quite sure what my responses were. Often students would meet me afterwards, or in non-institutional settings, and would ask me what do I really think about, say, *The Quiet Man*? Surely I don't take it seriously as a good film?

It's more important to present a range of responses than to identify any one exclusively your own. You have to simulate certain positions and perspectives with a view to making people think beyond clichéd responses. This may involve acting as devil's advocate. You have to be a ventriloquist of sorts, conducting a dialogue even with yourself.

When I taught English and History in secondary school, one of the main things I tried to do was cross-cut the two subjects, showing how, for example, reading narrative texts could enhance an understanding of history. There was a historical romance series on television called *Poldark*, set in Cornwall, which the school kids kept mentioning, and so I began to deal with issues based on it. It was not just a matter of illustrating history, but asking why the stories took the form they did, discussing plot structure and narrative, without putting it in so many words. I then tried to show how similar story structures were often at work in history; for example, Columbus's discovery of America being treated as if it could only have a happy ending. And why so few Irish stories have happy endings, or indeed endings at all.

I put together a short anthology of contemporary Irish writing that seemed to work purely through trial and error, with bits and pieces from Paul Muldoon, Frank Ormsby, Seamus Heaney and from the 'New Irish Writing' page in *The Irish Press*. For example, Paul Muldoon's wonderful poem where he compares the snail to a hovercraft. That poem had them thinking a lot about how images hit off each other. In a way they were delighted with pieces that would make strange, chance connections with their own lives. I used narrative and linguistic puzzles a lot, especially the type of enigmatic stories George Orwell used to include in his journalistic articles. They were trick short stories in which the meaning of the events couldn't be explained unless you attended very closely to the way in which it was told. There's usually a catch at the end, but the catch only works because of the preconceptions brought to bear on the story; whereas if the reader slows down, and listens carefully to each word, it will become evident that the meaning was not hidden but was out in the open all the time. Only prior expectations prevented the reader getting it.

There was in the 1970s a very useful publication by *The Irish Times* called *The Education Times* which had a young people's poetry page, and it was interesting to look at these with students. To see even one image in what might otherwise might be a poor poem could provide the flash of insight which might be built on next time round. This was not great literature, but I was trying to get across the idea that imperfection is not necessarily a fall from grace, but may be a stepping stone to something else. That's one of the difficulties with Matthew Arnold's idea of canonical touchstones, always teaching the best and only the best. It can end up intimidating and deterring those this side of paradise. They can become so aware of their own frailty, their own mortality, compared to those perfect well-wrought urns created by genius. Stepping stones may be better in the end than touchstones. 'Excellence' is better served as a terminus than as a point of departure, and it is not at all clear to me that students should be exposed to it at first.

One thing I'm constantly amazed at in more conservative English departments in universities is the way lecturers may be asked at the beginning of the year to teach, say, Spenser, Milton, Wordsworth and Yeats, traversing cultures and centuries at will, regardless of enthusiasm or even competence. Intellectual rigour is treated as a form of penance, the imaginative equivalent of Lough Derg. There is this relentless emphasis on textual purity, removing or rather repressing all 'extra'-textual factors as seductive distractions – theory, history, even the cultural context of a work. Many teachers of the old school see English as somehow beleaguered or threatened by anything other than textual purity, but in Ireland literature has always been suffused with politics and history.

One of the research projects I'm working on is a historical and critical enquiry into the absence of an aesthetic tradition in Ireland, in the rarefied sense of 'aesthetic'. This occurred not because people didn't appreciate texts or imaginative works, but because art was always the means of responding to something beyond the work. Life itself could not be lived without creative representations but the representations themselves had more to them than simply their own interiors. Some English departments are now talking about back to basics, which is a new form of textual fundamentalism. I have real difficulties with that because that's not the way literature manifested itself in this culture.

There is another irony in that many of the contemporary critical and political approaches that are condemned as imports are already part of the literary tradition in Ireland. For example, Irish literature didn't have to await the advent of post-structuralism to appreciate 'parody' and 'intertextuality'. The whole relationship to the English canon was parodic. Irish writers have tended to write endlessly about other texts, adopting at one and the same time a creative and critical relation to them. One of the best ways to learn criticism, in my experience, is to read the parodic sections in *Ulysses*. As I was saying about Francis Sylvester Mahony's poems, they are imaginative, but yet have the self-reflection of criticism. Flann O'Brien's writing also brings this out, with his irony, reflexivity and his pastiches of learning. It ill behoves conservative critics to argue that these wayward approaches to the untilled field of Irish literature are all being imported through postmodernism or whatever. One of the reasons these so-called postmodern theories even surface now is that peripheral literatures are making more and more impact on the canon and so the traditional modes of response have to give way. The back to basics approach is actually a way of removing the cultural specificity of literature in Ireland, and so far from getting rid of foreign theory, is actually endorsing critical stances that are themselves imperial imports, belonging to the good old days when English literature was central to the process of transmitting the glories of English civilization on other cultures.

The critical initiatives that I value most are the ones that acknowledge cultural specificity. To emphasize this does not mean simply supporting your local sheriff, come what may. Cultural specificity means precisely being aware of other horizons. It does not entail cultural enclosure of the kind that Daniel Corkery envisaged. What's most specific about Ireland is precisely its openness to other cultural projects and to other societies, for better or for worse. American culture and the American experience now suffuse Ireland, not just through cultural imperialism but through the diaspora and the emigrant experience, so that in some ways Ireland is at its most culturally specific when it is crossed by all those pathways going through it.

A very interesting initiative taking place right now in the humanities is the new distance education venture, Oscail, based at Dublin City University, but involving the most innovative departments in other universities. The literature course that has been devised for this stands in stark contrast to traditional English courses within the academy. One of the first questions you ask yourself in distance education is: how are someone's interest and motivation going to be maintained when thsat person is not within the privileged ethos of the university? The Oscail literature course makes contact at a level in which people can respond to literature, while doing other things with their lives. It is not just English literature, moreover, but involves translations from Latin-American writing, French, Russian, and so on. I have no difficulty with these kinds of imports in Irish culture; we can't have enough of them.

There is really a danger of treating literature as a museum piece, of doing to literature what museums do to memory. There is something to be said for preservation for its own sake, but not when it runs the risk of ossification, taking something out of the continuum of everyday life. If you use popular culture in your teaching you avoid some of that danger because the students know more about it than the lecturers. It doesn't mean that they have the monopoly of interpretation either. The interpretations are simply more contested when the students know as much, or even more about the original, than the lecturers.

The crisis of criticism as it has been traditionally conceived in universities was brought home to me when I heard a very eminent literary critic say, on being asked to write about a visit to Ireland, that it was preferable to write about texts. Experience had to be tidied up and ordered through art before a response could be ventured. Life itself was too messy and too inchoate. The role of the artist, on this reckoning, is to come in and save the critics the trouble of having to risk themselves, and then the role of the critic in turn is to save everybody else from the extremes of art. Or indeed the extremes of life itself.

It is interesting that having used texts as a prophylactic against experience, some of the top American literary academics are now reverting to confessional writing. There is a belated discovery that there is something beyond the text; usually it's themselves. It is interesting that, having used texts as a shield against the vagaries of life outside the academy, there comes a point where you realize that the texts are only as good as their ability to help you negotiate your experience. Criticism in this sense should not just bear the trace of one's own voice, but should be a matter of opening up one's experience to many voices. We are back, I suppose, to ventriloquism again.

Tom Mullins

Tom Mullins lectures on the teaching of English language and literature in the Department of Education, University College, Cork. Main research interests are the teaching of literature and curriculum revision. His ambitions are to write some books and walk on many mountains.

The Top Button on My Pyjamas

WHAT IS DISTRESSING about the students I teach is that many of them appear not to have any interest in verse at all. I ask them, 'Do you read poetry regularly?' and they look at me in astonishment, as if to say, what's that got to do with anything that's real? They see it just as study material for examinations. It's got nothing to do with them and their lives. This is a disastrous stance for people who are preparing to be teachers. It's not as if they're seventeen and just coming into college. One of the depressing and frightening things about many teachers I encounter is that they don't read. Many English teachers don't read. Now the curriculum has been radically changed in Ireland hopefully it might move them to read a little bit more here.

But I must say, the attitude that many people come out of the university English course with is a problem. I don't know where the blame lies. It's too simple just to point at one factor. They come out of a system which emphasizes texts and tests, and it's very difficult to know how we can rescue people from that when they see the achievement of their education being equated with a number of points. In that particular kind of packaged commodity system, the status of verse, except for the exceptional teachers, is going to be very reduced indeed.

There's another problem: defining the nature of English studies. In the school system it was certainly defined in terms of the great canon and New Criticism, and if you didn't have a response to that particular tradition of poetry, then you were incapable of having a literary experience. That was the assumption prior to the revision of the curriculum which was begun in 1990/91: literature was in a confined and decided space, and literary experience was also within that space and outside that there was something that wasn't literary experience. It's very hard to move people from that position. That's certainly one of the huge challenges we're facing in education: how to develop people's confidence in their own imaginative reconstruction of books, and their ability to be happy with this enriching of their imagination, which may not be approved of by the establishment, but is wonderful for them.

The first quality of the good teacher of literature is that he/she loves literature and continues to read it. You teach out of what you are, and in English you teach out of what you read as well. If you're not coming into the classroom – at any level of education – saying, 'Listen to this, I've just read this poem,' or, 'I've just read this novel and there's this great scene,' then I think you're failing your students, because it's out of that passion that they say, 'There's something here I must get into.' The Americans have the great phrase – it's also an ugly phrase – that the teacher must 'animate the symbol'. That kind of enthusiasm animates, if you like, or it invites the students into an encounter and a stance with literary experience which is the foundation stone of any development. That's the first thing. It's not just loving *Jane Eyre* or loving Shakespeare – of course that's wonderful – but it's an up-to-dateness, a sense that this is still going on and I am still excited by this, it's part of my life, part of my consciousness; this is what really animates and enriches the students. As Michael Oakeshott said, introducing people to literature and the writers of the past is introducing people to the conversation of mankind. I think that's what the good teacher of literature does. The students see him or her involved in that conversation and want to get involved themselves. Conversation between the teacher and the student follows on from the conversation between the teacher and the book.

Another important thing is an approach to the students which respects where they are. The characteristic stance of many in education tends to be that really I (the teacher) know and you (the student) don't, and you need to get what I have. I find that depressing. What we need to do is step out of it and *invite* students in in some way. I'm not saying it's easy, but you're down here to methodology, and your conception of the teacher's role, at whatever level of education. The teacher as dispenser of information seems to me a useful but a controlling role, whereas the teacher as instigator, as facilitator seems to me much more useful. The methodological skills needed to do that may be taught at second level but not at third level. There's a professionalism needed. Third-level teachers pick it up as they go along. Some are gifted but some obviously don't care. The third-level system also promotes the idea that if you've attained a certain level of knowledge, as guaranteed by your PhD, then you are therefore fit to transmit that knowledge. It identifies your ability to write academic English, but says nothing of your ability to speak about literature intelligently in a lecture room, which is not the same thing at all.

The first thing in inviting students to participate in literature would be to develop confidence in themselves, in their own response, in their own ability to read. First, you have to give them the confidence that their insight, their choice of word and their attempts to talk about a phrase or word in the poem are all fine. You have to help them see that they don't have to read in a linear way, or understand every single word, or use academic vocabulary to talk about it. You need to rescue them initially from those parameters which tend to produce a kind of paralysis in the mind: when I go through a poem in a linear way the thing dies in front of me; when I can't make a reference to a range of critical theory which appears to be necessary – then I can't read this poem. That method is always tending towards completion. Students think they must have closure, that there's always an answer to a poem or a novel, and when they think they've got the answer, they feel relieved that they can then forget it. That's a huge problem, so you have to get them away from that.

The first thing I might do in a class is have the poem read by the student, or by the teacher, and I tell them they're simply to underline the one word that surprised them in the poem, that's all, or the one phrase. I collect all the words they've chosen and put them on the blackboard, and then I chat about what kind of surprise did it give you. Also you can say things like, 'Is there any particular pattern in these words? Can we connect one word to another here in some way?' Almost invariably of course there is a pattern, and then suddenly the poem begins to open up. Each word chosen was a key entry point for the students. The poem, if it's any good, can be entered from any of those points. You don't have to start at the first line; you can start at the last word and gain entry to a poem that way.

There's one very important aspect to the introduction to a poem. The most frightening question in education at any level is: Why? I've noticed this over and over again in class. At first the student hasn't a clue why. That is a very important thing to learn. You don't ask why early in the class; you ask why after fifteen minutes when the thing has gone around and people are beginning to feel comfortable. An abstract question like that thrown in too soon is just going to chop off that sprout, no doubt about it. They don't know why they responded as they did, and then they feel that their response is in some way devalued. So what we need first is space to grow through the word or phrase they've chosen, so the imaginative pattern around that grows and grows and grows. Then suddenly the poem opens up and they begin to give you the answer to the why question without your even asking it.

A more challenging technique with the same kind of approach is to ask students to write down two or three questions about a poem that they don't know the answer to. People hate writing down questions they don't know the answer to. I've done this over and over again with teachers when I do in-service courses. Teachers, perhaps because of their role, are worse than most people because they always know the answer. Our culture expects them to know the answer, so when you ask a teacher to write down a question, they don't know the answer to, they look at you in absolute horror. Everybody knows a teacher because they always *tell* you things. Children have always said, 'Well, I try to guess the answer in your mind, because you know it and I don't.' The nineteenth-century model of a teacher has pretty much continued in the popular imagination, so for the teacher not to know is to enter into an area where knowledge, not definitive, is an absurdity.

So those are two very simple techniques which allow students to come in with their questions, feelings and images relative to a poem, and which are useful in moving towards that tension which lies at the centre of a poem, that friction from which you feel its energy. Once you get that sense of conflict going, then students get very interested. They like conflict. One of the problems in teaching poetry is that students are into narrative, they have no problem about narrative, but poems today don't tend to be narrative. So when you can get a sense of tension generated, this is a way of getting them interested, they can go hunting for more elements of it. They start to use more aspects of their own personalities, their own sense of what tension is or what generates tension, which is getting them unwittingly into unknown areas of themselves.

I like to do group performance of verse with students. In performance, the half-understood becomes realized when you put it literally into your mouth. Students won't read aloud one at a time, and even if they will, the rest of the class are instantly bored because they're not experiencing the pleasure of the words in their own mouths. Whereas if you get the whole lot to do it initially together, there may be a bit of a giggle and some people would probably not actually be saying anything, but it's like people who start to sing in a pub, and then five sing and then six sing and then seven sing when they think they can't be heard. I'm a great believer in the sensuousness of verse, and for that you do need performance.

After the first reading, I manoeuvre them into groups, give each group the same poem and say, 'Read it again one at a time in your groups and then you decide which of the group reads it the most interestingly.' Then that person is invited to say it to the class, or the group is invited to say it together as a choral performance. That works extremely well because they're taking possession of their own reading of the poem. They're talking about it: 'What are you trying to achieve here? Why did you read that word with greater emphasis than the other word?' Then of course you're into interpretation and the poem begins to open up again – not at the beginning, they'll all be very careful at first – but eventually they give very diverse interpretations. The important thing is to have short poems, so you can hold them quickly in the mind; ten or twelve lines will work fine. Recording it is always a very good thing to do, especially in secondary schools. That gives them motivation. It's always very gigglish, but the end is not a John Gielgud performance; the end is simply the process of doing it, so that they allow the sensuousness of the verse to take possession of them.

Louise Rosenblatt makes a distinction between what she calls 'efferent' reading and 'aesthetic' reading. Efferent means to carry away information, and she says that is the dominant reading of our time, where you simply see through the words the information they carry. In aesthetic reading you are conscious of your own response, conscious of the language in which the text is written. Many students don't have that focus. They find it hard to ask, 'What's happening to me while this is going on?' Whereas in other areas of life, like watching TV or movies, or listening to music, they find it easier to have that sort of response. There's an awareness of what they feel – Eliot's phrase about having the experience and missing the significance? I'm not saying that everybody shows a critical response through this method, but while they're reading, they're aware now and again that there's something happening in them. At certain moments you are aware that you are distressed or excited, and you're paying closer attention to the language, rereading a phrase for some reason. That experience is one that I don't think students have been allowed or invited to talk about.

So that would be what you might call the participation approach, which can get students involved in a poem and invite them to reread, which they've otherwise no interest in doing. I don't actually suggest that they learn by heart, but in the context of performance it happens by the way. I'm glad I learned a lot of verse, but I don't inflict it. I wouldn't like to provoke that, 'Oh no, not twenty five lines of Shakespeare again tonight' kind of response. That seems to me to be quite an inappropriate way of doing it. It can be done certainly, but again it involves a cultural shift in how we expect to teach verse. If for example, we equate good teaching with silence, which many people do, especially at second level, then we run into difficulties because this kind of creative involvement is not quiet. Nor should it be. I suppose it's organized chaos really and out of that comes something worthwhile.

Two other approaches that would be useful are the use of drama and the use of visuals. The drama is obvious enough. Performance begins the dramatic involvement. I like to get two students to freeze-frame part of the poem and choose a title for it. That technique works extremely well, though it involves a lot of management. The other one is to invite students to illustrate the poem. You learn so much about their response that way, though the teacher must be able to interpret the picture and show the student that what they have drawn is a particular viewpoint on the poem. A couple of years ago I had a meeting with some teachers here doing Seamus Heaney's poem 'The Forge', and they said, 'But we can't draw,' and I said, 'That's alright, just draw.' We discussed the fact that some of them were inside the forge in their drawings and some of them were outside looking in, and some of them drew objects from the forge in no particular setting. From that we teased out their various responses to the poem.

The teacher has to see the different framings that have gone on. So you need a basic sense of what is on the page; for example, a simple comparison between inside and outside, and what these choices say about your experience of the poem. This is extraordinarily liberating for students. It makes them realize that they do have a stance, despite themselves. Students find it very difficult to articulate what they want to say about a poem; they don't have the language. I'm not talking about academic language here, they don't have *any* language. But despite the fact that they can't draw, somehow or other they get something down visually and that is a beginning. I also like to ask them to put the poem into terms of colour, or a colour sequence, or to put the poem in terms of an abstract shape or a line. Recently in a school in Tipperary, the teachers found it very exciting to put down the sense of a poem in terms of colour. They said they couldn't believe the quality of the response they got. Things they had tried to talk about verbally with students – like trying to tell them this poem had a depressed mood – now the answer was screaming out at them: here was a black verse.

What we need to do is to develop a series of different languages to talk about literature – dramatic language, performance, visual, colour, line – that will rescue the poem from the prison it's in at the moment. Academic language has helped imprison it. I'm not saying it need necessarily be that way, and many people find it useful, but it is limited and sometimes dangerous. You're back to basic questions like, 'What is the purpose of teaching the poem?' 'What do you want to end up with?' I know what I want them to end up with is the ability to read verse with a certain degree of pleasure and a kind of personal recreation. I would like it to energize them in some way, to make life a little bit richer for them. At the end I do not want them to be an authority on critical approaches to Ezra Pound's work. I want them to have a sense of love and passion about the verse and that's all. So if they're going out to be teachers that's where it is, that's where it should be at, that students can come back to them afterwards when they've left school and say yeah, I still read Emily Dickinson. And that's it; then they've won in some way it seems to me.

The last area is that you want to invite them to write. I'm very much for that. It's important because they take the skill of verse for granted. When they begin to have a go themselves, they learn how difficult it is, and also that it isn't so remote from themselves. I stress to them that everybody has what you might call poetic experiences of some kind, in which their imagination is so engaged and so intense about some object or experience that it's worth writing or talking about. Many students don't respect their experience at all. They say, 'Well, I never have things to write about,' or, 'I've no imagination.' I invite students to remember three things from their childhood which they know are unique to their world. I emphasize it can't be anything vague, like the seaside; it must be an object. It's very important for the teacher to model, to liberate them. I choose, say, a rocking horse, a hot press door, or the Sacred Heart light at home. Then I say, 'Right, they're my three; you can't use those, off you go,' and they write down their three and then I say, 'I want you to choose one of these and I want you to describe it for me, using at least three of your senses.' They're always astonished by what they produce. Almost invariably the objects they pick have an intensity for them because they are unique to them. Then when they begin to write about them, they write with a certain amount of respect which perhaps they've never done before, and suddenly we have a roomful of potentially very good verse. Then I invite them to read it.

The only advice I give them is: write about it in terms of the senses. I might suggest that they write a sentence on it, so I deliberately go away from the sense of conscious poetic form. I'm trying to get them into the idea of concretizing, to suggest that the imagination works in terms of the sensuous, that it's not something vague and woolly. You can move on from objects to places, people, and then the whole thing begins to open up. At that stage you must decide what you do with all this extraordinary material. I invite them to put it into a little book and publish it for themselves. They get great delight out of this. It's just for themselves really, there's no big deal about it, but in the process of doing it, I think they grow in their respect for themselves and their experience.

It's very moving what people write. I just did this exercise in Tipperary the other day and it was wonderful. One lady said, 'The top button on my pyjamas. As a child I had a kind of silvery button on my pjyamas and before my father turned off the light, the light always reflected in the kind of silvery button.' Another lady said she always had rag dolls and this was the first doll with porcelain, and it was just sitting on the chair for Christmas and somebody threw a bottle and broke the doll; and the lady was crying in front of me in this in-service course. It was great that they could get so intense about a broken doll fifty years later and go on to write about it. I don't really respond when people get very moved like this. I keep quite distant and say, 'We all have things we want to write down and which are worth talking about.' And that's all it's left at. I think just the act of talking about the memory, the fact that they have now shared it with somebody is immensely enriching for them.

It's my firm belief that poetry is play, and playing with language needs to be an important thread all the way through the teaching of verse. This should be emphasized as much as possible by all kinds of gamey, funny poems. There are surprising revelations when you start playing with words. I would tend to use what they have been inculcated with – the much-despised canon, Wordsworth for example. It's not necessarily to devalue the poetry, though you demystify it certainly. I say to the students, 'Let's see can you write in that particular style.' And the teacher must do it too, in front of the students. If it's a mess, it's a mess. Perhaps the first time you go in you do have your parody prepared in case you're going to be a complete failure, but then as it goes on you say, 'Look, I prepared it last night and I'll have a go off it here and see what happens.' The teacher really should get up there and do it. I think that's where really good teaching goes on, where students see you in-the-process-of as well; they see your difficulties and your choices – including the wrong ones – and from that view of you structuring and constructing, they learn how to structure and construct, if not to do it better. Doing it better or worse is not the point. They see the teacher thinking in front of them and they see that he or she is uncertain, and that it's hard work for teachers too. I think that is immensely liberating for students.

I've mainly talked about teaching poetry, but I do teach the other genres too. In the past I think we have been very dutiful, certainly at second level – and third level to a certain degree too – in taking that awful linear approach to novels. For example, you know, begin in October at chapter one and finish in late March at chapter thirty-five. Nobody reads a book like that. I think we need to replicate in the classroom the way we read books out of the classroom. I'm all for selective reading. I take passages and do a lot of detailed work on those. The questions that arise to which the students don't know the answer, they must go away and think about, read what comes before or what comes after. That's how books are read anyway, you're always pitching forward and backwards, trying to explain this, trying to explain that.

I say to students that they should read novels as fast as possible initially to get some sense of shape, and what I always recommend is that they should keep some kind of response journal while they're reading. Now some of them view this as a pain – another thing that he wants us to do. I'm not saying you must write pages, just jot down something. It's exactly the same technique as finding the surprising word in a poem, or writing down the question you don't know the answer to. This response journal is for nobody but yourself; it doesn't have to be highly intellectual, or analytical; it might be remembering the top button on your pyjamas again. It might be a phrase from the novel that you like, and want to write down, or it might be, 'I hate that character,' or, 'This character reminds me of my aunt.' Then I say, 'But what you'll find very interesting if you continue with this, is how your response evolves relative to the narrative line, relative to characters. You get a real sense of your own reading graph, or reading feelings if you like, when you go back to this response journal. When we'll be discussing it here, what you'll find very interesting is to see how your stance is different from somebody else's and how it changes as we begin to explore the novel more fully.'

This works very well with some students. It depends how you put it to them, of course, and on your relationship with them. I give students as much space as I can. I think you have to be a good performer. Students have a range of responses to teachers and the first thing they would look for is: is this person serious? Do they believe in this stuff or don't they? Students, no matter how much they dislike your material or dislike you, if there's a sense of seriousness about your work, they respect that. They say, 'He's an awful bore, but he knows his stuff.' They respect the fact that you're professional about your material. They also respect enormously when you give credence – I don't mean that in a condescending way – to where they are and welcome them to where you are, when they see that you're happy for them to be there and you're delighted they have a response. It's very hard to get students to move from 'respect for the knowledge' to where they're coming from. They like doubt and humour because both of those create space for them and deny space to the teacher's authority. This allows growth and therefore allows them to be educated in the best sense of the word. Generally speaking I think we have had a good creative dialogue over the years. I get a great buzz from meeting young people. They remind you that you were there once and you should keep it going. I find that a privilege.

Linsey Abrams

Linsey Abrams is the author of three novels, *Double Vision*, *Charting by the Stars*, and *Our History in New York*. Her short stories, reviews and essays have appeared in such publications as the *New York Times Book Review*, *Christopher Street*, and the *Review of Contemporary Fiction*. She is a member of the faculty at Sarah Lawrence College and writer-in-residence in the graduate programme of the City College of New York. She is founding editor of a new magazine of fiction, poems and essays, *Global City Review*.

To Champion the Human

FIRST, ALL THE texts that were commentary on the original literary canon have now become the canon and, second, most interesting literary texts produced since then are considered peculiar or eccentric – gay and lesbian literature, women's literature, science fiction – and therefore not universal. I'll leave these ideas to the people driven by them. My own sense of being well read is to know certain stories that are really the source material of literature, and then to look at how the telling of the story has changed over time and with history. An example of that might be – and I would have a tendency to discuss this more with my graduate students than with my undergraduates – to have them read a part or all of the *Iliad*, and then, depending on which translation you use, talk about the issue of war-making, the issue of women as property, the issue of the journeyer, or conversely of the hermit who never leaves home. There's a lot of issues central to that text that it addresses by inclusion and exclusion. All important literature works this way.

I feel that to read certain canonical texts is still extremely important for that reason, though what matters is how you read them. You don't read them in the context in which they were written and you certainly don't read them in the context of the way perhaps a traditional literature teacher might teach them, which is historically, i.e. patriarchally, and within the history of criticism and now theory. I think you teach students to read within an informed emotional and mental world that is personal and expanding! Suzanne Gardinier recently published an essay in *The Kenyon Review* on the new translation of the *Iliad* which was a collaboration by two men, Robert Fagles and Bernard Knox. Lattimore was the translator into English of the original standard text, but then there the Fitzgerald translation and there's now this new one. The Fitzgerald text was heroic, thus very metaphorical. This new text – and Suzanne Gardinier talks about the translation in detail – is much more physicalized. It's really about what the blows are like, you know like, wham, he hit him over the head with a truncheon and split his head open. It makes you look at the act of war-making in an entirely different way. There's also a sense that it's really an act, a very intimate act the two men are performing with each other. Neither is it devoid of eroticism.

So I would then ask even my undergraduate students, who know a lot, for an essay like: talk about different ways an original text has been looked at over the course of time, depending on who's doing the translating, from what era, and within what perspective. Then, I might also ask them, for instance, to read Christa Wolf's *Cassandra*, which is the retelling of the Trojan War from the standpoint of the woman who told everyone at the beginning that it was all going to turn out badly and that no one would win, and so they locked her in a cage and buried it. Sound familiar? One of the interesting things about *Cassandra* is that it's a fairly short retelling of the actual story in which the women's lives are brought in. The people who do not participate in the war-making are made part of the story. It tells how in a way it was the splitting off of the women's story that allowed the war to be conceived and waged in the first place. There are also four essays in Christa Wolf's book. One describes why she wrote the book. Another describes actually going to the physical place where *The Iliad* was set, like a travelogue, so that she clearly functions also as her own secondary source. She puts the entire narrative in a context that explains why it's going to be read a certain way, how it *should* be read, how she personally came to do it, so that the author is introduced – a crucial inclusion.

As I've said, one of the things I try to do in teaching reading is to take to primary sources about very important issues. At the same time, I like to bring in other books that give a different angle on why a story is told the way it is told, and how that story can be changed by a different story-teller, because of course that's really the story. Similarly, in teaching writing I often give an assignment that I call 'the beach story'. I tell the students it happens at exactly noon; there is a vendor on the beach; there is a woman with a child – she may be the mother, she may be the babysitter, she may be the aunt, we don't know what their relationship is, it isn't defined – and by the end of the story the child has to ask the vendor a question. Then I make them all write that story. Now, it's all the same information; it's basically the same plot, and the characters' roles are defined but of course everyone comes up with a completely different story. How many people foreground the vendor? Almost nobody. Two students in two hundred foreground the vendor. That's interesting and that's something. That's why fiction is endlessly interesting and informative about being human. As my philosopher colleague Elfie Raymond commented on recent intellectual wars between literature and theory, while theory is ultimately self-referential, literature enduringly makes reference to all of life.

Another novel I might teach is *The Ravishing of Lol V. Stein* by Marguerite Duras, a circular story about a woman to whom something terrible has happened. Each time you circle around the story you get to know a little bit more. It appears that the story is being told in the third-person because it's all 'Lol did this', 'Lol did that', and then you find out halfway through the story that it's a man who's obsessed with her, telling her story, which then throws the story into another perspective. The objectification of Lol has happened above all in her own mind; she's lost. So you begin to question why she's lost herself. Had it something to do with a humiliation with a man? The man who is telling the story? No, as it turns out. But the issue of who's telling the story is again the key to it.

Then I might introduce some of Freud's case histories of 'hysterical' women, like Dora – and there's a number of interesting secondary texts by feminist psychoanalytic critics that can plumb more gracefully than I can some of the stylistic and psychological intricacies. I myself create the commentary on all these commentaries – as do my students. Together, we talk our way toward complex, overlapping truths, toward a kind of clarity that includes ourselves as well as our characters. This creates a kind of fierceness of intellect, of self, which life, as well as art, demands.

Nothing is without its literary antecedents. You can start with something that's a much earlier historical story, like Native American birth myths, or the Oedipus trilogy, then talk about a form that comes later. I usually work with novels rather than stories because a novel is with you for so long that it starts to get under your skin and infiltrate your thinking, whereas with a story you can be in and out of it sometimes before you know what it was. You can think of a piece of fabric, and then there's the dye that goes into that fabric. You can't miss colour in a novel and that seems to me, in reading and writing, what you're teaching people to look for. There's an emotional texture and an emotional fabric that you live in because of that dye. It's like life. As a writer, you're looking to put that part of yourself on to the page, and as a reader you're looking to enter into that on the page. Sometimes people think that literature is so different from life, and it isn't, it's just a rendering of it. Whether you use realism or you don't use realism, you want the reader to walk into a room and say, 'This is just like life.' And yet if you read five different novels in a row and each of them seems just like life, then clearly it's something else that's operating, so it's not *equivalent* to life. It's something that the language does.

But in order to be able to write at all, you have to work directly from life, from that very strong voice that each of us has, from that very emotionalized room that each of us knows holds our own life and that you're looking to find as you start to create your own work as a young writer. As a teacher, I try to pick books that are very clear in that way. If I were going to, for instance, teach younger students, first-year college or high school, I would pick books where there's an enormous amount at stake. I would take Toni Morrison's *The Bluest Eye* in which two little Black girls became the central characters of a novel for the first time in mainstream literature and a novel that, not incidentally, had incest at the heart of it. It's a hard book for people to read, but I never feel that 'hard' is the problem with students.

With young people, you've got open minds, unless they've been brainwashed. That's why I love teaching, and first year is almost my favourite kind. A lot has happened to those students. You do not have a sheltered life at seventeen or eighteen now. Everything has happened to you or someone you know. The amounts of violence, the amounts of drug addiction or terrible parenting or alcoholism or AIDS or just the turmoil of adolescence which you're barely out of –

which I'm barely out of! There's a tenderness to that state, which a writer needs. I'm never afraid of teaching something that has real subject matter. They love that, that's their best thing. I find that in their writing when they get off-track they write about the stuff that doesn't really matter and nothing's at stake, but the minute they start reading, they really get involved, whether it's a published novel or each other's work. When a writing class really starts cooking, it's catching, and the writing catches too. Everyone's hair is standing on end.

I tend to like to do contemporary literature, but I like usually to back up to the sixties or the fifties where certain ideas were emerging, like in James Baldwin's *Giovanni's Room*, about a gay man whose lover is in prison and is going to die and there's that sort of slide down into it, but there's a voice that cuts through the silence or the darkness or the void. There's great necessity in the telling.

Another book I like to teach is Camus' *The Stranger*, which is a beautiful, beautiful book about a feeling that never gets felt. It's a classic because of that and it will always be one. Some people will say, it's a book in which there's a gun and somebody shoots somebody and it's nihilistic. Or, it's existentialist; let me tell you about existentialism. One of the things that as teachers we're up against is that every time you mention anything, you're also giving sort of a précis of philosophical history and psychological, literary, even scientific history. You're constantly bringing in as much as you can, but you can't assume that certain terms or certain ideas are within a student's intellectual vocabulary. So you're teaching everything. In a way those of us who are teaching literature are lucky in that these things are built into conversation; at least the space is available, whereas maybe if you're teaching physics you also long to say some of these things but you have to get to, you know, this point and this point first. I guess if you get further on into physics, you're freed up again but there's a lot you have to get through to think more broadly in science, whereas in literature you can think broadly more from the beginning. I could be wrong here.

One way in which writers who teach literature are let off the hook is that, although some novelists who teach writing have PhDs, we're judged instead on our books. Susan Sontag once said that writers are free to be more instinctive, even stupid. And, in a way this ignorance frees us up to concentrate on the book itself. At the same time that I like to put a book in context, I also approach it the way I approach a piece of writing when I'm working with a student. What is it within itself? In other words, I'm looking within the confines of the book, not outside. If reading concerns how much of it can you hold in your head and feel in your feelings, then writing concerns how much you can invent and make known to others. Roland Barthes talked about friendship as a resonant space, and I think of the classroom as that same resonant space. Also that's the relationship you have to a book that really speaks to you – if you're really a reader – that there are so many sounds and there's so much coming at you, you feel like you're with a person. That's what a brilliant book is: it's a form that can hold enough of life and enough of language to be of great meaning.

I teach as a tenured member of faculty in both a Master of Fine Arts programme and an undergraduate programme at Sarah Lawrence, and as writer-in-residence at the City College of New York in a masters programme. My greatest inspiration in my teaching and my writing are my colleagues, my students and sense of community in a larger world of like-minded writers, young and old. We are very lucky at Sarah Lawrence in that it was a progressive school from its very inception in 1928. About fifty per cent of the faculty are women, which automatically makes an enormous difference. We teach, among other influences, from the knowledge of our sex. We also had lot of intellectuals who left Europe during the war who were a wonderful senior faculty for a long time, and they had a profound influence. Most of them are now pretty much retired. We also had the first women's history programme in the country and the president and both deans are women. My own sense of feminism is not women first; it's that no group has centrality, that there's a kind of multiplicity and an attention to fairness regarding all viewpoints. The most important thing that we've been doing in the last ten years is to become more culturally diverse and specifically trying to increase the African-American faculty.

City College is part of the great public university in New York, and has been a leading institution for generations in educating immigrants, minorities and the underprivileged. This is an inspiring legacy. But I think that everybody everywhere is in the same boat, that the world is really shrinking and all these different people are trying to coexist with very little elbow room. The issue of what you teach and how you teach it has become such a political one. In a way it's important and in another way it's a kind of red herring because to a certain extent people who really teach literature usually teach books because they love the level of truth that a book goes to, a truth so hard to get to in life. Those professors are committed not just to their own personal truth but to the different truths that make up the world. Similarly, as a writer you're really responsible for seeing your characters as *clearly* as possible. That's also my definition of love. Loving someone is to know who they are and to take them in wholly and completely. To be a good teacher now means to look further afield.

I think I'm lucky in that I run into more readers than non-readers because Sarah Lawrence and the courses I teach at City College tend to attract readers. But I have also taught in other places and under certain circumstances to people who weren't readers and to get them interested I tried to get books that would drive them nuts! When I started teaching at City in the '70s I started out teaching Remedial Reading 3. I had the lowest of the low – and by that of course I don't mean the lowest of the low humanly, I mean they were the most remedial of 1, 2, and 3. Of course they gave the class to someone like me who had no idea how to do it, but that's the way life is – the lowest gets the lowest – so I was the lowest and they were the lowest. They were of all different races, English was mostly their second language, and they all disagreed with each other. I used Grace Paley's first book of stories, *The Little Disturbances of Man*, half of which were so obviously Jewish and of a certain milieu and time, which were not the milieu or time of one of these students. Well lo and behold, that did not matter. They got into these wild discussions about what happened to the characters in the book: she should not have slept with him because they weren't married, he was too old for her, she was a cheapskate, the monkey was the best character, etc. We just started from what happened in the stories and who was outraged and who wasn't and then I sort of slipped in things. I spoke in the way that I always speak but I maybe repeated certain things more often and I stayed at a certain level for a longer time. I don't believe that in that time I made readers out of everyone in that class, but I know they were very interested in those characters, and those characters lived for them.

You hear some people talk about how they teach literature and you think: it's not only how they teach literature that's the problem; it's what's been done to the world. We're all going down the tubes, God help us, and the more you carry through this mechanistic sense of reality, which they even have managed to apply to novels and poems, the harder we'll fall. Literature is so arousing and emotional; it has such elasticity. Language is not music but it's the closest thing we have to music. But it's also connotative, so that it's the language of our rage, our passion, it's the language for everything we have, an explanation of what's human. If they can take that and make it mechanistic, then I'm really worried.

On the other hand, think of teachers passing things to their students, who in turn pass them along again. I remember Grace Paley once telling me something very important. She said, 'Honey, you never know when something you say is going to make a difference. Students call me up and say, "You remember seven years ago? It was a Thursday and we were under that magnolia tree and it was spring and you said to me x, y, z?"' Of course she doesn't remember. (Actually, sometimes she does.) 'Well,' the student says, 'I just got what you meant.'

The other truth is there is a whole network of people who are other teachers or who are readers who go off into the world in whatever way they do and pass on a love of literature. You know how people come to people in constellations and that constellation is what helps that person find him- or herself and form the life that's going to be lived – not necessarily what they do in life, a career, but the way they live in the world. The fact that there are other people doing it with you is a great relief because if you ever thought you had to do it yourself, what would you do? You'd pick up a golf club and go and whack people with it. And that's the genteel version.

Walking down a hall outside certain classrooms sometimes I hear this kind of talking that sounds like the New York poetry school, a particular way of droning that some poets unfortunately have taken on. Of course there are other marvellous poets in New York and elsewhere who don't read like that, but there is this eerily elevated discourse going on that I was just thinking about the other day, and when I heard it I thought oh my God, I'm getting a headache and I'm only in the hall. I don't know what it would be like to be in the classroom and listen to someone talk like that. Or maybe I do.

I feel that my entire life as an artist is about a kind of subversion. The life of an artist is to always champion the human and to bring things back to the specific. So that my goal is to help students find their language, and I say right out: voice is the most important issue. In the United States we live in a culture of advertising which is a different kind of voice, a voice that's selling you something. The government speaks in a voice that's always appearing to tell you something that is not anything, it's just taking up time. There are so many young people who have no idea who they are or what they think about the world because everyone keeps saying, 'Shut up.' I say, 'Talk,' and 'Keep talking.'

Often at the beginning of class I ask if anybody has had anything interesting happen, or anybody has a story to tell. The students do feel that certain of their teachers are much closer to the issue of the spoken word and oral storytelling. I feel very much aligned with the poets in that regard. Although I am deeply interested in certain ideas of narrative and the text, my self-knowledge and knowledge of the world comes through listening with my inner ear. It's like having a deaf ear, that is people's problem. I try to cure that. Sometimes in class we'll take an Edna O'Brien novel like *Night*, in which the whole story of a woman's life is told over one night, and we'll read it out loud so that we have the language in the air. Then people will say, 'Oh I don't know how you can only really write about one thing,' or, 'I don't know how you can get all this into one form.' I feel that if people aren't talking in class then they don't know that, in fact, you can.

Performance? Yes. There's performance in small classes as there is in large classes, but what matters is that it's a performance of genuineness. I think perhaps that may be a teacher's most important role. And another question is, How hidden is the teacher? Is the teacher the teacher or is the teacher this person who has a life which isn't so different from the student's, with the same trials and tribulations? I do think the issue of intimacy is extremely important whether you're talking about a class of 300 or a class of fifteen. I never had a class of 300, so I may be dreaming. But reading is a relationship of intimacy and talking is a relationship of intimacy. Talking is something students get trained out of all along the way. Teachers often think it will be your death if you admit anything about yourself or if you show your real self and of course it's just the opposite: it will be your death if you don't admit anything about yourself.

I know how lucky I am to teach under the circumstances that I do. I used to go to the conference of Associated Writing Programmes. People from huge universities all over the country are teaching writing in less sanguine circumstances. Say what you will about New York, in this city everyone on the subway has a book. It may not be a book *you'd* read, but this is a haven for readers. Also whenever you do a woman-in-the-street interview, where somebody sticks a microphone in your face, New Yorkers talk like crazy; everyone has an opinion, unlike Boston, where I came from, where everyone is trained not to reveal anything. So I feel lucky being in New York. I have talked with teachers who are in very different circumstances from myself, who are fighting incredible odds. To be able to generate your own spirit in those circumstances is an amazing thing. For those people, books are their friends, too.

I grew up in a pine forest, although now I'm an inveterate city dweller. The relationship I have with nature, in the sense of that fullness with which I respond to it, to me feels like the same part of myself that lives in literature. That's another thing that is horrible for a lot of young people now, they've never had a relationship with nature. Even when they live in it, they don't have it; they have video games and TVs and computer networks. Something essential has moved elsewhere.

The only way you know who you are is to have a place, is to have a mirror for the soul. That can be other people, that can be a painting, that can be an ocean, that can be a bird – but decreasingly. There's something missing in you if you have not gone through that process. It's a form of individuation. Reading a book is a form of ritual, it's a re-enactment of the self, in some way. It's a process that people over centuries have gone through that fewer and fewer people are going through now. There haven't been a lot of readers throughout history, but there have been other things or other ways. I wonder if the level of violence we have in the US might be related to this? I always consider that we're in the forefront of what could happen to everyone else and will, though I hope it doesn't.

A bunch of my friends was saying just the other night, 'Well, why does anybody bother to do anything? Art? Letters to the Editor? Write a book? Make breakfast?' And we said a) it's your life and b) we didn't want to get blamed if the world went all to hell; we didn't want it to be our fault. But teaching is like writing: you cannot control the consequences, you can be responsible only for the act. And the act can be shared.

Jean Valentine

Jean Valentine was born in Chicago in 1934, and has lived most of her life in New York City. She has taught writing workshops since 1968 at many colleges and universities, including Hunter College and Sarah Lawrence College. She is the author of six volumes of poetry, most recently *The River at Wolf.* She is presently living in County Sligo, Ireland, and a volume of new and selected poems, *Dog Skin Coat* is forthcoming.

What is Mayhem?

WHEN I WAS teaching in New York, first in City College and then at Hunter College for five years, I would teach poetry, fiction and non-fiction writing to a class of about thirty kids who had graduated from high school but weren't qualified to be in college. It was open admissions time in New York. All the colleges were required by law to take anybody who had graduated from high school, but they weren't really qualified because the high schools weren't that good. It was something arising out of the civil rights movement about people being entitled to the best education there was, but the teachers hadn't prepared them so there was a gap and a lot of us were brought in to teach reading courses. When I started to talk about poetry they were so embattled, so turned off. One of them came up to me and said: 'Listen here, Miss Valentine, let's get this straight before we start: I hate poetry.' She was just saying out loud what everybody else felt.

Almost all my teaching has been on a college or a university level – eighteen to twenty-two-year-olds and some adult students. These were mostly poetry writing workshops so they're people who volunteered. At Hunter I taught remedial courses where people had to take them and that was something else. I tried to get them to write in certain forms like poetry, stories, essays – if these forms meant anything to them – and it was very difficult. When I'm in my ordinary job at Sarah Lawrence College, which is to teach people who have come actually wanting to do this, they're still often frightened about poetry. One of my favourite things is a student who had taken a fiction course and came along and told me she was scared to take the poetry course. I said, 'Why?' and she said, 'Because in poetry you have to tell the truth.' I loved telling my fiction friends that. But I think there's something in what she was saying. People are afraid now that we're not in the days of poetry which justifies the ways of God to man, now that we're writing more out of our lives, not usually about characters with other names than I, or maybe You. You obviously have to be just as truthful in fiction, but as a beginner you might feel you could hide more in fiction. People are very scared of poetry because they think it's going to involve their feelings and they're scared of their feelings, but they're also bored with poetry because it's so boring, you know? A lot of poetry. I think a lot of everything is very boring but I think a lot of poetry that's boring has been held up as rather great poetry and if that's great poetry then I don't want it.

The two things that I think help people to want to read poetry are if you write it yourself and if you meet some real poets. I taught on the most wonderful course once; it was a very expensive course, but maybe we could figure out a way this could be done that wouldn't be expensive. It was a course that a woman dreamed up. She worked at something called the Academy of American Poets and they brought in poets to read every couple of weeks or so in New York. The course was for high school teachers. One week we would read the poetry of, say, James Wright, and the following week James Wright would appear, read some of his own poems, hopefully some of the same ones that we had already studied, and then they would get to talk to him about the poems and about anything they wanted. The class lasted two or three hours and there were about twelve or fifteen people in it. The other thing we did when we could was look at their poetry because they were all writing poetry it seemed to me. They also had an incentive to take the course because they got a pay raise if they got credit and it was a credit course. I thought it was wonderful because the teachers then go back into the schools and they're no longer frightened of poetry, in fact they're very enthusiastic about it, about their own and about other people's, and then of course it's infectious. It was very, very good, that course. I did it for a couple of years. Every poet who came through New York was on it. We didn't pay them much. They didn't mind. Poets mostly like to talk to people. I think that was the best teaching experience I ever had.

I don't think that course continued. I think she had a grant for about five years and I taught it for two or three and then someone else taught it and now I don't think it's taught any more. They do have a sort of similar thing at the Y on 92nd Street. It could be happening everywhere though. Writers, until they get very famous, do want to talk. Most of us want to talk to people and want to change things.

The other thing is to get people to write themselves because they can't be afraid of poetry when they're writing it themselves. Even if it isn't good, or classic literature that we're talking about, it's no longer frightening. Even if almost none of them go on writing they should be turning into better readers. Do they though? Do they go on and read poetry? I don't know. We have so many writing students now in America it would be interesting to get a survey and see if they still read poetry. For instance, poetry writers of twenty or thirty years ago, do they ever read a poem anymore? Probably they don't write one.

When I teach writing I ask them to memorize poems. A student came this spring and said she had memorized a poem by Emily Dickinson. She said that it was very interesting because she hadn't understood the poem and when she finished memorizing it she realized she understood it. She realized, in the way you do – 'oh, that's what that means' – just by getting it into her memory. That was very interesting to me and really confirmed my idea that it's good to memorize things. I was taught to memorize, but not as much I think as most people of my generation. I had to memorize some Shakespeare in school and I was glad of that. I try to memorize things when I'm asking my students to, and I try to memorize things that I love if they're short because I love having them with me. But I think that's a very good way of getting people to write too, because then you get the sound in your bloodstream.

In my choice of texts I stay pretty much with contemporaries but I get them to memorize anything but contemporaries. They don't have those twentieth-century rhythms in their heads, so I try to ask them to memorize pre-twentieth century poetry, and get rhyme and metre. But I read with them mostly contemporary work. I do that to persuade them to come in the door of poetry. I give them things that I think will reach them, that they will be liberated by, and say, 'Oh you can write poetry about that.' I give them for instance somebody like Sharon Olds because she's so immediate and so accessible and has written about experiences that everybody feels even if they haven't had quite them. Everybody's had a family, God willing, some kind of a family. I get them to read people who I think are the most alive because so much of what people are given as poetry is, at least at first, so distant from them. So I don't teach them for instance to read much English poetry when I'm teaching in America. I give them mostly American poetry, stuff that's close to their doorstep if I can. I taught once a course on Dickinson and Bishop and I thought, well, they'll find Dickinson hard but they'll love Bishop. It was just the other way around. It was funny. They didn't like Bishop at first, they found her quite difficult, but Dickinson didn't give them any trouble at all. She has a way about her, there's no doubt. Maybe it's the apparent informality – here's somebody who writes with dashes, who doesn't know about punctuation. I had a student at MIT and I said, 'What brings you to take poetry?' and he said, 'Well, you don't have to use any grammar.' So it could be that. Emily Dickinson does have that urgency too, and lots of death and despair and eroticism, all good subjects for any age. Those are things that aren't so much in Bishop, at least not on the surface.

If I were going to teach Dickinson, say, I'd start with the poem always. Grace Paley would get students who wanted to – this wasn't for credit or anything – to sit around at the table and read out loud. She liked them to hear the language of the King James version of the Bible, so she would pass that around a table and we would all read passages for a while. Grace was very much of an authority. She would say we'll read the Psalms or we'll read Job or whatever, but if they had had an idea she would have probably done that too. We did poetry too: Milton, Blake, Dickinson. There was no talk at all, just the text. We would meet, we would read and we would go. I remember there was a young woman who was quite a scholar who came and sat in when I was doing this with Dickinson one day and she couldn't stand it. She just couldn't stand it. After a while she interrupted and said, 'Well, we can't do this.' She was a very nice woman, but she just was so trained to teach by explication and search.

When I give readings of my own work I like to say to people: 'Don't try to understand this. Just let it be like rain, or sunshine for that matter. Let it be just something that comes down over you. Don't worry about it if possible because it's not going to get into you if you worry and if you think. If it gets into you it will have to be through a more unconscious part of yourself than your thinking brain and your rational brain. It will have to come through your intuitive side. So it would be more like listening to music. Don't try to say A equals B.' But that's very, very hard for a lot of people and it must be one of the things that makes literature hard for people as well. And all art, in fact.

If my own work were being taught in a university, I would be afraid that it would be taught badly. I'd be flattered, but I'd be afraid of a grid of interpretation being put on anybody's work. I almost never read criticism because almost none of it helps me. It's not that I don't need to learn; it's not that at all, it's that I don't learn that way. I sometimes find criticism by poets helpful, but scholars I don't often find helpful. I think it's because, even if they say something interesting, it's not in the poem, it's about the poem. I might think it was interesting but it wouldn't have anything really basic to do with what I'm reading. I went to a private high school which was very, very conservative and very, very excellent. So was Radcliffe, where I went to college. Although it was a wonderful world in a lot of ways, where ideas were really what people cared about, it was in the wrong sense. I came away feeling that I would love to know how you can give somebody an experience of a book without talking the way they talk in universities. That to me is really deadly. It takes you away from the book and away from the author instead of closer to them.

George Steiner wrote a very long and erudite piece about Simone Weil and at the end of it he said, she's a schlemiel. I liked that. Good for him. James Baldwin said that when he was a little boy he went into the library in Harlem and started reading books and he found other people like himself for the first time. That to me is what we should be talking about. How do we find other people like ourselves for the first time except in books? But how can the teachers give us that instead of coming between if they don't know who we are and if they don't know how to give us a book? For instance, I was never given – and I was given a great deal, so I've no complaint – nor were any of us given, any books outside this now famous white male canon. That's why I object to a word like literature or poetry. It's as if somebody decides what is civilization, what is mayhem, what is poetry, what is literature, and that is what we were given. Of course that's a political question, a very deep one. How well do we know each other, all of us?

My education certainly gave me some confidence – I was very much a woman in a man's world, especially at Radcliffe – so it gave me confidence that I could read, but it also gave me very much the message that I was a second-class citizen who couldn't even go into the library. That was shocking. There was also Bloom's idea of the anxiety of influence, that you could never be as good as the people who went ahead of you. I didn't feel that, but I felt I could never be like them. Then you begin to think, well, maybe I'm different, and then you begin to think, well, am I crazy? So it's not the ideal education. It's excellent in its way but it isn't ideal for a writer. I don't know what the ideal education would be for a writer. Maybe they don't need an education in that sense. I was just driving down here with Camille Souter, the painter, and she said that she didn't think that people should have any education at all while they were young, or no education in the imagination. She said she was very grateful that she had very dull teaching as a young child because she felt that you should come upon everything yourself. At Harvard they were very, very strong believers in there being a way you look at a thing and they had it and you didn't and they would give it to you, that was what they were employed to do. I suppose that is still the educational system that we have, is it?

One of the things that writing classes offer is some sort of community, where people can become better human beings by listening to one another. There isn't much of that in America. I don't think there are many places where people can be in that little community, even for four minutes. But when governments start talking about transferable skills, how can you say that would be a transferable skill, listening to one another?

I remember when I was at Radcliffe and I said that I was studying English literature people said, what are you going to do with it?

I had no idea. All I knew was I didn't want to be a teacher. And yet I did become a teacher and I sure have loved it. But I don't know if I would have loved teaching literature. I did have one wonderful teacher at Radcliffe who might have made me think about teaching. Bill Alfred had a writing class and he felt so sorry for us, for our shyness, that he read all our papers himself, which would have been awful in somebody else, but he was so kind that it wasn't awful. He had a beautiful reading voice so that when you heard your poem read by him you really did have a feeling that maybe you were quite good. But he was inspiring to me because he loved literature and because he was a fine person. Now again it's unquantifiable, but he was a really inspiring person. Not that he didn't have flaws, but you felt that he was a good person and so you wanted to be like him. What he liked was literature, what he loved was literature. He was writing poetry and drama when I knew him. What was inspiring to me was that he was very encouraging to everybody. I didn't ever see it, I don't think so strongly anyway, in anybody else that teaching could be a good human thing; it didn't have to just be a new lecturer thing, it could be an extraordinary way of loving people, a way of being in the world with other people. I always tried to think of him when I was teaching. He was very, very encouraging to everybody. He was able to give close to unconditional love to his students and that's what I thought was wonderful. I guess I wanted a mother, and he was just about like that. Sometimes he was very smart, he was very learned, but he was very loving and that's what I wanted. I don't think that would be what everybody wants but it was crucial for me. Later when I thought about who I wanted to be like as a teacher, I always thought of Bill Alfred and that was very helpful. Also he encouraged me about writing at a crucial time, when I was twenty, and he made me feel that I could do it. I always wanted to be that kind of person for students. I saw what a difference it could make – even if they don't go on to write. Some of them might go on to be lawyers, doctors or waitresses who read poetry.

The way you come across to students is incredibly important, the way you talk. We are in a position of authority as teachers, for good or bad. At Sarah Lawrence you spend most of your time talking one to one. You spend just a couple of hours in class every week but you spend many, many hours talking to people individually. It's conversation and it's informal. By the time the teacher has to write an evaluation of the student's work, the students know so well what we think of everything, because we've had so many hours going over their work together, that for us to write these things is not very useful. But they had to have that for their records. It's a strange place, maybe all avant garde places are like this, it's rather unbending in some ways. But they're very flexible to their writers certainly, and they have a lot of writers. They have about four, five, six poets at any given time and I think about ten or twelve fiction writers and now they're trying to get a couple of non-fiction writers.

I don't think the proliferation of all these writing courses is a bad thing. I think it's maybe the same as people who say, well, so and so shouldn't have a book yet, she's too young, or he's too young. I don't think it does any harm. If it does harm in their case, it might be a temperamental thing, but I don't think there's anything wrong with it. I said that the writing classes offer some sort of community to people on an intimate level which is missing in America, very much so, so I think it's socially good. I really do. I also feel that you can't really write very long without writing about feelings, and if there are Americans coming out of writing courses who are going to be a little more reflective towards their own feelings, that has to be good in itself.

Grace Paley

Gentl & Hyers/Arts Counsel Inc.

Grace Paley was born in New York in 1922. She has taught at Columbia University, Syracuse University, Dartmouth College and Sarah Lawrence College in New York. She has written several books of short stories, reissued in 1994 as *The Collected Stories of Grace Paley*. Grace Paley lives in Vermont.

Different Places, Mysterious Places

PEOPLE ARE FOND of asking the question: 'How can you teach writing?' What they're really asking is: 'Are you going to make great writers?' They never ask a history teacher: 'Are you going to make a great historian?' They think they're teaching them history, that's all. But it's true that I don't expect to make great writers unless there are people there who want to be, who will do the work. The main thing is for people to learn what the making of literature is about, how it is to do the work, so that they can understand literature, love it better, and understand what they're reading by knowing what went into it.

I think I have more of a wish to make readers than most writing teachers. In the business of teaching writing you do a lot of reading. I not only do reading out loud, I don't let people have copies. I've never understood why poetry teachers hand out copies of the poems that people are going to read. One of the things I'm trying to do is make people listen. They have to listen because they're going to be called on to speak about the work. I've done readings myself where someone has taken out my book, and I deliberately change things, or else I say, 'I won't have it. Don't you dare do that.'

If the poem has any difficulty whatsoever – which it might – I'd expect the poet to read the poem a couple of times, and then I would have him or her talk about it. I like doing it without everybody having copies, because when they have copies they all start nit-picking, you know, going after commas. I want them to hear the whole work, and then to remember. I want to train people's remembering, help them to pay attention; in the classroom one way that you can do that is have people pay attention to one another, and to keep one another's work in their heads for forty-five minutes. If they're going to be writers they have to be intentioned writers.

There is no longer any way of knowing what people have read. I've taught students who really should have been reading and they don't, they say, 'Well, I don't like poetry.' One of the ways to get back into reading is to go back to nursery rhymes. If you go back to nursery rhymes they immediately know that they loved certain things and had fun with them, they accepted the mystery of it, and somehow at the age of five understood it – and loved it, were moved by it, excited by it. Then you go ahead with them little by little.

I think that writing classes are the best place for people who don't read to start getting involved in literature, even more than for students like those I've had at Sarah Lawrence or Dartmouth, many of whom think they're going to be writers. At the beginning of Teachers and Writers Collaborative that was the idea: they were working to get writers going into high schools and talking to the kids, helping them to write.

Then you had all these movements that really changed everything: the women's movement, and community centres, women going back to work, and to school. Those people weren't embarrassed to take writing courses because they wanted to tell, they had this longing to tell you something. Those people have it most naturally, whereas in my writing class at Dartmouth, I had to say to the students: 'You know it's all very well, but what you're giving me is something you think I want to see. Don't bother doing anything if it isn't something you wanted to tell, you needed to say, something that's really bugging you.'

I think that there's a movement away from the university and back to the high schools and then forward again to English as a second language. I read a poem recently written in English as a second language and it was absolutely stunning. The love of learning and the love of literature come from different places, mysterious places. It really comes from around the kids you teach, from underneath almost, from their mothers, from the development of the women's movement, which is full of people telling you stories – some of it very annoying, you could go crazy listening to all their stories. But these are people who really want to put things down on paper, and who really are your readers.

That's just one line of people who will sustain literature, who will sustain good writing and good reading in time to come. It doesn't all come through the academic system – though it would come if they had more writing classes.

I have been involved very peripherally in something called 'Four Cs', which is an association of all the people who have to teach composition in the first year or two of high school. Those are the people who really are in a position to talk about literature: the people who have to do all the grammar work in high schools.

I was at a Four Cs conference where there were a couple of Black women who gave talks on rap and also showed us a video. That's where the literature comes from, from the need to tell, the longing to tell, and then from some sense of music and language. But oh, the struggle! You have to fight with the people in administration. These Black women's fight was with allowing their students the freedom to tell their own stories, or their family's story, and the freedom then to be able to choose books which they then want to read because they just became writers! In making writers of people you make them readers faster. They become interested – I've seen that happen – they really want to know.

I went to a high school once which was mostly Puerto Rican with a couple of Black kids, and I gave them this book of Sandra Cisneros, *The House on Landor Street.* They loved it – it's a very fine book – and they proceeded to write stuff for me that was marvellous, all of them. They said, 'We can do this? We can tell about this?' Something has to open the door for those people, and it can be the teachers.

But in education it's going to be worse. They're cutting people out, putting in part-time people, and they're enlarging classes. As long as you have three hundred people in a class, it looks like a lecture on chemistry. Some people will take to it and some people won't. The best person in the world might not be able to handle three hundred people. You'd have to have a style, a way of talking, an aura, and a kind of performance level. I remember we had a teacher in Sarah Lawrence on Shakespeare who could teach four hundred people if he wanted to because he really had a way of walking up and down and standing on his head and doing this, that and the other. But I don't know how to teach four hundred students; I'd get too shy or do nothing but sit there and read out of *Richard III*.

Even at Sarah Lawrence where the classes are small and a lot of the kids really are quite serious, I notice a deficit in reading earlier poetry. I keep one hour a week when we don't have any discussion about the poems; we just run around the room reading for an hour, reading the poems. Some students come for the sheer pleasure of hearing people read. Of course if you're going to read out loud then you have to say to yourself, 'Listen, you're reading to others, you're giving a gift to everybody. Either give it to them or shut up.' People have to learn that reading aloud is a gift.

Where we are in Vermont, there's a country high school which has a Shakespeare Festival each year done by the kids. They don't do whole plays, they do readings and it's always wonderful. The kids just go wild, they love it, they love doing that.

I was invited to a high school once, as a writer, so that they could see a live writer. The kids had read a couple of my stories and they were interested. At one stage they were very critical because the kid in the story was killed, and they didn't see why I had allowed that kid to be killed. They said: 'You didn't have to kill him.' But then they realized that they were alive in this story. I think you have to really show them that. It's very hard to do because a lot of kids are not alive in western literature. Certainly a lot of women aren't alive in it. If you're beginning with people who can't really read, you have to begin with stories they're alive in: stories about the street, summer on the stoop. Then they proceed from that to write their own stories of their own street; and they read something else by the same writer, and then something else. Then they'll be able to broaden beyond their own experience. They'll be able to say: 'Oh my life is like this person's,' or, 'Oh I'm nothing like that.' They'll be reading books as news – that's what the novel once was; it's news, it's interesting.

I think you can do the same thing teaching older literature, you can see how their situation was similar – or really different from your own. It's very easy to find yourself in Flaubert, for example; everyone's been bored and had romantic longings.

There are a lot of stories that are very simple, and you have to start with those. Of course you have television, which is even simpler – we book people are under constant siege. Though I also don't think it matters if people don't read older literature.

I had a writing class at Dartmouth which I used to begin by having everybody read something they thought was good, something they'd chosen themselves. It had to be beautiful and they had to love it for some reason. One boy read from Keats and Shelley and nobody in that class knew any of these poems or the romantic tradition, but once they began to read them out loud they had some sense.

You have to remember where you come from is what you first loved – which may be some of the worst poems ever. I can still remember saying, as a kid, poems like 'The boy stood on the burning deck'. But they don't let kids read this stuff in school. You have to remember people come from different planes. A lot of the song, a lot of the rhythm of Black writing comes from the Bible, from childhood, from the preachers. A lot of people think there's nothing in their ear, but there *is* something in their ear, and it's that which is after all English literature. If it's the King James version, that's what we were all raised on, that's English literature we're raised on. People who think they know nothing about literature already do know something if they've been to church, read the Bible, or heard it read.

I used to be so mad at friends of mine in the English department for being impatient with the students. I used to say to them: 'You've read that book about fifteen times, you've been teaching it every other year for about twenty years, which means, being a conscientious fellow, you reread it. The students are reading it for the first time with no experience of anything that surrounds it.' I think a lot of teaching is very unfair in that way. A friend who teaches in the German department and the comparative literature department, told me she gave a course on a book she herself hadn't read before, and she said to the class: 'We'll read this together, all of us, for the first time and see what happens.'

I would say to teachers of literature that wherever your students are, you have to start there. You can't start ten years ahead of them, and you can't start three hundred books ahead of them. You shouldn't grade too much. A lot of schools and colleges just do pass/fail. Though I've been in places where the teachers agreed not to grade and the students all wanted grades because they wanted to go to graduate school; they thought we were being silly.

We in the writing department at Sarah Lawrence, we're in a situation where the English department is always mad at us. English departments have been in business a long, long time, and the writing departments are new – or were twenty years ago – and they really do get a lot of students. So it's competition, but also it's a kind of snobbery; the English departments feel they're doing the serious stuff. Yet I think we in the writing department get more people to read.

The problem between the writing department and the English department is that we're not really teaching their stuff. We're not teaching the canon because many readers don't see themselves in it. Some people never have the need to see themselves in what they read. But the women who suddenly saw that they weren't in the canon, that it was not about them at all, they wanted to put themselves in what they read, which meant reading contemporary writers and writing their own stories. The teacher can bring them towards finding themselves, towards putting themselves into literature.

This isn't the world of little English and Irish islands any more, it isn't the world of Western European culture. African Nigerian writers live in London and are writing in London, and in France, the French African writers. They may be small countries, but their histories of conquest have made it possible to broaden the curriculum – in the end to the good, you might say, in bringing the world closer and closer together.

Academics have a problem with some of these new books because they don't know whether they're good or not. We were watching the ice skating last night from the Winter Olympics, and they all looked so terrific I didn't know if they were good unless the commentator said so. Someone was telling me whether they were good or not, according to some extremely rigid and refined narrow strip of goodness.

To know which new books to choose you have to read them and see if they're well-written. If you're going to bother to read a range of new books you would have an idea of what is well-written. You'd be able to hear another voice or another rhythm, not British or American, or North-Eastern American, or Faulknerian. You'd be able to judge a little bit; it would be risky – you might like something that every other Nigerian hates, and you might be right and they might be wrong, you don't know.

What the teacher has to think about is: these other populations have stopped standing around and have begun to demand to be seen. In the US we have on every single border people speaking other languages who have moved into our culture, who live in our country. And not just on the border. Hispanic culture covers the South-west – it was always there – and then in New York you have the Puerto Rican culture, and the French Haitians, and the Dominicans. And then you have in great pockets all over the United States now, a native American culture speaking again.

It's a wonderful time for people who are really interested in paying attention. There are teachers and students who are saying: 'What story do you have to tell? Listen to what's happening in the world, because you're going to live in this world.'

I'm kind of thrilled about my stories being taught. I think it's so funny because I was always a rotten student and I have no degrees at all. I was an undisciplined kid. The teachers I adored at school were the ones who loved literature, who wanted to share it, not interrogate us. If they noticed that a kid even read a poem or two, they would help that kid expand. I really wanted to write poems. I really didn't want to go to school. People used to ask me about that thinking it was some big political event, but I simply didn't want to go. This was fifty years ago. I was perfectly satisfied to just do a lot of reading. I was a reader as a small kid, in a family of readers – everybody reading every night: reading, reading, reading. It was just normal. So I worked for a year and then I was quite happy to go to college for a year. I went to NYU, and then I got married, and then there was the war and that was absorbing.

Sometimes the idea of being taught seems ridiculous, like the way I was taught mostly seemed ridiculous. I couldn't bear questions like, 'What does this character mean?' and 'What was the motive?' I haven't thought about motive in a boxload. There are textbooks teaching stories with these questions at the end which seem wrong to me. They're too technical, they break the thing up. This is the sort of thing I had trouble with as a kid. When I teach I ask broad questions like, 'Do you like this story?' 'What do you think it's about?'

People finally read with their own intelligence, no matter what the teacher says. They approve and disapprove; like those students who said about a character in my story 'Knock on Wood', 'He didn't have to be killed.' I hadn't thought about it. Why did I kill him? I said: 'Well, he had to die, he fell between train cars, and besides which that's what I was interested in.' That's what I call an awkward story, about the loss of a child and the irrepressibility of that child. I realized I had to kill him because otherwise the mother would never say what she says at the end of that story. I explain a little bit about that to the students, but they still are amazed with it. It's so close to them because they've been doing the same thing – fooling around on subway trains – and they didn't want to be killed, they didn't care about the logic.

I remember reading at City College a story called 'An Interesting Life', in which a woman is abandoned by her husband and picks up with another guy but she never really forgets the first guy, and so on. A young Black girl in the class gets up and she says, 'I bet you think that girl Ginny was some heroine.' So I say, 'Well no, but she was pretty courageous,' and she says, 'Well I don't think she was a heroine, I just think she was one dope.' I didn't know what to say, I was too embarrassed.

Mostly the people who want to teach my stories are younger people and they're going to really think about it and try to sell the story to the kids. Some of them understand me perfectly. But I can't worry too much about that. If you're totally misunderstood then you're bad, and every now and then you're totally misunderstood. Then you feel sort of sorry and wonder if you could have clarified it, but it's there, you can't help it, it's too damn bad for them, you gave it away already. I have a kind of political belief that once I write a story, I've given it away to a person who accepts it and reads it; they have to make what they want of it. There's no exit; if I didn't want anyone to read it I shouldn't have put it in a book. A lot of people feel they own their work. They don't.

Howard Barker

Trisha Purchas

Howard Barker was born in London in 1946. His first plays were written for radio, and his first stage play was produced at the Royal Court's Theatre Upstairs in 1970. His best-known plays, premiered by the Royal Shakespeare Company, the Joint Stock Company and the Almeida Theatre respectively, are *The Castle, Victory, The Possibilities* and *Scenes from an Execution.* The Wrestling School, a theatre company dedicated to his work, was established in 1989. Howard Barker's work is performed throughout Europe and America. He is also the author of a number of books of poetry, the most recent being *The Ascent of Monte Grappa,* and the libretto for Nigel Osborne's opera *The Terrible Mouth.*

Education is Friction

My experiences of education have been entirely negative, at every level. I hold no one responsible for this. The classroom was a place of anxiety for me, but so was the tutorial. This reflects rather little on the institutions, much more on me, my own horrors and frustrations. Most of my energy in school was spent concealing myself. Most of my energy in university on finding a means to live in a society that was equally uncongenial to me. Both at school and at university I was self-effacing. I volunteered very little and as a consequence I was characterized as an uninteresting student. I do not think even the most gifted teachers could have discerned my state, for I was skilled in disguise. The only thing I could not disguise was my dislike of games, physical or intellectual. In both cases I simply absented myself. None of this is to say that I gained nothing from education, or that it was repellent to me per se. Certain ordeals are profoundly stimulating.

While I'm not at all academic, I have developed certain analytical methods with regard to my own practice in theatre. I don't see how any artist can fail to engage with theory at some point in his development, however natural and spontaneous he regards the imaginative life to be. In my own case, this articulation was forced upon me by the sheer weight of critical hostility that was directed at me, and the few champions I attracted in the first decade or so. I'm not a compulsive reader now, though I read widely and eccentrically in my youth, perhaps too much so. It was a substitute for existence, obviously, a refuge, but also a means of knowing the pain of others, of finding a comradeship of pain. Now perhaps I fear to discover authors who might seduce me. I do not wish to be diverted from objectives I have set myself.

My texts are not taught at schools and do not form part of examination syllabuses. On the other hand, students in higher education encounter them, largely through the passionate advocacy of certain teachers. The controversial nature of my reputation also ensures there is an equivalent counter-propaganda from other teachers. In odd cases this produces friction between university supervisors and advanced students who have chosen the largely uncharted territory of my texts for their research. There is evidence of considerable conflict here, around politically motivated attitudes on the part of higher education teachers. Some of the students have shown courage in resisting conventional interpretations of my *oeuvre*. This is valuable to me, because the urgent need for a new perspective in theatre criticism is startlingly obvious, and it can only come from these sources. It will never simply materialize in the columns of the press. When an artist is exposed to the unrelenting hostility of newspaper critics, the considered judgement of researchers on the one hand, and the spirited, self-motivated actions of students who react almost instinctively to the work, on the other, can generate optimism and confidence. No artist can function without a constituency, in the end. There is a limit to blind faith and arrogance, though God knows any mental attitude that an artist can fashion for his survival is legitimate. There are too many individuals with a profound hatred for the possible power of art, and the majority of them are in journalism.

I certainly think of my texts as literature and not solely, or even primarily, as pretext for dramatic performance. They are published and distributed by a publisher with an impeccable and enviable record for literary values. I am aware that in many foreign universities I am taught as English usage, as an example of style. This is not surprising, because I am not a naturalistic writer; I am not concerned with the reproduction of common speech but set out to create a poetic idiom in the way any poet would. This is a theatre of invented language, and requires a certain attitude both in spectator and reader. That they are intensely theatrical would be conceded by even the most hostile reviewer. But I am equally concerned with the line, the *mot juste*, even the layout on the page. I expect actors and students to work on the text, to understand it as an expression of life, not as truth, nor as information, message, propaganda for a posture, nothing but emotion turned into language. The fact that these texts are occluded, hardly ever transparent, makes the teaching of them in a conventional sense difficult; it calls up other resources. For example, it is impossible for a class to be expected to deduce, in my case, what the author is 'saying'. I don't *say* anything. I am in the text, but I am not saying. This complicates life, and education in the contemporary world hasn't the will for complication. There is a rage experienced by certain individuals coming to my work who, taught in certain ways, cannot contemplate contradiction, instability, in character or situation. They have to know, and by knowing, to control, the work of art. This diminishes both them and the work itself. It is profoundly transgressive not to be knowable, whether in public or private life.

The theatre of the last fifty years has been fixed in a phase of critical realism. The sources of this are Brecht and Shaw, but the Royal Court theatre and its influence have ensured that most drama teaching, as far as text is concerned, tends to discriminate against dramatists whose impulses are not in the socio-critical register. Students themselves have been the quickest to complain about this stagnation, which is not universal. Often these students are regarded as 'difficult', but these difficult students are the ones on whom a new theatre practice will come to depend. I've always believed that the true nature of education is friction, not really education at all, in the latinate form of the word, but conflict – not being led by an enlightened teacher, but the discovery that the teacher is flawed, possibly a liar, certainly a human being who is a repository of prejudices, with which one's own prejudices brutally collide. In the most profound sense, education should be something of a turmoil, therefore, not placid at all. But this turmoil cannot be institutionalized, obviously. Perhaps the thing we need to be most on guard against is the charismatic teacher, given the will inherent in most human beings to yield themselves to others. The charismatic teacher's innate vanity – his or her absolute awareness of the effect of performance – the ease with which an audience can be stimulated – the plucking of its cultural superficialities – sexual exhibitionism – all contribute to inducing a condition of acritical hypnosis in which the significance of the ideas is obscured.

Education is founded on a notion of obligation, that the student will examine texts he or she has no natural taste for. There is nothing wrong with this, and it may even be the foundation of the necessary skill in discrimination. But I feel some contamination of myself resulting from the knowledge that strangers are obliged to examine my texts against their will. It is somehow morbid; it is the opposite of the artistic experience, which is wholly seductive. The highest honour paid to me as an artist from students and others involved in education is their desire to mount the plays themselves, out of free choice, and yet further, that *untaught*, they discover the work, endure the difficulty of retrieving it from bookshops, and make it their own. I believe that the best thing extracted from strange literature is the way in which one can *possess* it, having struggled to own it, and to unlock its secrecy for oneself. It was so for me in discovering an illegitimate author like Céline, or a hidden poet like Jozsef. I think some find that so with me.

John Giorno

Philip Heying

John Giorno is the originator of Spoken Word and Performance Poetry, and one of the most influential figures in the world of contemporary performance. He created Dial-A-Poem in 1968, beginning a new era in telecommunications, mass media and Dial-A-something. He founded Giorno Poetry Systems which has brought out twenty-eight LPs and CDs, as well as four video packs. He has also published several books of poetry and has performed, both solo and with the John Giorno Band, all over the US. John Giorno lives in New York City.

Teaching Literature is an Oxymoron

I HAVEN'T TAUGHT because it's a great trap for a poet or writer to teach. It takes over your life and ruins it. You're influenced by the things you do every day and when you teach, you take it with you when you come home and it spoils you – it spoils your life and it spoils your work. I've got enough troubles! And then I've never had to teach. I lead a blessed life. I work all the time on whatever I want, and I travel a lot because I tour. I'm a gay man, I don't have a wife and children, which is always the reason why somebody has to have x thousand dollars a year, so I've been able to escape that pressure. However, it would be very sad if there were no literature teachers, since there would be no writers; just like if there were no mothers and fathers, there would be nobody else.

I think teaching literature in a school is an oxymoron. Great literature liberates the mind in an absolute way, frees it from concepts into the vast expanse of primordial mind. Whatever the intention, by their very nature, schools are the opposite. They're built on hierarchies, on conservative thought, they're built on money values and people getting tenure or supporting themselves. The purpose of schools – or a common denominator of them – is to control people, not to enlighten them, in order to serve the functions of an often ignorant culture or government. Poetry frees the mind; therefore to teach it in schools is impossible.

Though there are great teachers in schools and those few are like terrorists in the best sense. They liberate minds. I had two great English teachers, Deborah Tannenbaum and Philip Rodman, and they liberated my mind. That's probably why I'm a poet. I had them when I was fourteen to seventeen. They understood that what literature does is open the door, liberate the mind from obscurations, from restraints and repressions, from the rules and structures that imprison, allowing the natural clarity of the mind to flow free.

These two teachers introduced me to nineteenth- and twentieth-century poetry. Unfortunately it only went as far as T. S. Eliot and Pound – this was the 1950s – but they explained why James Joyce wrote *A Portrait of the Artist as a Young Man*, why T. S. Eliot wrote 'The Lovesong of J. Alfred Prufrock' and 'The Wasteland'. They opened Baudelaire and Proust to me. Then I discovered all those writers from Hemingway and Fitzgerald to Kerouac. Those teachers were terrorists, breaking the bourgeois bondage into which I had been born. Of course they didn't liberate everybody. I'm sure most of the class considered literature, like math, something just to get through. But there were a few of us, poets and writers, for whom they opened the door to freedom. I was very young and they introduced me at the right moment.

Literature teachers introduce concepts that liberate you from concepts. How they do it is the genius of each teacher. When I say great teachers are terrorists, it's their genius that makes them terrorists, that gives them the ability to explode a bomb in someone's heart and to free that person from stupidity and ignorance. A great teacher indicates the empty nature of all phenomena, and shows the wisdom inherent in each writer's work.

In 1951, when I was fourteen years old, I decided I was a poet. I was told to write a poem, as a homework assignment. I had an experience of great clarity and bliss. I kept on doing it and I said to myself, 'What I like best is writing poems.' I am very one-pointed and I stuck with it.

Then I went to Columbia University and I had all the great teachers of the 1950s: Lionel Trilling, Mark van Doren, Eric Bentley among others, and they were great, but they were often as boring as the worst. Lionel Trilling's mind was fabulous, but studying Proust and Kafka with him was so boring, but *so* boring, particularly when I had a hangover. Mark van Doren was a great poet, but I didn't learn anything from him, other than that he was a very kind man and a pleasure to be with. I was forced to read this great pantheon of books which maybe I wouldn't have read in that order. One of the faults of school is that you have to read three hundred pages a day for each class, and sometimes you don't read anything slowly and deeply, you just fake it to pass a test, which is often what I did. They were very brilliant men, but they were discursively brilliant. They introduced one to a lot of information but it wasn't the kind of liberating wisdom that I got from those two high school teachers.

When I was in Columbia in 1956, a friend came to visit that April during a spring break. He gave me a book of poems and three joints, and said, 'John, you've got to read this!' The book was Allen Ginsberg's *Howl*, which had just been published. One night about two weeks later, I got the book, smoked the joints, and read it. *Howl* completely changed my life. It was like being hit by a bolt of lightning. The weather had just changed and spring was warm and a pleasure. I had a sort of nervous breakdown. I started screaming and crying and I ran out from where I was living into Riverside Park, with *Howl* in my hand, running and jumping, screaming and weeping tears of joy. It was revolutionary that somebody had these same feelings as I had, and a poet who had written such a great poem. It was the first poem I read which was about *now*. Eliot and everyone else was about the past. This was the 1950s and I was one of those people who was liberated by Allen Ginsberg. Nowadays, *Howl* is just ordinary. It's a very good poem, but it doesn't liberate anybody any more. Many times when I tell the story about Allen Ginsberg to a kid or student or fan, they say, 'Well it's great that it did it for you, and it's a nice poem, but it doesn't do it for me.' *Howl* is required reading in every poetry class in America.

School was always horrible for me; it was always a prison. The golden years at Columbia were so depressing. It was the opposite of being liberated. At Columbia I majored in Literature and Creative Writing, and I minored in Oriental Humanities. It was special in the sense that Columbia was just inventing these survey courses (the curriculum then to be copied across America) on Buddhism, and all the other religions, as well as philosophy and art. The classes were six people around a table talking endlessly about philosophy. It too was an oxymoron. I was glad I was doing it, but I was unhappy doing it. Buddhism is about meditation practice, working directly with actually liberating your mind. The 1950s was before Buddhist practice became available in the West, before the great Zen teachers came, and before the Chinese invasion of Tibet in 1959, which had the effect of making the great Vajrayana masters available to us. Studying philosophy was hopeless; it did not change any of my problems. Through my suffering I finally found my way to India in 1970, and met my teacher, H. H. Dudjom Rinpoche, and began Tibetan Buddhist meditation practice. Dudjom Rinpoche, who was a great scholar, said, 'You have never heard of anyone becoming enlightened reading a book.'

I don't know how you deal with reading this vast body of literature any more. When I grew up, we had television, but I didn't watch it that much. It was before television addiction. I was of a generation that read as a source of release. I came from a privileged family, I had everything, was given everything, every problem was supposed to be solved. I was just as bound as if I was disabled and from a dysfunctional, under-privileged family. Anyway, I didn't have bad television habits, so I read. Now it's quite different.

That actually gave rise to what is my life work. In the early 1960s I came upon the concept that there were many venues through which to reach an audience, besides the book and magazine. At the point I didn't read very much; there was no point in reading, I had read everything I wanted to read. I watched television, listened to LP records, talked on the telephone, did anything but read. It occurred to me that all these were or could be venues for poetry, and that gave rise to Giorno Poetry Systems. In 1965 I started working with electronic technology, making sound compositions of my poems. Then I started Dial-A-Poem, poetry over the telephone, and we received millions of calls. We have produced twenty-eight LPs and CDs of poetry, and a half dozen video packs. When we release an album, we send four hundred to FM and university radio stations across America. The smallest one had a listening audience of ten thousand and they play it over and over again. The point is that there are many ways for a poet to communicate with an audience.

That doesn't mean that the written word isn't important. All my poems are written down first, as they are conceived. If they weren't written I wouldn't be able to memorize and perform them.

I don't perform spontaneously and it isn't babble. My poems are highly conceived, so the written word is very, very important. But the book is not the prime venue.

What has happened over the last twenty-five years is that poetry has changed. One hundred or two hundred years ago, when you were home alone at night, anxious and lonely and bored, what you did was read. You sat with a book, lit by a candle, and read. That has been the traditional venue for literature for centuries. Nowadays, when you are home alone, you watch television, listen to a CD, talk on the telephone. The venues for poetry are quite different, and poetry is quite different. A poem that is meant to be read in solitude is quite different from a poem that is meant to be performed.

In the 1960s it also occurred to me that poetry was seventy-five years behind everything else, behind painting and sculpture and dance and music. There was Andy Warhol and the pop artists and Bob Rauschenberg and Jasper Johns and musicians like John Cage and David Tudor and all the dancers, like Merce Cunningham and Trisha Brown. But poetry was still emerging from the nineteenth century.

Conservatism is actually beneficial because it requires you to constantly blow up the building. The poet must be the terrorist who breaks down the mental structures that inhibit and imprison the mind. Compassion is the active ingredient always arising in the poet, the terrorist of absolute compassion. That's the self-arising nature of poetry; it's spontaneous, it has to constantly happen. That's why teaching poetry is an oxymoron. Poetry always has to recreate itself. You can never be liberated once and for all in this world, and you can never be on easy street. You must constantly keep doing it.

There are always new dynamic forms of poetry. One of them now is rap. I particularly like the rap which is X-rated, that is not allowed on the radio here because it is too violent or demeaning to women. Those guys write from deep in their hearts, from the hard-core experiences of their lives, and through their suffering they manage to make these great songs. Like all poetry, some rap is great and a lot of it is bad. I think rap now is what rock 'n roll was twenty five years ago – against hierarchy, against structures that limit possibilities. Twenty-five years later, rock 'n roll is the hierarchy itself; it's entertainment. But rap is one of the cutting edges. It may be violent, but you can't criticize them for writing about their lives, saying it's too violent: their lives *are* violent.

It's very important to understand technology. You must know how to use your voice, develop performing skills, and to translate that, with or without music, into a recording. I think it is necessary for a poet to perform a poem, to empower it. I learned to use my voice by performing for endless years, through trial and error. Nobody taught me. There are melodies inherent in the words that aren't apparent when you first read them. When I'm writing a poem, I rehearse it. From the beginning I say the words aloud, then with a microphone; it's better with a microphone because it's clearer, you can hear pitch and resonance, and have more control of the subtleties. I bring out or develop the melodic qualities in the phrasing of the words. By the time a poem is finished, it's memorized and complete, like a song.

When I met William Burroughs in 1964 he was a famous writer but he wasn't very widely read. He was well-known because of *The Naked Lunch*, but his other books – *The Soft Machine, Nova Express* – are difficult reading. When I started releasing my LP albums, William had some work on each one, so people heard him reading his words, and once they got William's voice they could read anything he wrote and hear his voice. It made his work accessible. I've been told this by many people. I've released 28 albums with William on them, and, with the radio play, millions have heard him. The point is that the sound of William's voice is very important to the wisdom of his words.

In 1951, when I was fourteen years old, I saw Dylan Thomas perform *Under Milk Wood* at the YMHA in New York. Looking back I can see he really changed my life. Dylan Thomas came to New York and gave performances in 1951, '52 and '53, and I went to see him each time. He sat on a stool in the middle of the stage with three performers on either side performing the voices in *Under Milk Wood.* There was Dylan Thomas, drunk out of his head, performing with unbelievable energy, pouring sweat, and using his voice in this amazing way. The next year I got tickets earlier – this is when I was fifteen. They were in the second row and I was spellbound. When I was sixteen I did the same. Of course I bought the LP album and listened endlessly to it. I read the book that came with the album, but I wasn't focusing on reading; I was interested in the sound of the words, and seeing him perform in my mind's eye.

Willa Cather comes to mind: 'Don't let them ever teach my books in high school because they'll never want to read me again!' Maybe she would have been happier if teachers had just read her books out loud in high school; if teachers had performed them.

Acknowledgements

I WOULD LIKE TO acknowledge the influence of my conversations with Michael André, Ian Breakwell, Declan Kiberd, and Haydée Vitali. Their thinking is part of the body politic of this book. Also Marguerite Duras, whose book of edited conversations with Jerôme Beaujour, *La Vie Matérielle*, gave me the idea for the format of this one. And my students, who gave me the idea for the content.